SOUTHEAST ASIA IN THE 1980s

Southeast Asia in the 1980s: The Politics of Economic Crisis

EDITED BY
RICHARD ROBISON
KEVIN HEWISON
RICHARD HIGGOTT

ALLEN & UNWIN
Sydney London Boston

© Robison, Hewison, Higgott 1987
This book is copyright under the Berne Convention. No reproduction without permission. All rights reserved.

First published in 1987
Allen & Unwin Australia Pty Ltd
8 Napier Street, North Sydney NSW 2060

Allen & Unwin New Zealand Ltd
60 Cambridge Terrace, Wellington

Allen & Unwin (Publishers) Ltd
18 Park Lane, Hemel Hempstead Herts HP2 4TE England

Allen & Unwin Inc.
8 Winchester Place, Winchester, Mass 01890 USA

National Library of Australia
Cataloguing-in-Publication entry:
Southeast Asia in the 1980s.
  Includes bibliographies and index.
  ISBN 0 04 176012 3.
  ISBN 0 04 301289 2 (hardback)

  1. Asia, Southeastern—Economic conditions. 2. Asia, Southeastern—Politics and government. I. Robison, Richard, 1943–   . II. Hewison, Kevin J. III. Higgott, Richard A.

338.959

Library of Congress catalog card number: 87-70895

Set in 10/11 Plantin by Best-set Typesetters, Hong Kong
Printed by Kim Hup Lee Printing, Singapore

Contents

1 Crisis in economic strategy in the 1980s: the factors at work   *1*
  Richard Robison, Richard Higgott, Kevin Hewison

2 After the gold rush: the politics of economic restructuring in Indonesia in the 1980s   *16*
  Richard Robison

3 National interests and economic downturn: Thailand   *52*
  Kevin Hewison

4 The politics of economic policy in the Philippines during the Marcos era   *80*
  S.K. Jayasuriya

5 Economic crisis and policy response in Malaysia   *113*
  Jomo Kwame Sundaram

6 The rise and fall of Singapore's 'Second Industrial Revolution'   *149*
  Garry Rodan

7 Australia: economic crises and the politics of regional economic adjustment   *177*
  Richard Higgott

Notes   *218*

References   *221*

Index   *238*

Contributors

Kevin Hewison Formerly a Post-doctoral Fellow in the Department of Political and Social Change, Research School of Pacific Studies, Australian National University, and now a sociologist/political scientist working on a domestic water supply project in Khon Kaen, Thailand.

Richard Higgott Senior Research Fellow, Department of International Relations, Research School of Pacific Studies, Australian National University, on secondment from his position as Senior Lecturer in Social and Political Theory, Murdoch University.

S.K. Jayasuriya Research Fellow, Department of Economics, Research School of Pacific Studies, Australian National University.

Jomo Kwame Sundaram Associate Professor, Faculty of Economics, University of Malaya.

Richard Robison Senior Lecturer in Politics in the Asian Studies Programme, and Dean of the School of Humanities, Murdoch University.

Garry Rodan Lecturer, Social and Political Theory Programme, Murdoch University.

Abbreviations

ADB	Asia Development Bank
ANU	Australian National University, Canberra
ASEAN	Association of South East Asian Nations
AWSJ	*Asian Wall Street Journal*
BS	Barisan Sosialis, political party in Singapore
ECAFE	Economic Commission for Asia and the Far East
EOI	export-oriented industrialisation
EPZ	export processing zones, in the Philippines
FEER	*Far Eastern Economic Review*
FTZ	free-trade zone, in Malaysia
GATT	General Agreement on Tariffs and Trade
GDP	gross domestic product
GNP	gross national product
GSP	Generalised System of Preferences (trade advantages) of GATT
IBRD	International Bank for Reconstruction and Development
ILO	International Labour Organisation
IMF	International Monetary Fund
IMP	Industrial Master Plan, in Malaysia
ISI	import-substitution industrialisation
LDC	less-developed country
LNG	liquefied natural gas
NAP	National Agricultural Policy of Malaysia
NEDA	National Economic and Development Authority of the Philippines
NEP	New Economic Policy of Malaysia
NFPE	non-financial public enterprise, in Malaysia
NIC	newly industrialising country
NIDL	new international division of labour

NTB	non-tariff barrier
NTUC	National Trades Union Congress, in Singapore
OBA	off-budget agency (now known as non-financial public enterprise, NFPE), in Malaysia
OECD	Organisation for Economic Cooperation and Development
OPEC	Organisation of Petroleum Exporting Countries
PAP	People's Action Party, political party in Singapore
R&D	research and development
SAL	structural adjustment loans of the World Bank
TNC	transnational corporation
VAT	value-added tax

RICHARD ROBISON, RICHARD HIGGOTT, KEVIN HEWISON

1
Crisis in economic strategy in the 1980s: the factors at work

Ten years ago the countries of Southeast Asia were being hailed, together with the 'newly industrialising countries' (NICs) of Asia and Latin America, including Hong Kong, Taiwan, South Korea, Brazil and Mexico, as the shining lights of the international economy. All were maintaining high rates of growth, and industrial deepening was taking place. According to a number of theorists, and especially those associated with the World Bank and the International Monetary Fund (IMF), they were showing the way forward for the less-developed nations—industrialisation was possible, and a new generation of industrial nations was in the making (Garnaut, ed., 1980; Kreuger, 1982).

The past decade, however, has seen the lights dim somewhat. Little is heard of the Latin American NICs—their development has stalled as debts have mounted to huge levels. In Asia the NICs have also taken an economic battering (*Far Eastern Economic Review* (*FEER*), 26 September 1985), and the same is true of the Southeast Asian countries, where the economic downturn has been almost as spectacular as their growth over the previous decade.

One of the results of this economic downturn has been the increased pressure, from both domestic and international sources, for the states of the region to engage in major structural adjustments of their economies (Bello et al., 1982; *FEER*, 27 September 1984). The political and economic implications of the crisis and proposed structural change are so fundamental that they have introduced a new note of urgency and confrontation even to the point of open conflict, as in the Philippines.

It is our intention in this book to analyse and explain the nature of the pressures for structural change and the processes by which responses to these pressures are formed. In particular we will be looking at the interface of the international political economy and domestic political and economic interests, in an effort to understand the dynamics of policymaking. The cases to be examined are Indonesia, Thailand, the Philippines, Malaysia, Singapore and Australia.

The countries under investigation have been chosen for quite specific reasons. Not only are the first five the major partners in ASEAN (Brunei is not considered) thus giving their selection a regional logic, but they present an interesting spread of politico-economic systems for analysis. Singapore is a highly organised city-state, dominated by a single party and one that for two decades been committed to the development of industries manufacturing goods for export as its economic backbone. Indonesia has the world's fifth largest population, the vast majority of whom remain peasant farmers. It has a military-dominated government and has directed its economic strategy primarily towards the creation of a broad, self-sustaining import-substitution manufacturing base. Thailand has a political system somewhat similar to that of Indonesia except that the military has not been able to create political and ideological institutions as systematic, pervasive and dominant: parties and parliament are relatively more significant. It has been the region's quiet economic achiever, although it has no resource base other than primary agricultural produce, in contrast to Indonesia's oil reserves. In the Philippines, a parliamentary system existed to 1972, dominated by the major landed families. President Marcos' subsequent attempt to build an authoritarian, corporatist regime collapsed in 1986, by which time the Philippines had become the poorest country in ASEAN and a member of the big league of international debtors. Malaysia has maintained parliamentary democratic political structures but faces greater problems of religious and racial tensions than any of its ASEAN neighbours. In the past few years it has attempted to move away from its reliance on primary exports towards the Japanese and Korean models of export-oriented manufacture.

Australia's inclusion in this analysis is no mere exercise in ethnocentrism on the part of the authors. One of the world's wealthiest states and a functioning liberal democracy, it will be nevertheless demonstrated to have economic problems, as well as a geographical proximity, sufficiently similar to those of its neighbours to warrant comparative discussion. Many of Australia's current economic problems stem from the pursuit of economic policies prior to the Second World War, not dissimilar to the early import-substitution policies of the ASEAN states in the early phases of the post-war era. As an exporter of primary commodities, Australia, like ASEAN, has been hit by price falls on world markets. But a consideration of Southeast Asia together with Australia is primarily justified because it is increasingly clear that, for Australia at least, the economic future lies in a much more systematic and intense cross-flow of trade and investment. To this extent their problems and prospects are intertwined.

Policy legacies in the region

For the Southeast Asian region, economic planning and state involvement in investment and production were a central characteristic of the 1950s and 1960s. Partly the result of current economic thinking, partly the consequence of nationalist economic ideologies and also a response to the absence of a strong private sector, state involvement has continued to exert a dominant influence.

In Indonesia the successive governments of the 1950s and the Sukarno regime in 1959–65, in particular, developed their economic policies around a drive to create an industrial base for the economy. The state took a leading role in establishing industry by direct corporate investment, provision of fiscal policies and creation of economic infrastructure. It intended (albeit unsuccessfully) to establish a full range of industrial activities including steel mills, metal refining, engineering and shipbuilding. Although interrupted in the mid-1960s as a result of political and economic collapse, the drive under state leadership towards an economy based upon domestic industry was to continue in the 1970s.

Thailand's government, under Field Marshal Phibun, moved to heavy state involvement in industry, with relatively large investments in sugar, textiles and food and beverages. With a large number of military and other state officials involved, some of the wealth created was siphoned off into political machinations, and many of the projects proved ponderous and top-heavy and incapable of generating surpluses that could be reinvested. By the late 1950s local investors were complaining that they were being squeezed out by the state, and a military coup in 1957 led to a greater role for private investment in industrial development.

In Singapore the attempt to promote industrialisation in any concerted way did not occur until after self-government in 1959. Colonial authorities had little interest in diversifying Singapore's economic base beyond entrepot activities, and the domestic industrial bourgeoisie was economically and politically too weak to force the issue. Upon taking office in 1959, however, the People's Action Party (PAP) gave priority to the development of industry as a means of addressing the declining growth in entrepot trade and the increasing problem of unemployment. The initial strategy of import-substitution industrialisation (ISI) was premised on access to markets in the Federation of Malaysia.

The Philippines experienced a long period of import-substitution manufacturing, beginning in the early 1950s, facilitated by import and exchange control measures adopted to overcome a serious balance of payments crisis in 1948–49. The strategy, as practised in the Philippines, enabled joint exploitation of a protected home market by

US and Filipino capital and thus met little resistance as it led to a very rapid industrial growth in the 1950s Mainly confined to textiles and other consumer goods, light engineering and agricultural processing, by the end of the 1960s the economy was slowing down as the easy phase of ISI ended. However, there was not a concerted move towards export-oriented industrialisation (EOI), and throughout the 1970s, despite rhetoric to the contrary, the basic structure of industry remained predominantly ISI.

Malaysia began its move away from the colonial agricultural export economy in the 1960s with increasing state investments intended to facilitate the growth of ISI. Because of the limited domestic market the ISI phase in Malaysia broadened quickly beyond consumer goods into capital and intermediate goods. Along with the Philippines, Malaysia moved into the export-oriented phase in the late 1960s as trade deficits grew and the domestic market became more constricting.

Australia's colonial experience differed from that of its regional neighbours. As a federation of former colonies settled by Europeans it always saw itself as a partner in the (British) Imperial experience rather than a victim of colonialism. As a consequence of its status as a 'far-flung' outpost of Empire, it created inward-looking, highly defensive state structures that attempted to nurture a domestic Australian industry. The intentions behind such policies were strategic, their consequences were economic. Australian governments erected highly protectionist barriers and provided vast subsidies to secure the growth of a labour-intensive manufacturing sector that would have failed to develop in the face of external competition.

These policies in Australia, brought to full bloom throughout the inter-war period, gave it a standard of living second to none and made it quite distinct from its regional neighbours emerging from colonial rule in the era after the Second World War.

Import-substitution industrialisation (ISI) gives way to export-oriented industrialisation (EOI)

Import-substitution strategies for manufacturing dominated economic thinking in the 1950s and 1960s, not only reflecting the orthodoxy of development economics at the time (Agarwala & Singh, 1958) but also appealing to both nationalist sentiments and the interests of nascent capitalist classes. By the early 1960s the thrust of economic policy, especially as it related to industrial development in the countries under study, had moved clearly into the import-substitution industrialisation (ISI) phase, protected by tariff walls, bans and quotas, as well as import licensing. Although initially concentrating on production of consumer goods, pressures to create cohesive circuits of industrial production led to the beginnings of expansion into intermediate and capital goods production. In terms of the range and depth of ISI, Australia was by far the most advanced, having established steel, shipbuilding and petrochemical industries in the interwar years and moving strongly into automobile manufacture and textiles immediately after the war.

By the mid to late 1960s, however, the ISI strategy was beginning to reach saturation point, particularly in consumer goods, in a number of the countries of the region, and calls were being made for a greater emphasis to be placed on industrial production for export. Ironically, such pressures were not to emerge in Australia until the late 1970s.

The 1960s also saw a series of new factors beginning to intrude into the processes of capital accumulation in the advanced industrial countries. While transnational corporations (TNCs) had expanded considerably in the post-war period, and many had established affiliates to manufacture behind tariff walls in the Third World and Australia, a number of factors converged to encourage an even greater internationalisation of capital.

In broad terms, the large manufacturing corporations of the advanced industrial countries experienced both a crisis of accumulation and significant technological advancement. The crisis of accumulation was related to the tendency of wages to rise in the industrial centre, which, together with increased productivity and technological advancements, allowed for the disaggregation of some important production processes (e.g. in electronics). This meant it became possible and relatively more attractive for TNCs to transfer certain industrial production processes to the Third World. This was, however, not a process given its dynamic solely in changes that occurred in the advanced industrial economies. As pointed out by Hamilton (1983), Jenkins (1984), Schmitz (1984) and Browett (1985), amongst others, the dynamics of change in the Third World economies were also important in that they determined whether these countries were able to respond to the opportunities offered by this restructuring within the capitalist system of production. Various Third World countries attempted to carve out a niche for themselves within this changing system, some basing their integration on large, cheap and repressed labour forces, others on skills, technical abilities, infrastructure and low taxes, but the common factor in the region under scrutiny here was a move away from ISI strategies towards outward-looking, export-oriented industrialisation (EOI) strategies.

By the 1970s, international corporate conglomerates were actively extending their operations beyond simple manufacturing behind tariff barriers for local markets to export-oriented production, including direct corporate investment in manufacturing in Third World countries for export, as well as subcontracting certain aspects of products to local manufacturers within the Third World. As mentioned earlier, it had become possible and desirable to decompose the production process and make decisions about the distribution of investment and production on a global scale.

The first wave of NICs substantially boosted their economic growth rates in the late 1960s and 1970s by moving into relatively labour-intensive sectors of manufacturing as the advanced industrial economies generally moved to higher value-added production. In trade, the NICs' growth rates were far in excess of those for the rest of the world, as much of their production was geared to export.

Dragging behind the structural changes in the international system of production, neo-classical economists rebuilt the ideologies of free trade and the free market, this time on an international scale. Economic growth, it was argued, could best be generated if each country exploited its comparative advantage, dismantled protective measures and submitted to the logic of allocative efficiency inherent in the free market (Garnaut, 1980; Kreuger, 1982). Significantly, free-market neo-classical economists began to establish their dominance in international banking and financial institutions and in the US government in the mid-1970s, thus establishing an institutional power base for their ideas.

However, the economies of Southeast Asia and Australia were not automatically subsumed into the new international division of labour (NIDL) as a consequence of these pressures. There were a variety of very important reasons why ISI continued to constitute the core of development strategy. Most obviously, the ISI structure had embedded within it quite powerful vested interests whose authority and position were predicated upon protectionist policies and active state intervention. These political and economic alliances included state officials and state managers of capital, party officials, domestic manufacturers and, particularly in Australia, organised labour.

A second factor that permitted ISI strategies to be at least partially maintained, particularly in Malaysia, Thailand, the Philippines and Indonesia, was the ready availability of international finance capital in the 1970s. Finance capital expanded rapidly during the 1970s due to excess international liquidity and the internationalisation of banking (Andreff, 1984; Griffith-Jones & Rodriguez, 1984). International financiers began to lend heavily to those countries that were most integrated within the world system of trade, and this included many of the NICs and the countries of Southeast Asia. The availability of finance allowed some Third World states and capitals to bear the cost of major investment and to sustain high-cost industries without the need for substantial export earnings from manufactures. While there were increases in manufactured exports, these were not significant. In

Indonesia and Malaysia, massive oil and gas export earnings and corporate taxes were the major source of funds for developing and maintaining huge ISI investment projects, but the countries of the region were also able to borrow heavily from the large stocks of petro-dollars available for lending in the US and Europe. Large amounts of this money also found its way into Australia during the 'mining boom' of the 1970s, although capital invested in the mineral exploration sector was not used for ISI strategies.

At the same time, long-term problems were acting against the viability of ISI strategies. Saturation of local markets was a substantial difficulty. However, this tended to affect the consumer goods sector and often simply acted as a spur to enter the phase of 'industrial deepening' or extending ISI to upstream and downstream industries in the intermediate and capital goods sectors. A second problem was stagnation in industrial productivity within the ISI regimes. It must be remembered that ISI is justified by both its theorists and apologists on the grounds that it, and its protective apparatus, is a necessary stage in the development of infant industries and their transformation into mature structures. But protection tended to become enshrined as a permanent condition behind which domestic producers were able to avoid the sorts of investments and developments in productivity and quality that were expected to take place in the infant stage. Domestic industries therefore became quite substantial burdens upon both the state and local investors.

It is not being suggested that the history of industrialisation in the region can be neatly divided into ISI and EOI periods. Export of industrial products in certain sectors (particularly textiles and processed foodstuffs) was common in Thailand, Malaysia and the Philippines in particular throughout the 1970s. Nor does a shift towards priority for EOI imply that ISI becomes inconsequential, as evidenced by the still-flourishing import-substitution sectors in South Korea and Taiwan. Nevertheless crisis points can be identified which may be considered to be crucial watersheds in the consideration of policy.

In the case of Singapore this point was reached in the early 1960s following the failure of the union with Malaysia and the destruction of any prospects for a domestic market of substance upon which to base ISI. Thus when separation occurred in 1965, Singapore's policymakers effected a sharp turnaround in strategy. Though scope still existed for the expansion of import-substitution industrialisation within Singapore, it certainly was not sufficient to sustain the sort of rapid economic growth considered necessary to arrest unemployment. By 1968, a range of comprehensive economic, social and political measures had been adopted to attract international capital to Singapore. The assumption behind the state's high profile was that it could shape the factors of production, most notably through the enforcement of low wages, to give Singapore a comparative advantage in having labour-intensive production. This was taking place, of course, at a convenient juncture in the development of international capital. The absence of politically powerful vested interests to defend the import-substitution strategy, so characteristic of many other countries in the region, also made for a swift transition. By the end of the 1960s dramatic results had been achieved in industrial growth and employment generation. With the exception of the 1974–75 recession, these results were consolidated throughout the next decade.

The so-called 'Second Industrial Revolution', the PAP's policy initiatives begun in 1979, was expected to usher in a new phase in Singapore's industrial sophistication. What we have seen, however, is that whilst international capital has been prepared to upgrade operations, and indeed introduce such processes as wafer diffusion, there are real limits to this. In the case of US-based capital, which has largely led the upgrading, the most sophisticated processes are still retained in the US or Europe, alongside pools of advanced R & D manpower and the markets for the finished products. In the case of Japan-based capital, there has been a considerable reluctance to upgrade operations. The primary concern to ensure access to the markets of Europe and the US has conditioned the evaluation of Singapore's production costs by the Japanese.

Meanwhile, Singapore's policymakers have had to face up to a longer term problem which is just beginning to emerge. Advances in automation threaten to undermine the essential attraction of Singapore as a production site, that is, cheaper labour. Recently, Fairchild returned its assembly operations to Portland when increased productive capacity in automatic bonding machines for electronic circuits negated the cost advantage of Singapore's labour. The potential for automation to extend to areas of middle technology poses a serious threat for the 'Second Industrial Revolution'. Moreover, the contradiction the PAP has to face is that the more successful its transition to higher value-added production, the less significance labour assumes in overall production costs.

For the other countries of the Southeast Asian region, apart from Singapore, pressures to shift the emphasis of policy from ISI to EOI were imposed by deepening crises in balance of payments and trade positions and in state revenues. These problems were largely the consequence of falling world commodity prices, which impacted upon traditional agricultural, mineral and energy exports. Not only did this shift towards export of industrial products become more urgent and necessary, but the decline in export income and company tax generated by oil and mineral producers severely affected the capacity of the state to finance the major industrial projects implicit in industrial deepening within the ISI framework. It also meant that there was a shift of political influence and power to the IMF and World Bank, which were increasingly called upon to provide loans for beleaguered governments and to prop up current account deficits.

The Philippines, heavily reliant on agricultural exports, was first hit by the crisis in the late 1970s because its export commodities were first affected. Thailand was also affected, but due to considerable agricultural diversification the impact was softened, at least until the early 1980s. Indonesia's massive oil exports were not hit until the 1981–82 oil price declines, while Malaysia, with a broader export base, including liquefied natural gas (LNG) and some industrial exports, has been more resilient. At the same time, these countries were faced with both a contraction in amount and an increase in cost of the loan funds previously so freely available from private banks in the United States, Europe and Japan as OPEC dollars available for investment began to dry up and the debt crises in the Philippines, Mexico, Brazil, Argentina, Poland and other countries began to suggest potential catastrophe.

In the case of Australia the notion of an *immediate* balance of payments crisis was not readily recognised in the early 1980s, and it was not until the mid-1980s that the magnitude of Australia's problems became apparent. A virtual overnight collapse in the value of the Australian dollar against a continuing backdrop of declining commodity prices by 1986 brought Australia to a position where its debt profile was similar to that of many of its regional neighbours and indeed worse than some.

The 1980s have been important to Australia as a learning experience. Cocooned for many years behind protectionist barriers, Australian manufacturing industries have become gradually, rather than dramatically, more inefficient. The strength of the Australian economy had never been in either export-oriented industrialisation or import-substitution industrialisation, but rather in the export of primary produce and raw materials. Structural change in the Australian economy was not from the primary sector to the manufacturing sector, which has remained largely static as a share of the economy. Rather, change has been in the preponderance of various subsections of the primary sector. Most notable here has been the decline of the agricultural sector at the expense of the mining sector as a major factor in Australia's export economy. Both are still vital to Australia, and the collapse of world markets for quite a few of the commodities from these sectors has caused major structural problems for the Australian political economy.

As the governments of the region encountered fiscal crises and the foreign debt problems escalated, the balance of power swung away from domestic states and capital to international financial institutions, and the balance of influence over policy moved from protectionists to proponents of neo-classical economic solutions. Policies of fiscal retrenchment stressing reduced government spending and the reallocation of state investment from ISI projects to provision of infrastructure for export industries were urged upon governments, and in some cases World Bank loans—the so-called structural adjustment loans (SALs) —were made conditional upon their acceptance. Whilst the demands of foreign corporate investment capital could be ignored during the period when foreign earnings from oil and other primary exports boomed and inflows of cheap finance were high, the new situation made foreign corporate investment more necessary.

Obstacles to restructuring

Despite the pressures upon countries in the region to move to the free-trade, export-oriented prescriptions of the neo-classical economists the very conditions that had enabled the EOI models (South Korea, Taiwan, Singapore) to grab a place in the newly evolving international division of labour were rapidly collapsing. High and endemic unemployment in the industrial metropoles, as well as the collapse of huge sections of domestic industrial capital as a consequence, real or perceived, of import competition from the Third World, placed intense political pressures on the free-trade strategies of the advocates of global structural adjustment. Governments were increasingly forced to raise protective barriers and to provide investment incentives for domestic industry. These protectionist pressures coincided with substantial declines in demand generated by recession in the industrial countries (Kaplinsky, 1984; Ofreneo, 1984; Cho, 1985; *FEER*, 26 September 1985).

We are also beginning to see a phenomenon, referred to by some as the fourth wave of global restructuring, that involves a flow of investment back to the old industrial centres. This 'fourth wave' is the consequence of advances in the technology of production which negate advantages formerly inherent in low-wage labour in the Third World. International capital is becoming much more selective about the sorts of productive processes it locates in the Third World for purposes of export production, as the case of Singapore illustrates.

Pressures to move from ISI to EOI strategies were therefore contradicted not only by political and economic interests vested in ISI and by ideological attachments to economic nationalism, but also by a growing realisation that the EOI route was less viable than supposed by the ideologues of the IMF and World Bank. The example of the difficulties of Singapore and the increasing protectionism of the US and

Crisis in economic strategy: the factors

Europe emphasised the fact that finding a niche within a rapidly changing system of production is a difficult prospect and a mere change of policy would guarantee nothing. What was also becoming apparent was the importance of the level at which countries were integrated: what their productive contribution would be. The levels of infrastructure, political order, administrative efficiency and development of local capital in Southeast Asia made it increasingly clear that their capacity to compete on world markets, despite low labour costs, was severely hampered by other costs and inefficiencies. The same factors meant that international capital was, in the final analysis, unwilling to see the region as any more than a marginal component in the world system of production.

Australia has been confronted by similar pressures to move into EOI and adopt free-market solutions to its economic problems. To a large degree its prospects are bound up with the process of industrialisation in the Asian region. It has been urged to open its doors to the import of labour-intensive manufactures and to abandon its own industries in this sector. Yet other than vague exhortation to move into high-technology sectors and the service sector it is not at all clear what is to replace these industries. Indeed, exactly where Australia's comparative advantage is deemed to lie is still a major question for policymakers on the island-continent.

Despite the markedly different situations prevailing within each of the countries there are certain important common factors. On the one hand, fiscal pressures on governments, rising debt levels and balance of payments problems have meant that they are now less able to finance movement beyond the limits of the first stages of ISI and develop integrated industrial circuits and the major intermediate and capital goods projects central to these objectives. On the other hand, movement from ISI to EOI is proving to be a difficult process, neither an automatic consequence of structural changes in the industrial metropole, as suggested by Frobel, nor simply a matter of introducing new policies, as assumed by Krueger and other neo-classical economists. More recent changes in the international division of labour are actually presenting difficulties for countries newly attempting to climb aboard. It is also becoming apparent that the special social and political conditions which provided the basis for the development of EOI in Singapore, Korea and Taiwan may not exist in Southeast Asia or Australia, and that even in the aforementioned countries these conditions may no longer exist or may need to be reshaped to fit changed international conditions. For example, we can even witness nowadays how NICs are establishing production facilities in Canada and the Caribbean in an effort to circumvent trade barriers established by the US.

As a consequence, the major Southeast Asian countries are caught in a bind, unable to sustain the existing ISI structures and facing real difficulties in moving into the sphere of EOI. Making economic policy in this situation has become an arena of bitter political struggle, and the outcome has fundamental implications for broader aspects of social, political and economic structures.

It is in the context of these considerations that this book will focus upon the processes of policy formation in the countries under review. In particular we will be arguing that not only is determination of policy a consequence of the balance of power and the outcome of conflict between competing elements within, and between, capital and labour and the state, but also that it is a consequence of these conflicts at both a national and an international level as well.

The structure of the book

In Chapter 2, Richard Robison looks at Indonesia where state-led ISI strategies and nationalist economic ideologies have had their fullest expression. State capitalism including heavy investment in basic industry has been a constant and dominant theme in the policymaking of governments of vastly different political hues over the past forty years. It is here that political, bureaucratic and capitalist interests have become most clearly fused together and integrated into ISI strategies. As a result, the difficulties of breaking down ISI and economic nationalism in Indonesia have been greatest. However, the extreme dependence of the ISI strategy on oil income meant that the collapse of oil prices has precipitated a dramatic political struggle over the future direction of industrial strategy.

Thailand, the Philippines and Malaysia are less extreme cases than Indonesia, but nevertheless, strong nationalist economic sentiments have underpinned considerable support for ISI strategies. Deteriorating balance of payments and debt positions precipitated political conflict over economic policy, resulting in strident intervention by the World Bank and the International Bank for Reconstruction and Development (IBRD).

In Chapter 3, Kevin Hewison examines Thailand, where economic growth has been especially rapid during the 1960s and 1970s but is now experiencing a downturn. Following a period of heavy state involvement in industrial development in the 1950s, Thailand's military governments of the 1960s embraced an ISI strategy which particularly emphasised the production of import-replacing consumer goods especially textiles and other relatively low value-added commodities. This emphasis saw the emergence of a reasonably powerful domestic class of capital and an alliance between bankers and ISI industrialists.

However, as the limit of domestic markets was reached, and as some industrialists moved beyond simple ISI, the pressures for a transition to a more export-oriented policy mounted. This pressure came not merely from industrialists, however, as state managers began to experience fiscal problems. The debate over ISI and EOI has raged for a number of years, with some participants changing sides more than once, and this confused situation is discussed.

In Chapter 4, Sisira Jayasuriya analyses developments in the Philippines which, from being at the forefront of industrialisation during the 1960s, has become the weakest of the ASEAN economies. The Philippines had a successful initial period of ISI but was unable to sustain the momentum. A switch to an export-oriented strategy was called for by technocrats in the late 1960s and also by the IMF and World Bank, especially in the Marcos martial law era after 1972. But there was no basic change in policy. The regime, balancing between different domestic and international forces, was unable and unwilling to confront and defeat the entrenched ISI interests. Major structural reforms and politically risky measures were avoided during the 1970s by recourse to heavy foreign borrowings which made the economy completely vulnerable to adverse international economic developments. Further, the narrow class basis of the regime and its inherently unstable character led to the phenomenon of 'crony capitalism' which saw major state intervention in the economy to enrich a small clique around the Marcos family.

The economic crisis was first expressed in the form of a balance of payments crisis, with the country unable to meet its debt obligations. This rapidly led to a major political crisis. A popular uprising and a split in the military brought to power a government that is a coalition of diverse forces, which inherited an economy in tatters. The developments of the preceding decade have, however, ensured the dominance of international finance capital in the Philippines, and the pressures for restructuring the economy with an EOI orientation are intense.

In Chapter 5, Jomo Sundaram examines the complex progress of Malaysian economic strategy. Despite the constraints imposed by the difficulties and costs associated with attempting to build up the capital ownership share of indigenous Malays, the government, through increasing oil and LNG revenues and foreign loans, performed well throughout the 1970s. Industrial production grew at a rapid rate, and the development of export-oriented industries appeared encouraging. However, declining commodity prices, the global recession, climbing interest rates and a sharp decline in foreign investment have presented the government with some real problems in the 1980s. In the face of fiscal difficulties and a gloomy balance of payments outlook the government has chosen to vigorously embrace, in rhetoric at least, the ideals of the market-oriented, outward-looking privatising strategies of Korea and Japan: the so-called 'look East' policy. This response and its success, and indeed the degree to which it is implemented, is a crucial test for the market-oriented model.

In Chapter 6, Garry Rodan examines the case of Singapore, the ASEAN country most completely incorporated into the new international division of labour. However, what sets Singapore apart is not, it is argued, any triumph of rationality over policy so much as a peculiar constellation of socio-political factors which have steered Singapore in this different direction. Historical circumstances ensure that, in developments leading to self-government in 1959, capital was not represented in the nationalist movement and, furthermore, that the successful People's Action Party came to office with a small elite of middle-class leaders in spite of its overwhelming reliance upon working-class support. Astute post-1959 exploitation of the state apparatus to isolate itself from any internal challenge assisted this elite subsequently to pursue an export-oriented industrialisation programme under the aegis of international capital. The absence of any powerful domestic industrial bourgeoisie capable of frustrating this effort was also a conspicuous point of contrast. In short, the People's Action Party enjoyed a degree of political autonomy which made incorporation into the new international division of labour a feasible political project.

Tracing the experience of Singapore in this new international division of labour, Rodan shows how the state has systematically provided social, political and economic conditions conducive to industrialisation through this export model. Having successfully moved out of the most labour-intensive, least-skilled forms of production associated with the division of labour, Singapore has encountered problems in moving further upstream. It is suggested that the difficulties encountered reflect the objective limitations imposed by the structure of the new international division of labour. In the Singapore state's reassessment of strategy and consequent moderation of ambition, a host of measures have been announced which are anticipated to restore Singapore's position as a rapidly expanding economy. However, Rodan's analysis of these measures contends that they carry with them economic and political costs in the longer term.

Finally, in Chapter 7, Richard Higgott looks at what is perhaps the most important and fundamental shift in the structure of the Australian economy that has occurred since the establishment of the import-substitution manufacturing sector in the earlier part of this century. Spurred by a long-term decline in the value of export commodities and the consequent deterioration in the balance of payments, the basic tenants of Australian economic life, including the regulated labour market, the tariff system and the tendency towards an inward-looking perspective, have come under threat. The welfare state, the union movement and the Keynesian orthodoxy have all been confronted by radicalised lobby groups from the private sector carrying the banners of neo-classical economics, privatisation and deregulation.

Whilst all groups agree on the need for a more outward-looking, export-oriented structure there is conflict over the way this can be achieved. For the radical Right it will be through the removal of structural distortions in the market: arbitration, tariffs, state intervention. For the Centre and the Left it can be best achieved by a more planned and coordinated strategy in which the state, the unions and business associations provide the institutional conduits and cement. For both, however, the crucial problem is to improve the currently dismal performance in the export of manufactures, where the burgeoning markets of Southeast Asia are both obvious and important targets.

A common theme emphasised in each of the chapters is the inseparability of economic, political and social factors. It is recognised that competing economic policies and industrial strategies are not simply abstract economic models but rather frameworks that encompass specific vested interests. Consequently, major policy shifts involve conflict of these vested interests: international versus national capital, manufacturers versus mineral exporters or bankers, state capital versus private. To this extent these chapters implicitly embody a critique of observations of structural change by neo-classical economists. At another level the studies implicitly take issue with the contentions of dependency theorists that the dynamic for global economic restructuring emerges from the advanced industrial countries, with the Third World countries virtually tossed around in a network of international economic relationships over which they have little control. What we argue is that the questions of economic crisis and conflict over policy can be understood only by looking at factors in both the sphere of circulation and the sphere of production, and in both the national and international arenas. Indeed, over the past decade, we would contend, the process of capital accumulation within Southeast Asia has enabled powerful domestic forces to impose their influence over policy formulation. The recent crises, which are the subject of this book, involve, at one level, disruptions to existing patterns of domestic capital accumulation and fiscal systems engendered by changes in international terms of trade. At another level they involve intense political and social conflict between forces representing class, political and ideological interests for whom changes in economic strategies and policies hold fundamental consequences.

RICHARD ROBISON

2
After the gold rush: the politics of economic restructuring in Indonesia in the 1980s

To understand the political and economic nature of Indonesia under the New Order we must comprehend the enormous significance of oil earnings and revenues. The consolidation of the power of the state and its officials, the process of industrialisation and the emergence of major domestic corporate groups have all been built around oil. Consequently the collapse of oil prices in 1981–82 and the more disastrous falls in early 1986 have posed fundamental threats to the fabric of power and policy in Indonesia.

At the heart of the upheaval has been the question of economic strategy and industrial policy. The currently dominant strategy which aims at creating an integrated national industrial base in consumer, intermediate and capital goods is enmeshed with the interests of the politically dominant state bureaucrats (politico-bureaucrats) and the major domestic corporate groups. With the fall of oil prices, the capacity of the state to provide the funds for such a strategy has been seriously eroded. Pressures for Indonesia to move its emphasis from import-substitution industrialisation (ISI) to export-oriented industrialisation (EOI) have been strengthened. This implies a greater integration with the new international division of labour (NIDL).

Whilst the outcome will in part be determined by such factors as commodity prices and the capacity of the state to resolve the fiscal crises produced by the oil price shocks, it is also a political struggle between, on the one hand, international corporate capital and financial institutions and also liberal reformist elements of the domestic technocracy who favour free-trade, outward-looking policies and, on the other, the bureaucratic and corporate forces whose interests are vested in the current industrial strategy. Pressures for change within Indonesia will also be exerted by factors emanating from the evolution of the division of labour at the international level. This means that as the capacity of the state to create a national industrial economy independent of factors operating at the international level declines, it will increasingly be forced to try to carve a position for Indonesia in the new international division of labour. The success of this will in large part be determined by what investment capital can be attracted in specific sectors and what Indonesian products can be sold on the world market.

Industrial strategy to 1981

Despite the fundamental shifts that have taken place in Indonesian politics since 1949 there has been a remarkable continuity in certain key aspects of economic policy. Two important ideological factors have underpinned this continuity. First, it has been generally accepted by successive governments that the state has a legitimate economic role and that market forces must be tempered by social objectives. Second, it has also been accepted that foreign ownership and control of the Indonesian economy be restrained, that the nurturing of domestic investment be a priority and that a significant degree of national autonomy be a basic objective in shaping the structure of the economy. This last element of economic nationalism has had important implications for industrial policy in particular, because it has meant that the drive to establish capital and intermediate goods sectors has been a central investment objective and one that has often come into conflict with the interests of international corporate capital and the ideological position of market economists in the World Bank and other international organisations (Anspach, 1969; Glassburner, 1971; Thomas & Panglaykim, 1973).

Reasons for the persistence of these dominant threads in economic strategy exist at several levels. At the ideological level, nationalism and social justice were powerful legacies of the anti-colonial struggle, and no matter how hypocritically these sentiments have been exploited by various governments, political leaders and economic opportunists, the vision of an autonomous, powerful, industrial Indonesia has been a driving force behind long-term economic strategy.

However, economic strategy has also been meshed with the interests of the dominant political strata: the politico-bureaucrats who exercise hegemony over the state apparatus, fusing political, bureaucratic and economic power. Economic structures and policy cannot be understood separately from these interests. State power to intervene in and regulate the economy has been subject to appropriation by politico-bureaucrats not only to shape the pattern of vast state investments but also to control the allocation of state concessions for the private sector. Because the state allocates import and export licences, oil drilling and forestry concessions, contracts for supply and construction, as well as even permission to invest, politico-bureaucrats have been able to use these levers to influence the position of firms in the broader market structure. This political control over the economy has provided the sources of revenues, patronage and power to underpin the dominance of state officials at both socio-economic and political levels (Robison, 1986).

Finally, policies of economic nationalism and state intervention have provided the basis for the emergence of major corporate conglomerates, both public and private. State corporations such as Krakatau Steel and Pertamina, as well as major private groups including those of Liem Sioe Liong, Willem Soerjadjaja, Ibnu Sutowo and, in previous years, Dasaad and Hashim Ning, have been built upon monopoly positions and preferential access to licences, supply and credit, all derived from the intervention of the state in the economy (Robison, 1986). Combined with extensive protection of these domestic groups through tariffs and restrictions on foreign investment in certain sectors of the economy, politico-bureaucrat intervention and economic nationalism (selectively applied) have been essential to the emerging domestic capitalist class.

In the formative years of the New Order, from 1965 to the early 1970s, a retreat from economic nationalism and state intervention was brought about in part by the bankruptcy of the Indonesian economy and hence not only fiscal crisis but also the inability of domestic capital, either state or private, to engage in programmes of investment. It was this growing economic crisis combined with intensifying political conflict between the Indonesian Communist Party, the propertied classes and the military that had precipitated the collapse of the Sukarno regime and destroyed the existing political basis of nationalist, state-led industrialisation. In the atmosphere of bankruptcy, hyperinflation and economic chaos, survival took priority over nationalist economic goals for the military and the urban middle classes. Consequently the state was forced to reconstitute the economy around foreign capital investment and foreign loans. By the mid 1970s, foreign capital constituted about 50 per cent of total investment in the non-oil sector alone, and focus on major industrial projects had been abandoned in favour of import-substitution production of consumer goods, notably textiles (Palmer, 1978).

In the early 1970s, however, the pendulum began to swing back, and from 1974 we see the re-emergence of state-led economic nationalism. This resurgence was facilitated by the dramatic rise in the price of oil in the fiscal year 1973/74, bootsed by further rises in the early 1980s. Oil and liquefied natural gas (LNG) constituted more than 80 per cent of foreign earnings by 1981/82, and a healthy current account and balance of payments ensued. In 1979/80 and 1980/81, Indonesia posted current account surpluses of US$2198 million and US$2131 million (see Table 2.2), and foreign currency reserves stood at US$10 000 million as late as January 1982. The oil bonanza meant a surge of funds for state revenues and therefore the state's capacity to invest. In 1969, oil and LNG taxes constituted only 65.8 billion rupiahs (Rp), or 19.7 per cent of total government revenues. After a period of steady growth, we see a significant leap in 1974/75, lifting oil tax revenues to Rp 957.2 billion, 48.4 per cent of total revenues. Between 1978/79 and 1981/82, oil tax revenue leapt from Rp 2308 billion to Rp 8627 billion, rising from 43.5 to 61.7 per cent of total revenues and from 54 to 70 per cent of domestic revenues (Table 2.5). As a result, state expenditure through the development budget was able to be increased from Rp 450 billion in 1973/74 to Rp 6940 billion in 1981/82 (Table 2.4).

However, the fact that the oil revenues were specifically used to reconstitute the drive towards state-led industrial autarchy reflected not only the persistence of economic nationalist sentiment at the ideological level but also the fact that such policies embodied the interests of the new dominant forces in Indonesia—the military bureaucrats, state managers of capital and the major domestic corporate groups—in the same way that they had reinforced the political and economic interests of their predecessors in the Sukarno regime. For the politico-bureaucrats, a centrally directed economy effectively concentrated economic power and domestic capital ownership in the hands of the state. For domestic capital, both state and private, absorption into a state-orchestrated, state-protected set of monopolies and oligopolies guaranteed their position.

Between 1969 and 1975, a major political struggle took place over the question of economic strategy between proponents of state-led economic nationalism led by Ibnu Sutowo, the director of the state oil company, Pertamina, and the technocrats of the National Economic Planning Board (Bappenas), who favoured the more open-door, free-market policies urged by Indonesia's creditors through the Inter-governmental Group on Indonesia and by the World Bank. As the terminal for the allocation of oil-drilling concessions and the collection of oil taxes, Pertamina was the strategic cornerstone of the Indonesian economy. Under the virtually autonomous direction of Ibnu Sutowo it constituted a centre of fiscal and economic power parallel to, and often competing with, the formal state apparatus and budget.

Contrary to official state policy, Sutowo was able to push ahead with the development of industrial projects (including the Krakatau steel mill) and the raising of foreign loans independent of the formal organs of economic and industrial policy and independent of the formal state budget. Under the Pertamina umbrella domestic business groups flourished with contracts and concessions. The generals were quite

Table 2.1 Indonesia's gross domestic product by industrial origin at current market prices, 1967–83, in Rp billion (and as a percentage of GDP)

	1967	1968	1969	1970	1971	1972	1973	1974	1975	1976	1977	1978	1979	1980	1981	1982	1983
Agriculture	457 (53.9)	1 069 (51.0)	1 339 (49.3)	1 575 (47.2)	1 646 (44.8)	1 837 (40.2)	2 710 (40.1)	3 497 (32.7)	4 003 (31.7)	4 812 (31.1)	5 906 (31.0)	6 706 (29.5)	8 996 (28.1)	11 290 (24.8)	13 643 (25.3)	15 668 (26.3)	18 772 (26.4)
Mining (including oil)	23 (2.7)	87 (4.1)	129 (4.7)	173 (5.2)	294 (8.0)	491 (10.8)	831 (12.3)	2 374 (22.2)	2 485 (19.7)	2 930 (18.9)	3 600 (18.9)	4 358 (19.2)	6 980 (21.8)	11 673 (25.7)	12 971 (24.0)	11 700 (19.6)	13 824 (19.4)
Manufacturing	62 (7.3)	179 (8.6)	251 (9.2)	312 (9.3)	307 (8.4)	448 (9.8)	650 (9.6)	890 (8.3)	1 124 (8.9)	1 453 (9.4)	1 817 (9.5)	2 420 (10.6)	3 311 (10.3)	5 288 (11.6)	5 822 (10.8)	7 681 (12.9)	8 918 (12.5)
Electricity, gas and water	3 (0.4)	9 (0.4)	13 (0.5)	15 (0.4)	18 (0.5)	20 (0.4)	30 (0.4)	52 (0.5)	70 (0.6)	98 (0.6)	106 (0.6)	118 (0.5)	149 (0.5)	225 (0.5)	288 (0.5)	380 (0.6)	503 (0.7)
Construction	14 (1.6)	45 (2.1)	75 (2.8)	100 (3.0)	128 (3.5)	174 (3.8)	262 (3.9)	406 (3.8)	590 (4.7)	813 (5.3)	1 023 (5.4)	1 242 (5.5)	1 790 (5.6)	2 524 (5.6)	3 118 (5.8)	3 507 (5.9)	4 434 (6.2)
Transport and communication	19 (2.2)	57 (2.7)	77 (2.8)	96 (2.9)	162 (4.4)	182 (4.0)	257 (3.8)	442 (4.1)	521 (4.1)	663 (4.3)	843 (4.4)	1 032 (4.5)	1 422 (4.4)	1 965 (4.3)	2 352 (4.4)	2 795 (4.7)	3 325 (4.7)
Banking	4 (0.5)	12 (0.6)	22 (0.8)	33 (1.0)	45 (1.2)	53 (1.1)	83 (1.2)	113 (1.1)	151 (1.2)	207 (1.4)	236 (1.2)	396 (1.7)	655 (2.1)	752 (1.7)	1 404 (2.6)	1 604 (2.7)	1 841 (2.6)
Other services	266 (31.4)	639 (30.5)	812 (29.9)	1 036 (31.0)	1 072 (29.2)	1 359 (29.8)	1 930 (28.6)	2 934 (27.4)	3 699 (29.3)	4 491 (29.0)	5 502 (28.9)	6 474 (28.5)	8 722 (27.2)	11 729 (25.8)	14 429 (26.7)	16 290 (27.3)	19 598 (27.5)
Gross domestic product	848 (100)	2 097 (100)	2 718 (100)	3 340 (100)	3 672 (100)	4 564 (100)	6 753 (100)	10 708 (100)	12 643 (100)	15 467 (100)	19 033 (100)	22 746 (100)	32 025 (100)	45 446 (100)	54 027 (100)	59 633 (100)	71 215 (100)

Source: Adapted from World Bank (1985b) citing BPS data

Table 2.2 Indonesia's balance of payments, 1973/74–1983/84, in US$ million

	1973/74	1974/75	1975/76	1976/77	1977/78	1978/79	1979/80	1980/81	1981/82	1982/83	1983/84
1 Net oil	641	2638	3138	3710	4352	3785	6308	9345	8379	5788	6016
2 Net LNG	—	—	—	—	93	225	667	1256	1382	1378	1355
3 Non-oil (net)	−1397	−2776	−3992	−4512	−5135	−5165	−4777	−8470	−12551	−14205	−11522
Exports (f.o.b.)	1905	2033	1873	2863	3507	3979	6171	5587	4170	3928	5367
Imports (c.i.f.)	−2938	−4341	−5090	−6167	−7241	−7543	−9028	−11837	−14561	−15824	−14346
Services (non freight)	−364	−468	−755	−1208	−1401	−1601	−1920	−2220	−2160	−2309	−2543
4 Current account (1 + 2 + 3)	−756	−138	−854	−802	−690	−1115	2198	2131	−2790	−7039	−4151
5 SDRS	—	—	—	—	—	64	65	62	—	—	—
6 Official capital (aid + loans)	643	660	1995	1823	2106	2101	2690	2684	3521	5011	5793
7 Official debt repayment (principal)	−81	−89	−77	−166	−761	−632	−692	−615	−809	−926	−1010
8 Miscellaneous capital	549	−131	−1075	38	176	392	−1315	−361	1140	1795	1191
Direct investment	331	538	454	287	285	271	217	140	142	311	193
Others	218	−669	−1529	−249	−109	121	−1523	−501	998	1484	998
9 Total (4 through 8)	355	302	−11	893	831	770	2946	3901	1062	−1159	1823

Source: Adapted from World Bank (1985b) p. 192, citing Bank Indonesia data

Table 2.3 Indonesia's exports by commodity 1975/76–1995/96, in US$ million (and as a percentage of total exports)

	1975/76	1976/77	1977/78	1978/79	1979/80	1980/81	1981/82	1982/83	1983/84	1984/85	1985/86	1986/87	1988/89	1990/91	1995/96
	Actual									Est.			Projected		
Export values at current prices															
Agriculture	1472	2347	2898	3199	5115	4273	2590	2398	3083	3229	3257	3709	4711	5950	10373
(% of total exports)	(20.2)	(25.5)	(26.7)	(28.1)	(27.6)	(18.7)	(11.3)	(12.8)	(15.6)	(16.0)	(15.7)	(16.2)	(16.0)	(16.4)	(18.1)
Metals and minerals	257	320	363	437	609	774	718	676	901	1023	1124	1207	1436	1676	2530
(% of total exports)	(3.5)	(3.5)	(3.3)	(3.8)	(3.3)	(3.4)	(3.1)	(3.6)	(4.0)	(5.1)	(5.4)	(5.3)	(4.9)	(4.6)	(4.4)
Manufactures															
—Plywood	—	—	—	—	—	—	199	324	579	660	732	842	1135	1705	4098
—Others	144	196	245	360	447	540	666	530	505	989	1403	1598	2151	3058	6886
—Subtotal manufactures	144	196	245	360	447	540	865	854	1484	1649	2135	2440	3286	4763	10984
(% of total exports)	(2.0)	(2.1)	(2.3)	(3.2)	(2.4)	(2.3)	(3.7)	(4.6)	(7.5)	(8.1)	(10.3)	(10.7)	(11.1)	(13.1)	(19.1)
Total non-oil exports	1873	2863	3506	3996	6171	5587	4173	3928	5368	5901	6516	7356	9433	12389	23887
(% of total exports)	(25.7)	(31.1)	(32.3)	(35.1)	(33.3)	(24.4)	(18.1)	(21.0)	(27.1)	(29.2)	(31.4)	(32.2)	(32.0)	(34.2)	(41.6)
Oil and products	5410	6350	7192	6858	10995	15187	16482	12283	12050	11051	10714	11769	15023	17752	22808
LNG	—	—	162	516	1345	2111	2343	2461	2399	3290	3539	3743	4997	6096	10762
Total oil and LNG	5410	6350	7354	7374	12340	17298	18825	14744	14449	14341	14253	15512	20020	23848	33570
(% of total exports)	(74.3)	(68.9)	(67.7)	(64.9)	(66.6)	(75.6)	(81.9)	(79.0)	(72.9)	(70.8)	(68.6)	(67.8)	(68.0)	(65.8)	(58.4)
Total exports	7283	9213	10860	11370	18511	22885	22998	18672	19317	20242	20769	22868	29453	36237	57457
	(100)	(100)	(100)	(100)	(100)	(100)	(100)	(100)	(100)	(100)	(100)	(100)	(100)	(100)	(100)

Source: Adapted from World Bank (1985) citing Ministry of Finance data

Table 2.4 Indonesia's central government budget summary, 1973/74–1985/86, in Rp billion

	Actual										Budget	
	1973/74	1974/75	1975/76	1976/77	1977/78	1978/79	1979/80	1980/81	1981/82	1982/83	1983/84	1984/85	1985/86
1 Domestic revenue	967.7	1753.7	2241.9	2906.0	3534.4	4266.1	6696.8	10227.0	12212.6	12418.3	14432.7	16149.4	18677.9
2 Routine expenditures[a]	713.3	1016.1	1332.6	1629.8	2148.9	2743.7	4061.8	5800.0	6977.6	6996.3	8411.8	10101.1	12399.0
3 Government saving (1–2)	254.4	737.6	909.3	1276.2	1385.5	1522.4	2635.0	4427.0	5235.0	5422.0	6020.9	6048.3	6278.9
4 Development expenditures	450.9	961.8	1397.7	2054.5	2156.8	2555.6	4014.2	5916.1	6940.0	7359.6	9899.2	10459.3	10647.0
5 Balance (3–4)	–196.5	–224.2	–488.4	–778.3	–771.3	–1033.2	–1379.2	–1489.1	–1705.0	–1937.6	–3878.3	–4411.0	–4368.1
Financed by:													
6 Counterpart funds[b]	89.8	36.1	20.2	10.2	35.8	48.2	64.8	64.1	45.1	15.1	14.9	39.5	70.9
7 Project aid	114.1	195.9	471.4	773.6	737.6	987.3	1316.3	1429.7	1663.9	1924.9	3867.5	4371.5	4297.2

Notes: [a] Includes debt-service payments
[b] Program aid
Source: World Bank (1985) citing Ministry of Finance

Table 2.5 Indonesia's central government receipts, 1973/74–1985/86, in Rp billion

	Actual											Budget	
	1973/74	1974/75	1975/76	1976/77	1977/78	1978/79	1979/80	1980/81	1981/82	1982/83	1983/84	1984/85	1985/86
Taxes on income	505.0	1228.7	1592.1	2046.6	2511.3	2996.3	5129.3	3230.3	10100.3	10009.9	11605.1	12968.3	14401.1
Corporate tax on oil	344.6	973.1	1249.1	1619.4	1948.7	2308.7	4259.6	7019.6	8627.8	8170.4	9520.2	10366.6	11159.7
(% of domestic revenue)	(35.6)	(55.5)	(55.7)	(55.8)	(55.1)	(54.1)	(63.6)	(68.3)	(70.6)	(65.8)	(66.0)	(64.2)	(59.7)
Non-oil taxes, including income and corporate tax, IPEDA and other	160.4	255.6	343.0	427.2	562.6	687.6	869.7	1210.7	1472.5	1839.5	2084.9	2601.7	3241.4
(% of domestic revenue)	(16.8)	(14.6)	(15.3)	(14.7)	(15.9)	(16.1)	(13.0)	(11.8)	(12.1)	(14.8)	(14.4)	(16.1)	(17.4)
Indirect taxes including taxes on domestic consumption and international trade	412.9	458.4	539.4	740.9	879.5	1078.4	1380.2	1681.0	1775.9	1972.8	2308.1	2566.1	3544.9
(% of domestic revenue)	(42.7)	(26.0)	(24.0)	(25.5)	(24.9)	(25.3)	(20.6)	(16.4)	(14.5)	(15.9)	(16.0)	(15.9)	(19.0)
Nontax receipt	49.8	66.6	110.4	118.5	143.6	191.4	187.3	315.7	336.4	435.6	519.5	615.0	731.9
Total domestic revenue	967.7	1753.7	2241.9	2906.0	3534.4	4266.1	6696.8	10277.0	12212.6	12418.3	14432.7	16149.4	18677.9
(% of total revenues)	(82.6)	(88.3)	(82.0)	(78.8)	(82.0)	(80.5)	(82.9)	(87.3)	(87.7)	(86.5)	(78.8)	(78.5)	(81.0)
Development Funds	203.9	232.0	491.6	783.8	773.4	1035.5	1381.1	1493.8	1709.0	1940.0	3882.4	4411.0	4368.1
(% of total revenues)	(17.4)	(11.7)	(18.0)	(21.2)	(18.0)	(19.5)	(17.1)	(12.7)	(12.3)	(13.5)	(21.2)	(21.5)	(19.0)
Total revenues	1171.6	1985.2	2733.5	3689.8	4307.8	5301.6	8077.9	11770.8	13921.6	14358.3	18315.1	20560.4	23046.0
	(100)	(100)	(100)	(100)	(100)	(100)	(100)	(100)	(100)	(100)	(100)	(100)	(100)

Source: Adapted from World Bank (1985) p. 207, citing Ministry of Finance data

prepared to allow these developments, given the fact that Pertamina was also effectively providing them with extra budgetary finance and sources of economic patronage (Crouch, 1976; McCawley, 1978; Robison, 1986).

Despite the fall of Sutowo in 1975–76 and the consequent restraint of Pertamina following disclosures of massive indebtedness, the momentum established by the availability of oil money and cheap foreign loans ensured the continuing dominance of nationalist economic policies. The forces that gave coherence to this trend were part of the military and intelligence network under the direction of General Ali Murtopo. The expanding domestic corporate conglomerates, closely tied in the centres of military bureaucratic power, including the presidential palace and the Murtopo group, were building their empires upon access to contracts, credits and monopolies made possible by state investment fuelled by oil income. Policies of state-led import substitution industrialisation had now become integral to the interests of the alliance of economic and politico-bureaucratic power.

Consequently the influence of technocrats who favoured a nationalist approach to economic planning was facilitated while that of liberal technocrats associated with the National Economic Planning Board (Bappenas) declined. With hard-line economic nationalists such as Suhartoyo and Soehoed in the Department of Industry now able to exert more influence there began a concerted move towards 'industrial deepening' and the creation of backwards and forwards linkages in manufacture designed to establish self-generating, mutually reinforcing, sectoral growth (Soehoed, 1977, 1981, 1982). This involved heavy state investment in steel and other metal industries, petrochemicals, oil refining and LNG production, fertilisers and machine tool production and the provision of infrastructure (Gray, 1982).

Although the basic aim of the industrial programme was to develop self-sufficiency with mutually reinforcing backwards and forwards linkages, a subsidiary aim was to increase the value added of production both in the ISI and EOI sectors. A primary example is the logging industry, where restrictions on the export of raw logs forced producers into wood processing, notably plywood (*Asian Wall Street Journal* (*AWSJ*), 20 June 1981, 21 July 1981). A sharp drop in the value of log exports was followed by a slow climb in the value of plywood exports, which by 1983/84 were worth US$579 million out of a total value of US$1484 million for all manufactured exports (Table 2.3). In this industry at least, the Indonesian government was able to enforce a shift in the global division of labour, moving the focus of log processing from the importing country (Japan) to the producing country (Indonesia).

At the same time, through the introduction of priority investment lists (DSP), the government reserved certain sectors, either partially or totally, for domestic investors. Foreign investors were increasingly restricted to those sectors that required special technologies and skills or large amounts of capital not available domestically, or were located in sectors with export earning potential (Rice & Hill, 1977; Suhartoyo, 1981).

In the period from 1967 to 1981/82 manufacturing value-added grew at a rate of 11.5 per cent per annum. From 1967 to 1975 this growth was essentially in relatively labour-intensive consumer goods, and the growth rate in this period, taking up a huge unfilled domestic demand, was 16.5 per cent per annum. With the ending of the easy phase in import-substitution industrialisation, the move into intermediate and capital goods, with state protection, subsidy and direct investment, provided the generator for further development. Consumer goods dropped from 80.8 per cent of total value of manufactures in 1971 to 47.6 per cent in 1980, whilst intermediate goods grew from 13.1 to 33.5 per cent and capital goods from 6.1 to 16.9 per cent in the same period (Roepstorff, 1985; World Bank, Indonesia, 1985b: 61–2). By 1982, manufacturing had grown to 12.9 per cent of gross domestic product (GDP) with a total value of Rp 7681 billion, from a base of 7.3 per cent of GDP with a value of Rp 62 billion in 1967 (Table 2.1).

The major domestic investors in the industrialisation process were the state corporations, especially in the major projects, but several important private domestic corporations also emerged in the fields of foodstuffs and beverages, textiles, cement, tyres, metal fabrication, engineering and automobiles. The rise of these private investors not only facilitated extensive state protection and subsidy but had a readymade market in the burgeoning state industrial and infrastructure projects (Robison, 1986: chs 7, 9 and 10). The state was able to provide the engine of growth through its huge investments in the face of disappointing inflows of foreign capital investment in the non-oil sector since the mid-1970s. At the same time, the extent of growth in state revenues was sufficient to enable it to provide significant inputs into the rural sector through special infrastructure projects, particularly in irrigation, and through grants to regional and local authorities for construction projects (schools, roads and bridges, hospitals). And there was no shortage of largesse at the top to be creamed off for political or private purposes by the various politico-bureaucrat factions and military commands which controlled the state apparatus (Robison, 1986: ch. 7). The politico-bureaucrats of the New Order were able to simultaneously generate broad economic growth, finance themselves politically and ignore outside calls for 'rationality' and regularisation. By the early 1980s it looked as if Indonesia was well on the way to developing a significant industrial base, despite the wastage and misuse of investments, because of the enormous avalanche of funds that

Table 2.6 Indonesia's gross domestic investment, 1974/75–1984/85, in Rp billion

	1974/75	1975/76	1976/77	1977/78	1978/79	1979/80	1980/81	1981/82	1982/83	1983/84	1984/85[a]
1 Direct government investment[b]	458	750	520	954	1249	1422	1908	3632	4223	2651	3987
2 Public enterprise investment[c]	768	1221	1346	749	989	1773	2093	2730	4143	4761	4914
3 Total public investment	1226 (68.2)	1971 (76.6)	1866 (58.2)	1703 (44.5)	2238 (47.9)	3195 (47.7)	3901 (41.1)	6362 (55.1)	8366 (64.1)	7412 (60.0)	8901
(as % of gross domestic investment)											
4 Private[d] investment	571 (31.8)	601 (23.4)	1339 (41.8)	2123 (55.5)	2433 (52.1)	3509 (52.3)	5584 (58.9)	5191 (44.9)	4690 (35.9)	4945 (40.0)	
(as % of gross domestic investment)											
Gross domestic investment	1797	2572	3205	3826	4671	6704	9485	11553	13056	12357	

Notes: [a] Preliminary figures
[b] Government savings, net foreign savings and borrowings less transfers to public enterprises
[c] Including transfers from Central Government, internal savings and domestic borrowing
[d] A residual figure: GCI minus total public investment

Sources: Adapted from World Bank analysis of the public sector capital account citing budget data, Bank Indonesia financial statistics and World Bank Debtor Reporting System (World Bank, 1985b, p. 180)

poured apparently endlessly into the economy. At the same time, the process of industrial investment and policy was specifically consolidating the power of the politico-bureaucrats and the economic position of their corporate clients.

These developments were consistently opposed in the 1970s both by international corporate interests and financial institutions that wanted access to the Indonesian market on their own terms and by domestic political forces opposed to the increasing consolidation of state power. It was not, however, until the decline of oil prices in the early 1980s that cracks began to appear in either the configuration of power or the dominance of ISI policies.

The fiscal crisis of the early 1980s

As a consequence of a substantial decline in the price of oil, Indonesia's total oil and LNG earnings rose only marginally in 1981/82 over the previous year, from US$17 298 to US$18 825 millions. In 1982/83 foreign earnings from oil dropped alarmingly to US$14 744 millions, sustaining further declines in 1983/84 to US$14 449, and in 1984/85 to US$14 341 (Table 2.3). Although improvements in non-oil export earnings were to offset this, the rapid growth in total export earnings was also brought to an abrupt halt. From a peak of US$22 998 in 1981/82 they declined to US$18 672 in 1982–83, climbing slowly to US$20 242 in 1984/85, still below the figure of 1980/81.

Consequently, Indonesia's balance of payments were thrown into some disarray. From current account surpluses in 1979/80 and 1980/81 of over US$2 billion, the current accounts fell into *deficits* of US$2790 million in 1981/82, US$7039 million in 1982/83 and US$4151 million in 1983/84 (Table 2.2). Although the deficits were cushioned by healthy foreign assets which had recovered to US$10 billion by 1984/85, Indonesia was nevertheless forced to call on more foreign loans. Between 1982/83 and 1984/85 external capital requirements averaged US$6.2 billion per year, US$4.3 billion of which was raised each year through public medium-term and long-term loans and credits. By 1984 Indonesia's total disbursed and outstanding debts stood at US$28.4 billion, with a debt service ratio of 21.1 per cent (Table 2.7).

The effect of the decline in oil prices on state revenues was also serious. Oil and LNG tax revenues remained fairly static between 1981/82 and 1982/83 at just over Rp 8000 billion, but due to improved performance from LNG they climbed again to an estimated Rp 10 366 billion in 1984/85 (Table 2.5). Expenditure on the major resource and industrial projects had been predicated upon the continuing exponential growth in oil revenues. A budget deficit of Rp 1705 billion was

Table 2.7 Indonesia's disbursed and outstanding medium- and long-term debt in US$ billion at current prices

	1981	1984	1990 (projected)
Public debt	15.9	24.6	41.4
Private debt	3.6	3.8	5.5
Total	19.5	28.4	46.9
Debt service ratio	10.4%	21.1%	23.8%

Source: World Bank (1985) p. 59.

incurred in 1981/82, Rp 1938 billion in 1982/83, Rp 3878 billion in 1983/84, and a deficit of Rp 441 billion was expected in 1984/85 (Table 2.4).

Combined with these fiscal difficulties, market contraction (both domestically and internationally) hit domestic manufacturers whose investments had presupposed continuing market growth, particularly from the state. For example, production capacity in cement rose from 5.8 million tons in 1980 to an expected 17.4 million tons in 1985, but expected domestic sales were only 10 million tons. In tyres, production capacity rose from 2.7 million units in 1978 to an expected 6.7 million units in 1985, but domestic demand was expected to be only about 4 million units. Other industries in the same situation include a wide range of consumer durables, notably automobiles and home electronic products (*FEER*, 20 January 1983; World Bank, Indonesia, 1985b: 7–8).

Responses to the crisis

The 1981 World Bank report, Indonesia, came at a time when the crisis was becoming apparent, and it was this combined with the critical nature of some of its prescriptions that made it a contentious and influential document. In general, the World Bank's response to the Indonesian situation in this and subsequent reports was similar to its response throughout the Third World, urging fiscal constraint and free markets. To balance the budget, the World Bank argued for the removal of extensive fuel and food subsidies and the immediate development of domestic revenue sources to replace declining oil taxes. It also called for a reduction in state investment in large resource and industrial projects. This latter recommendation was intended not only to ease fiscal pressure upon the state but also to correct what it regarded as an irrational pattern of investment and an inappropriate industrial strategy. According to the principles of comparative advantage, World Bank officials urged that the Indonesian economy be allowed to respond to the free operation of the international division of labour. Removal of state subsidies and protection would, it was argued, make way for the replacement of inefficient and costly industries such as automobile manufacture and steel production, by internationally competitive industries able to compete effectively on world markets. In conjunction with this change in strategy it was also necessary, according to the World Bank, to open Indonesia to unfettered investment by international capital (World Bank, 1981, 1984a, 1985b; *AWSJ*, 28 April 1981; *FEER*, 29 May 1981, 2 June 1983, 17 May 1984, 16 May 1985).

The Indonesian government's immediate response to the report was one of irritation. It was felt that the World Bank had not fully appreciated the social and political problems faced by the government and had taken no account of social and political objectives which must necessarily be built into economic strategy (*FEER*, 29 May 1981). At the broadest level of economic strategy the most powerful figures in the key departments—Industry (Hartato), State Secretariat (Sudharmono), the Capital Investment Board (Ginadjar Kartasasmita) and Research and Technology (Habibie)—were all to argue that real development could take place only on a firm basis of investment in capital, intermediate and even high-technology manufacture, which could be generated only by deliberate state intervention and would not be produced by free operation of an international marketplace in reality dominated by transnational corporations (Habibie, 1983; Hartato, 1985; *Kompas*, 24 August 1985).

However, the fate of Indonesia's economic strategy in the face of the oil price crisis was not to be determined by intellectual debate over the various merits of competing theories on the part of technocrats and economists. Rather the conflict has hinged upon the determination of vested political, bureaucratic and economic interests to resist pressures for change in the status quo brought about by declining oil income and general recession. A crucial factor in the struggle has been the degree to which the edifice of political and economic power vested in the existing structures and policies can be maintained in the face of structural pressures. How much of the existing system can be dismantled without causing fundamental damage to the regime and its social and economic base? How many of the peripheral elements of the power structure can be abandoned without bringing down the regime itself? On the other hand, the powerholders are forced to consider the consequences of doing nothing given the crisis in revenue collection and foreign earnings. With each policy decision the immediate political and social interests of the various elements of the ruling group compete with the need to maintain the viability of the broad economic framework in which their dominance is embedded at a more general level. In other words, as will be demonstrated later, contradictions began to develop in some instances between continued economic growth and the political and economic interests of the dominant forces.

Reformist moves

Reforms that had long been urged by the World Bank began to be adopted in the 1980s because the increasing fiscal difficulties of the Indonesian state and the deterioration of the trade balance made urgent action unavoidable. In 1983 the government instituted a devaluation of 27.6 per cent to boost non-oil exports, which had flagged since the previous devaluation of 33.6 per cent in 1978 (*AWSJ*, 4 April 1983; *FEER*, 14 April 1983). Various export incentives were introduced, and a counter-purchase scheme was initiated requiring foreign firms obtaining domestic government contracts in excess of Rp 500 million to purchase and export from Indonesia goods to the value of those imported under the terms of the contract. This last measure was a tactic that certainly did not please the World Bank or, particularly, the foreign companies forced to purchase the Indonesian goods (*AWSJ*, 11 and 14 December 1981; *Indonesian Commercial Newsletter* (*ICN*), 23 August 1982).

To reduce government expenditures, subsidies to basic food items and fuel to the value of Rp 608 billion were slashed in the 1982/83 budget and have been progressively reduced in subsequent budgets (Dick, 1982). Most important, it was announced in May 1983 that forty-eight large existing and planned public-sector project investments with a value of US$20 billion would be shelved, rephased or cancelled (*FEER*, 26 May and 4 August 1983).

To generate domestic sources of state revenue the government instituted changes in personal income and corporate taxes in 1983 and introduced a value-added tax (VAT) in 1985. As mentioned earlier these items had always constituted a disproportionately small part of domestic revenues. Personal income tax, for example, had slowly dwindled from 6.5 per cent of total revenues in 1968 to 2.9 per cent in 1983/84 (*FEER*, 1 December 1983; Rahardjo, 1985; Sjahrir, 1985a). To increase the potential for domestic capital accumulation it was announced in June 1983 that credit ceilings and interest rates imposed on private banks would be removed (Arndt, 1983: 23, 24; Booth, 1984: 12–17; *FEER*, 22 September 1983).

All of these moves, however outwardly benign, held implications for the structure of social and political power. Rapid price rises followed the removal of subsidies and constituted a potential threat to social stability particularly in the burgeoning cities. Introduction of new taxes held implications not only for those to be taxed, and for the general willingness of capitalists to invest, but also for the Department of Taxation and its officials—long considered a department where fortunes could be made. It would be necessary to impose rule of regulation and procedure in the Department of Taxation if the reforms were to succeed, thereby making inroads into the dominance of officials over the apparatus of the state. Finally, deregulation of the banking sector (which, incidentally, led initially to a surge of interest rates and hence a rush to deposit rather than borrow) restricted the degree of control over loan funds and their dispersal that could previously be exerted by officials through Bank Indonesia (Booth, 1984: 12). In some cases, reform required direct assaults upon the bastions of vested interests, and such assaults were indeed made in the cases of the state oil company, Pertamina, and the Department of Customs and Excise.

As mentioned earlier, Pertamina had long been the major source of extra budgetary funds for the military and various political factions, as well as a source of personal funds for individual officials, and for development projects beyond those funded by the normal development budget. Conflict between the various political appanage holders who controlled Pertamina and the technocrats who sought to make the oil giant more efficient and accountable has been a feature of the New Order period. The technocrats gained the upper hand in their long struggle to make Ibnu Sutowo accountable when in 1975 Pertamina was found to have debts totalling $10.4 billion largely as a result of its forays into financing industrial projects. Although the technocrats managed to divest Pertamina of its industrial holdings, they then lost control in the late 1970s as oil prices soared. But the decline in oil prices in the early 1980s once again reversed the balance, because continued expropriation and wastage of its resources now posed a direct threat to the state's major source of revenue and the country's major source of foreign earnings. With far less ability to absorb the impact of inefficiency and corruption, Pertamina was also faced with the new difficulty of competing for East Asian markets with newly available Chinese crude oil. To this was added the need to realise the vast sums ploughed into the refineries by successfully selling oil products overseas in competition with Singaporean and Middle Eastern refineries and by providing low-cost products for the domestic market.

The government's response reflected the urgency of the situation. Between 1982 and 1983, the board of directors, dominated by the technocrats Subroto, Sumarlin, Prawiro, Habibie and Secretary of State Sudharmono, gradually restricted the financial autonomy of the president-director, Judo Sumbono, and imposed more stringent accountability. In April 1983 three task forces were appointed to examine marketing, refining and auditing (*FEER*, 5 July 1984). Finally, in June 1984, Judo Sumbono was replaced as president-director two years before his term expired (Jufri, 1984). Given his political connections it was a remarkable step but one strongly indicating that, in the current oil price crisis, the vested interests of politico-bureaucrats and the long-term viability of the oil sector are becoming increasingly incompatible and that President Suharto has been forced to move against the interests of the former.

Under Sumbono's successor, General Ramly, pressures to extend efficiency and accountability have been maintained, led by a bevy of international accounting firms engaged to overhaul Pertamina's accounting and auditing procedures. A remaining challenge, however, involves regularisation of marketing procedures and channels. Under Sumbono several private oil traders had been given opportunities to market Pertamina crude allegedly sold to them at a discount as a means of bypassing OPEC minimum prices. To restore discipline, and hence Pertamina's strength in the marketplace, the ability of these companies to obtain and dump cheap Indonesian crudes, particularly in Japan, had to be halted. Given the political connections of some of them, this meant a very immediate test of the government's determination to regularise the oil industry (*FEER*, 19 July 1984 and 24 March 1985).

Perhaps the radical changes to customs and excise procedures embodied in Presidential Instruction No. 4 of 1985 (Inpres 4/85) most clearly illustrate the conflict between the interests of the politico-bureaucrats and structural pressures emanating from the economic crisis. Customs has been a department notorious for corruption, and the passage of goods through the godowns of the port of Tanjung Priok has long been an expensive and frustrating procedure. Jobs in the Department of Customs are renowned as lucrative posts. However, the persistence of corruption here has taken on a new dimension in the wake of the oil price crisis. As pointed out earlier it became essential for Indonesia to replace oil with non-oil exports. Unfortunately, Indonesian goods, despite low wages, were not low-cost goods. Part of the blame for this can be attributed to the high cost of moving imports and exports through the wharves in Indonesia (Sjahrir, 1985a) The centres of political power were sufficiently alarmed at the seriousness of the situation to adjudge the vested interests of the customs officials and their value as political clients less crucial than the threat their activities now posed to the economy as a whole. Finance Minister Radius Prawiro temporarily took charge of Customs, appointing a Swiss firm, Société Générale de Surveillance, to handle inspections and assessments and transferring collection of import duties to foreign exchange banks (*FEER*, 25 April 1985). Whilst there is often a gap between policy and implementation, Inpres 4 has the potential to divest customs officials of significant autonomous power over the movement of goods, to remove the competitive edge of politically well-connected companies at the waterfront and to save importers what has been an estimated US$200 million in bribes each year (*FEER*, 25 April 1985).

Inpres 4 is a fascinating and significant development. It expresses the willingness of the state to sacrifice whole sections of the web of patronage and expropriation that constitute politico-bureaucratic power under the New Order where these interests pose fundamental threats to the broader economic fabric. The questions to be resolved over the next year or two are whether these reforms will prevail and how far into the heart of politico-bureaucrat power will the reformers be able to pentrate? Will the need for the development of a domestic tax base, for example, mean that similar regularising procedures will be introduced in the tax-collecting apparatus?

Resistance to structural change

One of the major concerns noted in World Bank reports has been the proliferation of protected high-cost industries which produce expensive goods for domestic consumers and prevent Indonesia competing in world markets. In particular, the reports have pointed to areas where negative value added is produced, i.e. sectors where it would be cheaper to import than to produce in Indonesia. This category includes much of the high-technology production under Habibie's control as well as the more-established ISI producers in automobiles, motor-cycles, television and other electrical products, glass, tyres and various metal engineering products (Gray, 1982; World Bank, Indonesia, 1984a: 101; World Bank, Indonesia, 1985b: 66–71).

The 1984 report listed the following implicit subsidies to domestic producers:

Portland cement	US$156.8 million
Colour TV	US$ 43.6 million
Kraft paper	US$ 1.8 million
Synthetic yarn	US$ 24.6 million
Steel billets	US$ 74.8 million

In the 1985 report, the World Bank added more examples to the list:

Motor-cycles	Rp 53.2 billion
Cosmetics	Rp 67.1 billion
Motor vehicles	Rp 134.4 billion
Glass	Rp 37.5 billion
Sugar	Rp 137.6 billion

But opening these sectors to free international competition by removing quotas, protective tariffs and other constraints is no easy task.

Many such industries, notably steel, petrochemicals, engineering and automobiles are the key elements in the long-term strategy to create a nationally integrated and industrially based economy. It is also precisely in the negative value added industries that so many of the major domestic business groups are located and flourish under the protection of politico-bureaucrats and within the monopoly positions made possible by these political patrons. Hence a fundamental assault on the policies of protection and the network of monopoly and privilege in these sectors would threaten the corporate base of social and economic power which the leaders of the New Order have built for themselves over the past twenty years. Further considerations not generally taken into account by the World Bank are that removal of subsidies and protection offers the prospect of widespread collapse amongst existing industries, and it is justified only by an abstract hope that these would be replaced by flourishing and competitive industries in largely unspecified sectors. There is, of course, no guarantee that any Indonesian industry would flourish in a free-market situation, making major deregulation a risk that can be taken neither by domestic capitalists (including the generals amongst their number) nor by Indonesian policymakers. These considerations are quite apart from the likely catastrophic effect on existing patterns of employment and subcontracting, an effect that also has implications for political order.

World Bank recommendations included not only withdrawal from a protective trade regime but also the ending of discrimination between categories of investors at the corporate level. Despite some progress in tariff reduction, restrictions on certain categories of imports are actually being extended (World Bank, Indonesia, 1985b: 63). Requirements that foreign investors include a minimum of domestic equity remain intact, and the priority investment lists (DSP) continue to exclude foreign investors from a range of sectors, notably some of the still-lucrative import-substitution areas. Two fairly recent developments have, in fact, made further assaults upon free trade and equal treatment of domestic and foreign investors. The government's counter-purchase policy of 1982 (noted earlier) represented a technique to boost exports totally contrary to notions of comparative advantage and relying entirely upon the exercise of state power.

The state also took measures to ensure that domestic capital received a share of the substantial contracts for supply and construction generated by state project investments. The bulk of state project expenditure, it must be remembered, is comprised of imports. Under the requirements of Presidential Decision Keppres 14 and 14a of 1979 and 1980, Keppres 10 of 1980, and Keppres 29 and 30 of 1984, all state expenditures on projects in excess of Rp 500 million are scrutinised by a State Procurement Team under the authority of the State Secretariat and headed by Ginanjar Kartasasmita, Chairman of the Capital Investment Board and Junior Minister for the Promotion of the Use of Domestic Products. The provisions of the various Keppres require the State Procurement Team to give preference to domestic and indigenous producers for smaller orders and contracts (Daroesman, 1981: 15-16).

Whilst lauding free trade in principle, Ginanjar has explained the activities of the State Procurement Term as virtually an act of self-defence in the face of growing protectionist tendencies in world trade and the growing practice of dumping by multinational corporations. In any case, he noted, of the total of US$20 billion of projects processed by the team, US$413 billion were imported inputs (*FEER*, 10 May 1984: 72, 73). Of course, at a political level the Keppres 14, 14a and 10 give the State Procurement Board a strategic position at the interface between state and capital and therefore vest significant power in the State Secretariat, power that would be hard to wrest from it.

At another level the state appears determined to continue with the general thrust of investment policy towards the creation of capital and intermediate goods industries in contradiction to notions of comparative advantage. There are several concrete examples of the strength of this commitment, perhaps the most crucial being that of Krakatau Steel. Krakatau was begun in the early 1960s with Soviet assistance, revived by Sutowo in the early 1970s and completed in the late 1970s with a direct reduction plant, a billet plant and various downstream mills producing wire rods, bars, sections and hot strip slabs (Arndt, 1975). Reportedly, Krakatau lost about Rp 250 billion between 1977 and 1980 and had invested US$3.79 billion by the end of its current programme of investment. Reportedly Krakatau's liabilities to commercial banks had reached Rp 962 billion by the end of 1982 (*FEER*, 23 June 1983: 60-2).

In addition to pumping huge amounts of state money into the Krakatau complex, the state has moved to ensure Krakatau's position in the domestic steel market against potential competition from cheaper imports by giving Krakatau and other state trading companies the monopoly on the import of similar steel products. Consequently, the state is the sole importer of scrap, billets, wire rods, hot strip coils and sheets and is able to control the price and extent of these imports.

The most recent Krakatau initiative is a projected US$800 million cold rolling mill, a joint venture between Krakatau (40%), the Ciputra group (20%) and Liem Sioe Liong (40%). Equity participation will constitute 30 per cent of investment, whilst export credits and commercial loans will constitute the remaining 70 per cent. The participation of private investors is interesting, appearing to demonstrate the viability of the government's expectation that domestic private capital would play a much greater role in major investments in Repelita IV (the fourth five-year plan, 1984/85–1988/89). However, the movement of private capital, notably that of the Liem Sioe Liong group, into the notoriously inefficient steel industry must be understood in the broader context of Liem's corporate activities, which are heavily based upon government-conferred monopolies and special preferences (Robison, 1986: ch. 9). It would appear that the government agreed to minimise his risks by giving him the monopoly on the import of cold rolled steel products, thus enabling him to secure major profits on these imports before the mill began as well as control of prices in the domestic market afterwards (Hill, 1984a: 18).

Whilst Krakatau may be a millstone inherited by the government and one that it is politically difficult to unload, the government's decision to throw its resources behind the development of the strategic industries programme designed by the Agency for the Assessment and Application of Technology (BPPT), under Research and Technology Minister Habibie, is a new and calculated venture running contrary to both the notion of comparative advantage and the pressures for restructuring, emerging from the realignment of the international division of labour. What is more remarkable, the development of strategic industries is being prosecuted in the face of the state's declining capacity to invest.

Habibie has consistently argued that the capacity to develop and produce technology is essential for successful industrialisation. With the strong support of the president, he has established two major technology ventures in shipbuilding at Surabaya (PAL) and aircraft at Bandung (Nurtanio). In both cases large amounts of investment capital continue to be made available despite the large cutbacks announced in other industrial projects. Capital investment in Nurtanio is estimated by some sources to be US$250 million (Hill, 1984a: 20). Nurtanio manufactures aircraft (the CN 235) under licence to the Spanish company CASA, while PAL manufactures various types of ships, from tankers to patrol boats and hydrofoils, in agreements with foreign manufacturers. Despite Habibie's claims that operations have so far been profitable there is significant doubt not only about the mechanics of his calculations but also about the long-term viability of the projects. Overseas sales have been disappointing, and sales have largely been confined to domestic purchases by the armed forces, the state-owned airlines and Pertamina (Hill 1984b: 54, 55).

Perhaps the best recent illustration of how the state has sought to generate the development of its heavy and technological industries through policies of backwards and forwards linkages has been its strategy to reconstruct the shipping industry. To stimulate the shipbuilding industry the Department of Sea Communications, under the director-generalship of Habibie's brother, ordered the scrapping of all Indonesian-owned ships over thirty years old by May 1984 and ships over twenty-five years by January 1985. Further, it was required that the ships be scrapped in government-designated yards and sold to Krakatau Steel at fixed prices, considerably below the going international rate (*FEER*, 8 November 1984: 68). To replace these vessels, the companies were required to purchase Caraka Raya class vessels designed by BPPT, PAL (the state shipyard headed by Minister Habibie) and a Japanese partner—vessels built in Indonesian shipyards using Krakatau steel and other domestic inputs. The state shipyard, PAL, already building naval vessels and tankers for Pertamina, was expected to receive the bulk of the orders. Whilst shipbuilding is an attractive industry because of its labour-absorption potential and the linkages it offers, particularly with Krakatau, it is likely to produce expensive ships for the foreseeable future given the high costs of domestic inputs. Preliminary estimates include a price three to four times that of the most logical alternative replacements: used Japanese ships about three to seven years old. Foreign observers also doubt the technical and managerial capacities of the Indonesians in this field (*FEER*, 8 November 1984: 70).

Both the ship and aircraft industries are examples of the government's continuing preparedness to intervene in the marketplace through regulation and direct investment, to create a domestic industrial network in the face of market forces. It is continuing evidence that the political leaders of the New Order remain committed to the creation of an integrated industrial base and their continued scepticism of the long-term benefits of free market and comparative advantage policies urged by the World Bank.

A further example of the operation of this sort of industrial policy is the automobile industry. This industry had long been based around the sole agency—a monopoly to import particular automobile makes—in effect allocated by the government to well-connected corporate groups through the Ministry of Industry. Under Sukarno, such businessmen as Hashim Ning, Dasaad, Panggabean and Surwarma and the state company, Gaya, held import and assembly licences. With the rise of the New Order, new monopoly-holders were to include Sutowo, Wahab Affan, Willem Soerjadjaja, Liem Sioe Liong and Probosutejo, the president's brother (Robison, 1986: ch. 3). But the government began a programme in the 1970s to move beyond import and assembly to local content manufacture. Higher local content requirements combined with quotas and tariffs gave rise to a greater degree of local manufacture as well as a thriving domestic components industry. In 1982 the government had consolidated and rationalised the industry by reducing the number of participating firms and requiring that the major groups move into engine manufacture. Six new engine plants are being established involving Toyota, Daihatsu, Mitsubishi, Isuzu, Daimler

Benz, Sumitomo and their local partners (*ICN*, 14 September 1981 and 10 January 1983). It is a move that has been seen by most foreign observers as likely to produce yet another high-cost, and eventually, state-subsidised industry (Gray, 1982; Hill, 1984a) and by at least one of the Indonesian businessmen involved as not being the preferred commercial choice at this stage (Astbury, 1982: 21).

Long-term prospects for resistance to structural change

Despite enforced moves to develop domestic revenue sources, to cut back on public project investment and to begin a drive for efficiency and regular practices in some state corporations and departments, the Indonesian government has not yet been forced to surrender fundamental principles of economic nationalism or to dismantle the basic structure of politico-bureaucratic power. Economic strategy remains geared to creating a nationally integrated, industrially based economy rather than an economy structurally responsive to capital investment flows and division of labour operating at the international level. The state still occupies the commanding heights of the economy both as an investor and as a regulator. Within the state corporations the politico-bureaucrats continue to exercise ultimate authority, channelling state–capital relationships through themselves and the holders of appropriated state power.

In the long term, however, the capacity to avoid further and more fundamental change depends upon the future course of the oil market and the success of measures already introduced to alleviate the impact of oil price declines. This throws the spotlight on the effectiveness of such measures as Inpres 4/85, the drive to develop manufactured exports, the drive to develop a domestic tax base and to develop sources of domestic investment capital to supplement state investment.

The question of export earnings

After the dramatic slump in oil production and foreign exchange earnings in 1982/83 (discussed earlier), the trajectory of the decline, in real dollar terms, levelled off and was expected by the World Bank report of 1985 and Indonesian government sources to climb slowly again in the late 1980s and early 1990s (World Bank, 1985b: 33–9). Nevertheless, the relative position of oil as a foreign exchange earner was not expected to regain the dominance it held in the 1970s. Total production would flatten out, the domestic market would soak up an increasing amount of the production, while competition from the new Chinese crude for the Asian markets would place further pressure on sellers. It is already reported that Japan has cut back purchases of

Indonesian oil, forcing Indonesia to become even more active in the spot oil market, selling at prices lower than those on which income projections were calculated (*FEER*, 8 August 1985: 44, 45). In early 1986 the breakdown of OPEC pricing policies precipitated a further dramatic decline in the price of oil from about $28 per barrel to as low as $12 per barrel. The consequences of this are so devastating that they throw into disarray calculations and predictions made to this date and which, in the case of the World Bank, were based on a steady recovery in oil prices.

The drop in oil earnings from $16.4 to $12.2 billion in 1982/83 left a massive $7 billion current account deficit. Further damage was minimised by a significant rise of 37 per cent in non-oil exports in 1983/84 including an 80 per cent increase in manufactured exports (Table 2.3). Rises in non oil exports continued in 1984/85, including 15 per cent in manufactures. Total non-oil exports rose from 18 per cent of total exports in 1982 to 27 per cent in 1984. The balance of payments situation was also helped considerably by an 18 per cent decline in imports in 1983/84 and 1984/85 due to the government's project rephasing, failure to implement planned expenditures, increased restrictions on imports and strong performances in the agricultural sector (McCawley, 1985: 11–12; World Bank, 1985b: 20–1, 50–2).

As a consequence, the current account deficit was reduced to $4.2 billion in 1983/84 and $1.9 billion in 1984/85. Net foreign assets were expected to increase to $9.9 billion. Projections of recovery beyond the mid-1980s were heavily predicated upon expected increases in the value of manufactured exports at the rate of 100 per cent for the period 1984/85 to 1988/89 and a further 200 per cent between 1988/89 and 1995/96 to $11 billion, or 20 per cent of total export value (World Bank, Indonesia, 1985b: 173–5).

Yet there are serious doubts about the future of Indonesia as an exporter of manufactures. It must be remembered that manufactures still comprise just 8 per cent of the total value of exports (US$1.65 billion) while manufacturing contributed only 15 per cent of GDP in 1983, well below Thailand (21%) and Malaysia (18%) (Hill, 1984a: 8). Much of the growth in non-oil exports in 1984/85 came from a $900 million surge in LNG, while manufactured exports have been dominated by the growth of plywood production (Table 2.3). The value of textile exports increased from $180 million in 1982/83 to $500 million in 1984/85 but these have now reached the level where they are beginning to encounter protectionist barriers (McCawley, 1985: 12; World Bank, 1985b: 18, 52).

Despite low wage-labour costs the exported manufactures from Indonesia find difficulty in competing on the international markets because total production costs are generally higher than their competitors. This is due to a combination of factors, among them a low capital output ratio, poor infrastructure, wastage and the depredations of politico-bureaucrats and minor officials. As the urgency for non-oil exports has increased, so has the debate on Indonesia's high-cost economy come to the fore. In June 1985 the issue was first systematically and publicly debated in *Sinar Harapan* (24, 25 and 26 June 1985), but the most forceful attack came from Professor Sumitro, former minister in various economic portfolios in the 1950s, the late 1960s and early 1970s and architect of much of Indonesia's thinking on industrial strategy. In an address reported in *Kompas* (23 and 24 August 1985) he argued that import tariffs, import quotas and controls on investment, applied in an ad hoc and arbitrary manner, were creating and propping up inefficient, high-cost industries and preventing innovation and movement into areas where a more defined comparative advantage existed. Not only did this result in failure to compete on international markets, Sumitro argued, but it resulted in a saturation of the domestic market with expensive goods, effectively depressing real income levels.

However, the move out of the 'high-cost economy' from ISI to EOI is not a simple matter. It does not simply involve better management and production organisation, the development of infrastructure and the more effective application of technology, as difficult as that may be. It means nothing less than fundamental changes to the economic base of political and corporate power and a major challenge to the prevailing nationalist ideologies and strategies which underpin such power.

To begin with, as a consequence of decades of nationalist economic policies, the bulk of investment in manufacturing, both state and private, is located in sectors where there is little chance for export competitiveness: steel, petrochemicals, automobiles, shipbuilding, TVs, tyres, cement and glass, indeed in the very areas identified by the World Bank as being the worst examples of negative value added production. These industries were never intended to produce export goods but, rather, to form the core of an integrated national industrial economy. This commitment continues to be the central theme in economic strategy. The government's major economic spokesmen, including Habibie, Ginanjar and Hartato, defended the long-term efficacy of protectionist strategies, citing the examples of South Korea and Meiji Japan as countries that successfully used protectionist policies as an instrument for industrialisation. They also criticised the notion that free-trade policies would lead to a more efficient Indonesian export sector or, indeed, would result in anything but the obliteration of Indonesian industry at the hands of international cartels of state and private corporate capital dumping goods in the Indonesian market (*FEER*, 10 May 1984. 72, 73; *Kompas*, 24 August 1985).

The arguments are, so far as they go, powerful ones. The 'free market' and 'free trade' are utopian abstractions at the best of times, and successful exporting has been quite demonstrably related to the international collusion of state and capital in a way that certainly does not approximate the free-market, free-trade ideals of neo-classical economists. But none of this answers the immediate problem of Indonesia: to rapidly generate large foreign earnings from the export of manufactured goods.

Theoretically there is no reason why international competitiveness in particular industries cannot be nurtured behind walls of tariff protection. Comparative advantage is not an enduring natural phenomenon; it is the creation of people, as the Japanese have so clearly demonstrated in the steel industry, in shipbuilding and more recently in computers. This is precisely the case argued by Ginanjar and others. But the critics are asking how long this process takes (*Kompas*, 9 April 1985). In the case of Indonesia, there is little evidence to suggest that progress is being made behind the protective walls to produce efficient competitive industries able to storm the markets of the world let alone compete with foreign products in the domestic market. Protection has tended to be regarded and used as a permanent structural feature and not a temporary policy expedient.

Nevertheless, policy continues to reinforce and perpetuate inward-looking industries. As described earlier, various types of tariff protection and import monopolies protect Krakatau Steel, Pertamina and other state corporations, as well as a whole variety of private corporations involved in capital and consumer goods production, from import competition. Despite the government's announced tariff reductions in March 1985, it continues to give strong protection to a variety of industries, perhaps best illustrated by its attempts to build an integrated automobile industry in Indonesia through import controls and deletion programmes (*FEER*, 8 December 1983: 82, 83; *ICN*, 14 September 1981, 10 January 1983; World Bank, 1985b: 63).

The continuation of such policies is not simply the consequence of an ideological attachment to economic nationalism. Both the state and private domestic capital in Indonesia are also committed to maintaining the ISI structures simply because this is where bulk of the assets, the investments and property is located. Enormous corporate entities, both state and private, have been constructed within the framework of protectionist policies and political patronage, the termination of which would threaten the whole edifice of capital ownership. Nor is it a simple matter to shift direction. Moving out of the ISI sector would be feasible only if existing assets could be realised and reinvested in new export-oriented industries. But in a catch-22 situation, cement plants or automobile factories would be worth little on the Indonesian market without a long-term guaranteed framework of protectionist policies.

As a result, the bulk of the manufacturing sector in Indonesia is not only located in the ISI sector but is locked there. Moreover, those with interests vested in ISI are politically well able to resist pressures for their demise because they are not simply an isolated and politically weak national bourgeoisie but are comprised of officials and their clients, a crucial and constituent element in that fusion of political, bureaucratic and economic power that dominates Indonesia under the New Order. State corporate managers preside over corporations that are not only instruments of economic nationalist policy but have been major terminals of revenue, influence and patronage for politico-bureaucrat power-holders. Private capitalists have constructed corporate empires upon monopolies and concessions provided by political patrons, who increasingly are integrated with their corporate clients as shareholders or directors. Consequently, state protection and intervention represent the exercise of state power by politico-bureaucrats to secure their own financial interests as politico-bureaucrats, state managers of capital and private capitalists. It is these linkages, between particular centres of power and individual companies rather than simply between state and capital, that reinforce the influence of ISI capitalists and give rise to the patterns of arbitrary and ad hoc application of protection referred to by Sumitro.

The high cost of production in Indonesia is also a consequence of the particular nature of the relationship between politico-bureaucrats, the state apparatus and capital. The maze of regulations which govern the operation of capital in Indonesia are a mechanism by which politico-bureaucrats, as appropriators of state power, are able to extract extra-legal payments from companies or ensure a privileged position for their own or their clients' companies. Naturally these impose a high cost in extra-legal payments, free equity and directorships and in uncertainty and unpredictability. But to deregulate, to simplify the labyrinth of import and export licences, exploitation concessions, procedures for government contracts and investment would remove a set of strictures and mechanisms through which politico-bureaucrats exercise their economic and political domination. Such a set of relationships would find an open-door EOI system a much less fertile environment.

Consequently the dispute between the domestic critics of protectionist policies and the high-cost economy and their defenders is very much a political one. But whilst it is a political one, it is not one the critics are able to win politically because they, as mainly technocrats and researchers, do not have an independent power base. Their influence derives from their function as economic managers, but their authority is held at the discretion of the politico-bureaucrat power-holders. They exist to manage an economic structure in which, as the 'bottom line', the interests of the politico-bureaucrats and their corporate clients must be guaranteed. Their capacity to erode some of these structures becomes effective only at times when broader fiscal and economic crises force compromises and adjustments. This is not to suggest that all technocrats are advocates of open-door, free-market policies. Whilst this has tended to be true of those associated with the National Economic Planning Board (Bappenas) and the University of Indonesia, a powerful technocrat lobby group centred in the State Secretariat and the Ministry of Research and Technology are propagators of integrated national industrialisation strategies.

The key to any switch to export promotion strategies lies, therefore, in the direction of new investments into this sector. With manufacturers facing difficulties in a saturated market and the state no longer able to provide guarantees of lucrative profits through subsidies and monopolies, there are certainly pressures to restructure, but whether the liquid assets are there to respond to these pressures and whether they would necessarily be invested in Indonesia is doubtful. The problem of investment will be discussed in the next section.

The revenue crisis of the state

Declines in oil revenues in 1981/82 and 1982/83 led to a budget deficit of Rp 3882 billion (almost Rp 3.9 trillion) in 1983/84 and an expected Rp 4.4 billion in 1984/85. Together with appropriate foreign borrowing, the deficits have been kept under control due largely to an increase in LNG revenues, an increase of 12 per cent in non-oil revenues, further reductions in subsidies and government investments and failure to implement projected investments (Tables 2.4 and 2.5). The success achieved in fiscal management so far and the basis of projections for long-term rehabilitation of the revenue situation are heavily reliant on three factors: the development of non-oil domestic taxes, the increased role of overseas loans and restraint in government expenditure. This whole process now becomes at once more urgent and more difficult in the wake of the dramatic second round of oil price collapses in 1986.

The 1985/86 budget projects a decline of oil and LNG revenues from Rp 12.4 trillion to Rp 11.2 trillion but an overall rise in total revenue from Rp 17.9 trillion to Rp 18.7 trillion to come from a nominal 36 per cent increase in non-oil revenues, a third of which is to be generated by new value-added tax. Rp 777 billion is expected to be collected from taxes on domestic manufacture. Individual and corporate taxes are also expected to rise 40 per cent (World Bank, 1985b: 16). This places a great deal of reliance on the immediate effectiveness of the VAT programme and the buoyancy of hard-pressed domestic manufacturers. This is not to say that businesses and individuals did

After the gold rush 45

not pay taxes before; they did, but largely to the politico-bureaucrats through extra-legal arrangements. The problem now is that the state needs these taxes. This therefore requires the creation of a modern, efficient and regularised tax collection service: a further erosion of politico-burcaucrat power and a further example of the contradictions inherent in the policy options forced upon the New Order.

A second element in the government's revenue strategy has been the increased importance of foreign loans. Revenue from this source has increased from 12.3 per cent of total revenue in 1981/82 to 21.2 per cent in 1983/84 (Table 2.5). The World Bank expected that over the next three years Indonesia would require gross annual disbursements of medium- and long-term loans of US$5.5 billion (World Bank, 1985b: 54). Even before the second round of oil price collapses, disbursed and outstanding medium- and long-term debt was expected to rise from US$19.5 billion in 1981 and US$28.4 billion in 1984 to an estimated US$46 billion in 1990, with a debt service ratio of 23.8 per cent (World Bank, 1985b: 59). This in itself is not a dangerous situation and, given existing circumstances, the foreign borrowing programme does not threaten for Indonesia the same sort of fate that has befallen Brazil, Mexico, Argentina or Poland. Nevertheless foreign loans are a limited long-term solution because aid receipts are increasingly disbursed in debt servicing. McCawley estimated that in Indonesia foreign aid receipts net of repayments would begin to fall rapidly in 1985/86; foreign debt repayments would rise 32 per cent in 1985/86 from Rp 2.7 billion to Rp 3.6 billion, while net receipts would fall from Rp 1.7 trillion in 1984/85 to Rp 0.8 trillion in 1985/86 (McCawley, 1985: 18).

The third major element of fiscal policy aimed at controlling the deficit has been restraint in government expenditure. Initially the government attempted to contain this within the routine budget, focusing upon the reduction of subsidies. However, as mentioned earlier, the government was forced to make substantial cuts in its programme of investments in major resource and industrial projects. Given that the state is the major source of investment funds, the pressure upon the government to reduce expenditure has crucial implications for the level of capital expenditure in the economy as a whole. Indeed, gross domestic investment fell from 23.6 per cent of GNP in 1983, to an expected 21.8 per cent in 1984, and was projected in the World Bank report of 1985 to fall further in 1985/86 to 19.9 per cent before, hopefully, recovering. Gross domestic investment derived from government savings was expected to decline from a projected 9.8 per cent of GNP in 1984 to 7.2 per cent in 1985 and 1986 before once more rising (World Bank, 1985b: 41). Direct government investment and public-enterprise investment fell from Rp 8366 billion in 1982/83 to Rp 7412 billion in 1983/84, a 17 per cent decline in real terms (Table

2.6). The decline in government investment is even more precipitous if we consider productive investment as separate from investment in economic infrastructure and social services (Table 2.8).

The effect of planned changes in the sectoral composition of government development expenditure for Repelita IV will be to shift emphasis sharply away from the productive sector towards infrastructure and the social sector. Quite clearly the pattern is designed to transfer responsibility for productive investment increasingly to the private sector.

Nevertheless, in Repelita IV, the government is planning for increases in total investment from Rp 19 trillion in 1984/85 to Rp 40 trillion in 1988/89. This will require sustained and substantial increases in private investment from a planned Rp 8.7 trillion in 1984/85 to Rp 19.5 trillion in 1988/89, a growth rate of 20 per cent per year over the period. Of the total Rp 145.2 trillion of investment projected for Repelita IV, Rp 67.5 trillion, or 40 per cent, is therefore expected to come from the private sector (*FEER*, 26 January 1984; *Tempo*, 25 February and 31 March 1984). Domestic, non-government savings are also assumed, as part of the plan, to rise by an incredible 32 per cent per annum.

So far the government's expectations of the private sector have not been met. Direct private foreign investment continues to be sluggish. From a high of US$538 million of investment capital in 1974/75 it fell to US$140 million in 1980/81, then reached US$193 million in 1983/84. It is projected to rise to US$479 million by the mid-1990s. However, it is clear that foreign private investment will not come flooding back into Indonesia until it is able to invest in sectors it considers appropriate— i.e. until the priority investment lists (DSP) are withdrawn—and until a greater degree of reliability and predictability are introduced into the physical and administrative infrastructure.

Domestic investment has also performed poorly. It has been hampered by slackening domestic demand (due in no small measure to declining state investment in the industrial projects), overcapacity, the uncertainty of new taxes and, most importantly, huge debt servicing burdens for those who borrowed heavily in US dollars during the oil boom, as a consequence of devaluation and the continuing strength of the dollar. Early data suggest that the hopeful targets set for the private sector are not being met. In the first six months of Repelita IV, the Capital Investment Board (BKPM) reported only Rp 923 billion of an anticipated Rp 3.9 trillion had been invested (*FEER*, 27 September 1984; World Bank, 1985b: 4–5).

In one extremely important case it has transpired that, rather than private capital coming to the rescue of the government at a time of fiscal difficulty, private capital has fallen into an even deeper hole and it has

Table 2.8 Indonesia's development expenditures, by sector (%)

Sector	Repelita III period of the third 5-year plan (actual)	Repelita IV fourth 5-year plan 1984/85–1988/89 (planned)
Productive sectors:	27.1	17.5
Agriculture	7.9	6.8
Industry	12.0	7.5
Mines	7.2	3.2
Economic infrastructure:	25.5	30.7
Irrigation	4.5	5.9
Energy	7.9	12.2
Communications	13.1	12.6
Social sectors:	16.0	23.0
Education and culture	10.0	14.7
Health and population	3.5	4.5
Housing and resettlement	2.5	3.8
Other sectors:	31.5	28.7
Total	100	100

Source: World Bank (1985b) p. 78, citing Repelita III & IV and Ministry of Finance

been the government that has had to do the rescuing. I refer here to the government's celebrated purchase of shares in Liem Sioe Liong's Indocement group.

If any domestic, private corporate group had the potential to play a leading role in the privatisation of investment it was the Liem group. By far the largest of the private corporate conglomerates, the Liem group enjoyed close relations with the Suharto family, many of its companies having Suharto family members as shareholders and directors. Between 1965 and 1975 it secured dominant, often monopoly, positions in trade (notably clove importing), flour milling, cement manufacture and automobiles with generous access to licences and state credit. Most recently Liem expanded into the milk and cooking oil industries, assuming almost a monopoly position in the latter. In the early 1980s he completed several spectacular takeovers in trade and banking in Holland, the USA and Hong Kong (*FEER*, 7 April 1983 and 26 April 1984; *Tempo*, 31 March 1984; Robison, 1986: ch. 9). His rise to international status was followed in Indonesia by a series of moves which suggested he was to be the spearhead of privatisation. His joint venture with Krakatau and Ciputra in the cold rolling mill has already been discussed. After the government's decision to privatise several public corporations, Liem made a highly publicised takeover of Semen Madura. However, from this point things seemed to turn sour; Liem's huge Indocement group, with a capacity to produce 8 million tons of the country's total capacity of 12.3 million tons in 1985, confronted serious difficulties in the form of a slack domestic market and soaring servicing burdens on its overseas borrowing. It was at this stage that the state stepped in to rescue the flower of Indonesian private enterprise.

Under Regulation 32 of 25 June 1985, the government purchased a total of 35 per cent of the shares of Indocement at a cost of Rp 36 333 840 000 (about US$350 million). Indocement was also to receive a government loan of US$120 million from four state banks. In effect, the state is paying off Indocement's expensive dollar debts and replacing them with rupiah debts at, reportedly, favourable rates of interest (*Kompas*, 14 August 1985; *Sinar Harapan*, 22 August 1985).

At one level the Indocement case might be seen to constitute nothing more than the use of state power and resources to rescue an ailing investment of the Suharto family. Of course it must also be said that states in general are loath at allow the demise of major national corporate groups whatever their relationship to powerful political leaders because of the broader economic implications of collapse especially for international business confidence.

At another level it demonstrates the dependence of major domestic business conglomerates on the resources of the state applied through both general policy and bureaucratic patronage. Contrary to the belief of free-market ideologues, domestic private capital is sustained by state intervention. Private capitalists are all too aware of this fact, and several have spoken out recently against the clamours for the removal of protection. In particular, we should note the pleas of Fritz Eman, a prominent businessman and member of the Chamber of Commerce, who not only argued vehemently against free-market policies but urged the government to extend to other companies the type of assistance it gave to Indocement (*Kompas*, 14 August 1985).

As the capacity of the state to finance, subsidise and provide markets to private domestic capital declines, along with its capacity to guarantee profitability to certain companies through allocating of monopolies and privileged market positions, so has private investment become increasingly cautious. If indeed domestic private capital is not able to fulfil the optimistic targets set for it in Repelita IV, Indonesia will either have to settle for lower investment and growth rates or make some more fundamental adjustments to its investment policy to attract foreign direct investment.

The impact of the oil price collapses of January–February 1986

The 1986/87 budget was introduced by President Suharto in January 1986 before the latest oil price shocks had occurred. Even at this stage the budget, based upon what transpired to be an optimistic forecast of US$25 per barrel, was 7 per cent down on 1985/86, the first decline under the New Order. The development budget declined a substantial 22 per cent, with serious implications for investment, GDP growth and employment. Despite falling imports, the government predicted a current account deficit of US$2.2 billion (Glassburner, 1986).

However, oil price declines proved to be far in excess of predictions. US$15–20 appears to be a more reasonable medium- to long-term prospect than the expected US$25. As Glassburner has noted: 'Each drop of $1 in the average price of Indonesia's exported oil implies a loss of roughly $400 million in export earnings and Rp 300 billion in oil tax revenues; thus export earnings and tax receipts for the new fiscal year (1986/87) could decline by 25% or more as compared to the 1985/86 budget.' (Glassburner, 1986: 1).

It will be some time before the precise impact becomes clear, but what is certain is that the pressures that emerged from the 1982 price decline from $36 to $28 per barrel will be intensified. Balance of payments problems and foreign debt will increase, and even the 1986/87 budget debt servicing was expected to rise to US$1.77 billion, up from US$1.29 billion in 1984/85. The state's revenue crisis will deepen, forcing either further spending cutbacks with their depressing effect on growth and employment, or expansionary policies with growing budget deficits and inflation. Increasingly the business community is becoming aware that pressures to resort to the hard choices—spending cutbacks, devaluation, deficit budgeting and increased foreign borrowing—could be lessened if the state apparatus was made more efficient. Their increasingly vocal stance on the issue of efficiency will further erode the hegemony that officials exercise over the state apparatus.

Concluding remarks

As outlined in the introductory chapter of this collection, new factors in the process of production have made it both desirable and possible for international capital to decompose the process of production globally according to corporate criteria of efficiency and profitability. This has involved the relocation of many labour- and energy-intensive manufacturing industries to the Third World (Adam, 1972; Frobel, 1982; Jenkins, 1984). At the ideological level, this new international division of labour is explained and justified by its proponents, corporate and academic, as a rationalisation of the world economy: an application of the principles of comparative advantage and allocative efficiency. Export-oriented economies such as those of Singapore and South Korea are held to be illustrations of the benefits to be gained by integrating with the new international division of labour, by switching from inward-looking to export-oriented industrial policies (Keesing, 1967; Garnaut, 1980; Balassa, 1982).

Indonesia's policies over the past four decades generally run counter to the objectives of both international investors and free-market economists. By restraining international capital investment and internally financing investment projects in all sectors of the manufacturing industry the Indonesians have attempted to create an autonomous industrially based economy outside the logic of the new international division of labour. However, over the past five years the capacity of the Indonesian state to resist absorption into the new international division of labour has been diminished by severe falls in the prices of its main export earner: oil.

With the fall in oil prices, international pressures for Indonesia to abandon its nationalist economic policies, to abandon ISI for EOI policies, have gained real force. Whereas the oil bonanza allowed for general economic growth *and* the sustenance of politico-bureaucrats and their capitalist clients, the decline in oil prices has meant that the vested interests of the entrenched political and economic forces run increasingly counter to the viability of the economy as a whole. As well, the leverage available to international forces has grown with Indonesia's increasing need for external sources of loans and investment capital. But resistance to structural change has been considerable. It has come partly at the ideological level from the strength of nationalist feelings, from distrust of international capital, and from the belief that submission to NIDL and abandonment of the state's protective and supportive role for the domestic economy would destroy existing structures and enterprises and leave the economy vulnerable to international cartels, monopolies and manipulative trade practices.

At a more concrete level, resistance has come from the dominant political and domestic corporate groups whose interests are integral to policies of state intervention and economic nationalism. To keep the nationalist state-led economy intact in the face of falling oil prices the government has been forced to seek alternative sources of foreign earnings and revenues. To the end of 1985 it had achieved remarkable success in avoiding a revenue and balance of payments crisis. But to achieve this it has had to adopt policies which, ironically, are corrosive to the continuation of politico-bureaucrat hegemony over the state and the pursuit of a nationally integrated industrial economy. The further Indonesia is forced to borrow externally, to increase productivity and efficiency of industrial production, to develop a domestic tax base, to expand domestic private sources of investment capital and savings and to restrain state expenditure, the more it weakens the position of the vested interests, the hegemony of politico-bureaucrats over the state apparatus and the integrity of the nationally conceived economy.

The outcome is not likely to be confined to either integration into the new international division of labour as an export-oriented producer or successful defence of the integrated, inward-looking industrial model. Entry into the new international division of labour is not simply a matter of adopting different policies. A complex range of specific economic and political factors underlay the successful entry of South Korea, Taiwan and Singapore in the 1960s and 1970s, as explained in the introduction to this collection. Further, there is also the question of the level at which countries would participate. Certainly Indonesia could not expect to keep its automobile or steel industries. With the accelerated decline of oil income and the weakness of domestic capital, Indonesia may prove to have too little to offer investors to enable it to play a significant role in the new international division of labour and too little in the way of independent resources to underwrite autonomous industrialisation. In other words, economic stagnation is a real possibility. Whatever the case, the outcome will be determined not only by pressures emanating from structural changes in capital accumulation at the global level but also by development of economic forces within Indonesia and the process of political conflict between vested interests in response to threats and opportunities posed by structural change.

KEVIN HEWISON

3
National interests and economic downturn: Thailand

Not so long ago Thailand was described as the Association of Southeast Asian Nations' 'dark horse' in the economic stakes (Bowring, 1982: 85). Its potential, according to this interpretation, tended to be underrated because its high and sustained rates of economic growth since the early 1960s were overshadowed by the more spectacular growth rates achieved by newly industrialised countries (NICs) such as Singapore, South Korea, Hong Kong and Taiwan.

Thailand's average annual growth rate was in excess of 8 per cent throughout the 1960s, more than 7 per cent during the 1970s and ranged between 4 and 6 per cent for the first years of the 1980s. Even in per capita terms the rate of growth in the gross national product (GNP) for the whole 1960–82 period has been 4.5 per cent (Mackie, 1985: 42). Such growth has brought considerable change to the economic structure of Thailand and to the daily life of the people.

In 1960 agriculture employed the bulk of the population, and primary commodities were the major exports. This situation was to rapidly alter. Table 3.1 indicates the changes that have taken place in the productive structure since 1960. It is evident that the significance of agriculture, in national production terms, is declining as the importance of manufacturing and the financial sector has increased.

Manufacturing has grown rapidly since 1960, with growth rates generally exceeding those for the whole economy (Thailand, *National Income of Thailand*, various issues). Exports of manufactures have expanded from just 1 per cent of total exports in 1960 to about 30 per cent by the early 1980s (*Thailand Investment Bulletin*, 5, 1, 1980: 1–14; Bangkok Bank, 1983: 8). While most people are still engaged in agricultural pursuits, in percentage terms there has been a decline from 82 per cent of the economically active population engaged in agriculture in 1960 to 70 per cent in the early 1980s. Concomitantly, there has been

Table 3.1 Gross domestic product of Thailand, by industrial origin, selected years, 1960–83 (%)

Sector	1960	1971	1980	1983
Agriculture	39.8	29.8	24.9	23.5
Mining and quarrying	1.1	1.5	1.6	1.2
Manufacturing	12.5	17.5	20.7	21.0
Construction	4.6	5.5	5.7	4.5
Electricity and water supply	0.4	1.8	1.9	2.2
Transport and communications	7.5	6.7	6.4	6.9
Wholesale and retail trade	15.2	17.1	16.5	16.6
Banking, insurance, real estate	1.9	4.2	6.0	7.0
Ownership of dwellings	2.8	1.9	1.5	1.5
Public administration and defence	4.6	4.3	4.2	4.2
Services	9.6	9.7	10.6	11.4

Sources: Data for 1960 are from Ingram (1971: 234)
Data for 1971, 1980 and 1983 are from Bank of Thailand, *Annual Economic Report* (various issues)

an increase in the proportion involved in the manufacturing sector, from 3 to 8 per cent (Hewison, 1983: 190–1). While statistically small, these changes are indicative of the development of a more industrially based economy. This is confirmed by the fact that the occupational status of the population has moved more in the direction of wage-labour, with almost a quarter of the economically active population now in this category.

An examination of output also emphasises the significance of the industrial sector, for it is here that productivity is highest (see Table 3.2). Increased industrialisation is also reflected in data on trade. Figures for the 1960–83 period indicate that there has been a gradual decrease in the import of consumer goods, but an increased inflow of capital goods and crude materials (*Bank of Thailand Monthly Bulletin*, various issues). Such a change is consistent with the expanding technological base associated with industrial development.

By the early 1980s Thailand had emerged as a rapidly industrialising country with bright prospects for continued growth and industrialisation. There were four reasons for this optimism. First, industrialisation was being built on a base that was largely owned by domestic capitalists, and the dominance of the financial and industrial fractions of this class meant that they had a large stake in the industrial future of the country (Hewison, 1981, 1985; Krirkkiat, 1981; Kraisak, 1984). Second, despite the international recession and a series of oil price rises, Thailand's growth rates had remained relatively high. Third, unlike many other developing countries, Thailand did not face a crippling debt burden, having followed reasonably conservative borrowing

Table 3.2 Output and productivity in the Thai economy, 1977

Sector	Value added[a] $US million	Value added[a] %	Labour force[b] No. (millions)	Labour force[b] %	Average value added/worker $US	Average value added/worker % of average
Agriculture	5 169	28.5	13.4	71.4	386	39.9
Industry	5 125	28.2	2.0	10.7	2 652	265.3
Services	7 865	43.3	3.4	17.9	2 313	239.5
Total/averages	18 159	100.0	18.8	100.0	966	100.0

Notes: [a] Estimates, at market prices
[b] Estimates
Source: International Bank for Reconstruction and Development (1980: n.p.)

policies. Fourth, a degree of stability had entered the political sphere following the turbulence of the mid-1970s.

However, the mid-1980s saw this optimism wane, giving way to more cautious assessments as the economy experienced its first serious downturn since the mid-1950s. Before we consider the crisis of the 1980s it is first necessary to assess the strategies that have promoted Thailand's rapid economic expansion in the previous two decades.

Industrialisation strategies

Prior to General Sarit Thanarat's 'revolution' in 1958, the military-dominated government led by Phibun Songkhram had emphasised industrialisation as a means to 'civilise' Thai society. It was believed that progress came through industrial development of the European and Japanese varieties. An added consideration was that the leading ideologues of the regime saw the Chinese in Thailand as a potential threat to ethnic Thai control of the economy. The result of this combination of nationalism and developmentalist thinking was that a series of uncoordinated attempts were made to develop selected industries such as textiles and food processing. These efforts took place without much official thought being given to their direction, the state being seen as a necessary leading force, due to the dearth of private (Thai) investment. However, there was no discernible pattern to the investments made by the state, with planning seldom extending beyond individual industries (Hewison, 1985: 275-6). Under the Sarit regime this changed.

The new administration trumpeted its support for industrialisation, but in terms of planning there was little initially that would have distinguished Sarit's regime from its predecessor. It was only the emergence of balance of payments and trade problems which induced the government to seek a reduction in manufactured imports. Import bans were introduced but resulted in considerable opposition as they led to a variety of shortages. To overcome this problem the move to an import-substitution industrialisation (ISI) strategy appeared promising, especially as it had been advocated by the influential World Bank report (IBRD, 1959: ch. 3), the Bank of Thailand (1960), a United Nations mission (van Rijnberk, 1961) and the Commission for Asia and the Far East (ECAFE, 1964).

In general terms ISI aimed to establish industries that produced goods that would otherwise have been imported. But, as an ECAFE study (1964: 14–15) noted, it was not necessarily expected to reduce total imports. Rather, ISI aimed to save foreign exchange in order to allow for the expansion of capital goods imports or certain basic consumption goods. For many political leaders, however, the perception in the 1960s was that total imports would be reduced, aiding the trade and balance of payments problems (*Nangsuphim ho kan kha thai* henceforth, *Nangsuphim*), 14, 3, 1960: 98–9). A successful ISI strategy demands that domestic manufacturing be protected by various import bans and tariffs, and from 1960 the Thai state began to erect such barriers, despite some opposition from 'free traders' (*Bangkok Bank Monthly Review* (*BBMR*), 3, 6, 1962: 1–3; *Nangsuphim*, 15, 1, 1961: 102).

The state did not simply decide, of its own accord, to adopt an ISI strategy. According to contemporary reports, domestic industrial capitalists exerted strong pressure for protection. When announcing increased tariffs in late 1960, the minister for finance stated that the decision had been taken following strong representations from local industrialists. Banjurd Cholvicharn, a prominent banker, president of the Thai Chamber of Commerce, and close to General Sarit, was outspoken in his criticism of the lack of control placed on merchants he believed were creating a 'terrible' trade imbalance, and he urged import controls (*Siam Rath Weekly Review*, 1 November 1962: 4). Part of the reason for the trade imbalance was the fact that traders had accumulated considerable wealth during the Korean War boom, and, unwilling to invest in unprotected industry, they were limiting their investment to commercial activities and especially to importing consumer goods. Once ISI policies emerged, even some traders were prepared to move to manufacturing activities.

The logic of import substitution remained predominant throughout the 1960s, being strongly supported by the Board of Investment, the National Economic (and Social) Development Board (NESDB), the Ministry of Industry, the Bank of Thailand and local manufacturers.

Their position was reflected in the first (1961-66) and second (1967-71) development plans, where the majority of capital invested with government promotional privileges in the 1960s went into ISI areas (Ingram, 1971: 288-9).

The available assessments of ISI indicate some successes, such as textiles, but also note a number of emergent structural problems, such as inbuilt disincentives to exports (Sidhiphol, 1972: 429-39; Narongchai, 1973a, 1973b). In terms of political economy, however, there were significant developments. First, important structural changes occurred in manufacturing, where there was increased production of consumer goods. During the 1960s the manufacturing sector's contribution to GDP rose from 12.5 to 17.5 per cent (Table 3.1), wih its annual growth rate averaging 11 per cent (at constant 1962 prices) over the period (Richter & Edwards, 1973: 35). Second, high rates of protection encouraged domestic investment. That is, the development of domestic manufacturing advanced the whole process of capital accumulation, especially for the banking and industrial capitalists (Trairong, 1970: 52; Amnuai, 1978: 149-68). Banking capitalists, notably the Bangkok Bank and its principals, the Sophonpanich family, took advantage of ISI policies to expand into industry, greatly enhancing their corporate power (Hewison, 1983: ch. 9). During the period when ISI was in full swing, the co-operation between industrialists and bankers provided a strong economic and political base, which allowed them to override the interests of consumers and traders who were more interested in liberal trade policies (Pasuk, 1980: 152). However, by the end of the 1960s the expansion of manufacturing, concentrated in conumer goods, was bursting the seams of the ISI strategy, having outgrown the relatively small domestic market in crucial sectors such as textiles and motor vehicles.

The decline of ISI was hastened by domestic and international developments. Within Thailand excess capacity had become a major problem, and growth in the manufacturing sector dropped to 7.5 per cent a year in the 1970-72 period, and there were corresponding falls in manufacturing investment (IBRD, 1974: 103-4; *Business Review*, December 1972: 116). Agitation amongst groups of local capitalists had emerged in 1969, with the president of the Thai Industries Association urging both increased protection for domestic industries and more incentives for exporters (*Bangkok World* (*BW*), 15 October 1969: 17). Simultaneously, growing trade deficits forced the government to examine export-oriented industrialisation (EOI) strategies. EOI was to be based on a nation's 'comparative advantage' in producing commodities for a world market, bringing in valuable foreign exchange and achieving a trade balance by 'doing what comes naturally'.[1] Internationally, higher inflation in the West and exchange rate fluctuations made Thai manufactures potentially attractive on the world market. These changing circumstances began to be recognised, and in 1971 the Board of Investment announced incentives for export. These benefits were enhanced in 1972 when the Investment Promotion Act was revised and export targeting introduced (*BW*, 2 March 1971; 15; *Business Review*, December 1972: 120). The icing on the EOI cake was the formal recognition of the strategy in the third plan (1972–76), even though it was also conceded that ISI was not to be completely jettisoned (Thailand, 1975; C68).[2] The value of manufactured exports began to expand at an unprecedented rate, rising from US$40 million in 1970 to US$270 million three years later (IBRD, 1974: vii).

The fourth plan (1977–81) continued the emphasis on EOI while again indicating that ISI would be maintained in some areas. However, export industries were to receive special state promotional privileges (*Business in Thailand*, January 1979: 22). As will be discussed below, this emphasis on export was close to the World Bank desire for labour-intensive, export-oriented industries. As ISI had seemed in the 1960s, so a number of political leaders saw EOI as the magic formula for development in the 1970s, as the state attempted to reduce trade and balance of payments deficits by expanding exports.

The emergence of a more export-oriented strategy also reflected developments within the capitalist class. Under the insulated conditions of ISI, domestic industrial and banking capitals were able to expand to a stage where, in some cases, capital was developing a more international character. These large, highly concentrated corporate groups were demanding a more outward-looking development strategy, for they had outgrown the Thai market and were seeking to expand their accumulation on an international scale. Consequently, the priority given to EOI may be seen as an indication of the increased influence of big capital within the Thai political economy (Hewison, 1983). At this juncture it is appropriate to examine the patterns of investment and accumulation within the economy under both ISI and EOI development regimes.

Investment and accumulation

As noted previously, investment by the state became an important factor in the 1940s and 1950s. Initially state investment was required for the reconstruction of a war-damaged infrastructure, but there was also state capital in manufacturing, transport, finance and trade (Sangsit, n.d.; chs 3–4). While total state investment remained comparatively low compared to other countries of the region (ECAFE, 1959: 77–8), both domestic and foreign capitalists, facing an economic downturn following the Korean War boom, felt they were being squeezed out by state investments. This was especially so in the manufacturing sector where the proportion of investment accounted for by the private sector had declined (van Rijnberk, 1961: 9). While a number of local capitalists made their fortunes during this period (Kraisak, 1984: 140; Akira, 1985: ch. 3), there also developed a number of serious economic difficulties.

With the end of the Korean War boom, commodity prices stagnated, resulting in substantial trade deficits as imports of consumer and capital goods continued to expand. If it had not been for US aid contributions, the Thai balance of payments would have recorded a deficit for the entire 1952–58 period (Chira, 1971: 115–33). In addition, the government continually spent more than it collected in revenues (IBRD, 1959: 285). The central bank was highly critical of the government's administration of its economic responsibilities, charging that budget deficits were the result of overspending on large-scale industrial projects and arguing that poor fiscal policies were fuelling inflation and depleting foreign exchange reserves. The bank also claimed that budgetary procedures were inadequate and poorly co-ordinated, leading to injudicious expenditures (Bank of Thailand, 1955: 20; 1960: 13–14). For both foreign and local capitalists such problems cast a shadow over their ability to expand accumulation. However, General Sarit's seizure of power brought an end to the state's role as a major investor in the manufacturing sector.

Within the new regime's general support for private enterprise, the move to an ISI strategy, with state investment being concentrated in infrastructure, was satisfactory to both local and foreign investors, for it unleashed the private sector and coincided with the drive by trans-national corporations (TNCs) to establish enterprises around the globe (Hymer, 1975: 43–8). The Sarit government, primed with World Bank and UN advice, saw TNCs as a source of capital which could replace state investment but continue the drive for expanded industrial activity. TNCs were also seen as a source of technical and entrepreneurial skills, and the promotion of foreign investment became a pillar of state economic policy. Indeed, a recent study by Akira (1985: 4.20) suggests that about half of the TNCs operating in Thailand established their operations between 1963 and 1972.

While there were many domestic capitalists who opposed foreign investment, fearing increased competition (*BBMR*, 3, 6, 1962: 1–3), the big capitalists amongst the banking and industrial fractions were keen that such investment be accelerated (*BBMR*, 3, 2, 1962: 2). This latter group felt that Thailand required skills and capital, but it should also be noted that the promotion of foreign investment, and especially joint ventures, provided political protection for local capitalists. While state officials might have been willing to nationalise or harass a wholly Sino-Thai enterprise, they would be more reluctant in the case of a joint venture. Big capital thus felt it had more to gain from increased economic activity than it might lose from increased competition.

Despite the efforts made to attract foreign capital, it is important to realise that domestic capitalists retained considerable control over the Thai economy. As can be seen in Table 3.3, while direct foreign investment increased considerably during the 1960s compared to gross fixed capital formation, direct foreign investment actually decreased in percentage terms.[3] Indeed, total foreign capital inflows as a percentage of gross fixed capital formation fell considerably during this period. Therefore, the rapid economic growth during this period, whilst benefiting from foreign capital inflows, was due primarily to investment expansion by local capitalists.

Significantly though, in the 1970s there was a general rise in total capital inflows, even if these inflows have been relatively low when compared to other countries of the region (Hill & Johns, 1985). The increased inflow has been associated with a more footloose and eclectic phase of international capitalist development. Some TNCs have become increasingly interested in taking advantage of such benefits as cheap labour, protection, generous taxation concessions, bans on organised labour and growing domestic markets in the Third World when considering the location and relocation of industrial investments.

Table 3.3 Thailand's capital inflows and gross fixed capital formation, 1960–83 (in millions of baht)

Period	Gross fixed capital formation (1)	Direct foreign investment (2)	% $\left(\frac{2}{1}\right)$ (3)	Other inflows[a] (2 + 4) (4)	Total inflow (5)	% $\left(\frac{5}{1}\right)$ (6)
1960–62	7 980	337.8	4.2	2 372.9	2 710.7	34.0
1963–65	42 780	1 591.3	3.7	2 830.9	4 442.0	10.3
1966–68	60 620	2 704.7	3.9	1 990.1	4 694.8	6.7
1969–71	94 690	2 775.4	2.9	3 586.9	6 343.3	6.7
1972–74	137 960	6 868.3[b]	5.0	8 134.3	15 002.6	10.9
1975–77	238 032	5 522.7	2.3	22 404.5	27 927.2	11.7
1978–80	278 716	5 874.5	2.1	72 637.4	78 511.9	28.2
1981–83	207 133[c]	18 710.1	9.0	87 501.2	106 211.3	51.3

Notes: [a] This figure includes loans and credits to government and private enterprises, trade credits and portfolio investment.
[b] Included in this figure is a 1974 oil concession fee of 1 070 million baht.
[c] 1000 figures are estimates.
Sources: Various issues of: the Bank of Thailand's *Bulletins* and Thailand, *National Income of Thailand*.

Others have sought to have component manufacturing carried out by local firms in the Third World. More recently there has been a pronounced trend towards money transfers as transnational financial institutions have invested in and lent more to the Third World, and especially to the NICs (Andreff, 1984: 62). This restructuring of international capitalism has provided new opportunities for international capitalists and also for the expansion of accumulation by domestic capitalists in the Third World (Petras, 1984). This is so because as the forces of production expand, they do so for both domestic and transnational capitals (Bryan, 1983), a point often neglected by those who argue that domestic capital is generally dependent upon foreign capital.

The fact that the move from ISI to a more export-oriented approach did not seem to result in any dramatic upsurge in direct foreign investment during the 1970s was primarily because of the recession in the West. Nevertheless, the Thai economy continued to grow, despite the oil price shock of 1973, due mainly to the rapid increase in financial transfers as loans and credits. While such capital flows do not involve the same level of control over the investment decisions of individual capitalists and companies as does direct investment, the supply of large loans and credits by international agencies and private transnational banks gives them a considerable stake in the direction of national development and provides international finance capital with a stong stimulus to influence development policies.

The large capital inflows were, in part, a response to balance of payments problems, but also served to stave off the worst effects of the world recession until the early 1980s, despite a deteriorating economic situation. It is noticeable, in Table 3.3, that the 1981–83 period represents a turning point for the pattern of capital flows. Firstly, gross domestic capital formation is seen to have decreased for the first time. Secondly, despite this fall, both direct foreign investment and total capital inflows increased considerably. It seems clear that the recession had finally caught up with domestic capital. This crisis of accumulation amongst domestic capitalists is confirmed by data on bankruptcies, where the total number of cases before the courts rose by 15 per cent between 1978 and 1979, but leapt by almost 47 per cent in 1980 and more than 30 per cent in 1981 (Thailand, *Statistical Yearbook*, various issues). At the same time, with the worst of the recession passing in some of the countries of the West, transnational capital began to move back into Thailand.

While the impact of increased capital inflows will be discussed in more detail below, it must again be emphasised that the Thai economy continues to be dominated by domestic capitalists, despite the crisis of accumulation that confronted them by the mid-1980s.

The crisis of the 1980s

By 1985 the Thai economy faced its first major crisis since the late 1950s. The initial focus of concern was the mounting debt problem, but the crisis was much broader than this. A conference, which brought together academics, economists and political and business leaders, produced the following pessimistic assessment:

> Thailand's future does not look rosy with the economy in the worst shape it has ever been in, a lack of political and national leadership, a misguided educational system, a stagnant bureaucratic system, and dwindling natural resources. [*Bangkok Post* (*BP*), 22 July 1985: 1]

Meanwhile, the government was assembling a 'no-growth' budget, business confidence was ebbing, and draft economic growth estimates in the sixth plan (1987–91) was being revised on almost a daily basis. By year's end, this pessimism had become entrenched, with NESDB Secretary-General Snoh Unakul stating that even low predictions of 4 per cent may not be achieved (*BP*, 28 November 1985: 15). Bankruptcies were reported to have increased by almost 27 per cent in the first nine months of 1985, and investment and factory approvals were both down (*BP*, 26 November 1985: 19; 27 November 1985: 20). At this time a number of companies were reporting significant declines in profitability. Thailand's two largest banks, the Bangkok and Thai Farmers banks, indicated big drops in their profits (*Nation*, 13 November 1985: 17), while reports of losses, efficiency drives and retrenchments became common. For example, the large Saha Phattanapibul group recorded its first loss in several decades (*Nation*, 3 December 1985: 17).

This crisis did not confront only capitalists and state managers, for while the statistical data on the impact of the economic downturn tend to mask the real effect on average people, it became clear that workers and peasants were suffering. Throughout 1985 farmers' groups protested the decline in prices they were receiving for their crops, with falling commodity prices having a severe effect in the countryside (*BP*, 5 December 1985: 3; 12 December 1985: 3). Urban dwellers were not immune either, with officials putting unemployment at two million (10 per cent being university graduates)[4] and warning that it was rising rapidly. The Board of Trade reported 100 000 lay-offs in the first half of 1985 (*BP*, 20 November 1985: 1).

Thailand's economic problems fell into a number of overlapping categories but may be emphasised by an examination of foreign debt and trade, current account, and budget deficits. Prior to a discussion of these areas, however, it is useful to place the crisis of Thai capitalism within its international context.

As noted previously, the world recession had been slow to have an impact on Thailand, mainly because Thailand was able to borrow overseas, thus cushioning, for a time, the effects of the recession. Indeed, while the Organisation of Petroleum Exporting Countries (OPEC) oil price rises had a marked effect on the import structure of many Third World countries, the major impact for many countries was to be on fiscal policies. The oil price rises brought huge amounts of money capital, as petrodollars, on to the world financial markets, and when combined with the already large outflow of dollars from the United States, due to its trade deficit and low corporate demand for loans during the recession, international liquidity was at an all-time high. A number of Third World countries found that this enabled them to borrow quite freely on favourable terms (Bhattacharya, 1980: 157–64). The flow of private funds to the Third World rose substantially. In 1967 the private component of Third World foreign debt was 28 per cent, but by 1977 this had jumped to 48 per cent and as high as 54 per cent in the 1977–80 period (Green, 1980, 117; Andreff, 1984: 64). The total external public debt of the developing countries rose from US$276 000 million in 1977 to $634 000 million by 1983 (World Bank, 1985d: 176).

At the same time, EOI has not proven to be the Messiah of development predicted by the prophets of the 'free market', despite the example of the East Asian NICs during the 1960s and 1970s. Based on their so-called comparative advantage in cheap labour, it was assumed that a relocation of labour-intensive production into Third World countries would take place almost 'naturally'. However, relocation has not been a major trend, except in certain industries such as textiles (Jenkins, 1984: 43), and cheap labour has proven to be something of a mirage as TNCs chase it from one country to another. Also, technical innovations have so increased the productivity of wage-labour in industrialised nations that often increased capitalisation within the major markets of the West can offset the savings offered by cheap labour in the Third World (Kenichi, 1985: 10; Cho, 1985: 78–80).

In addition, what has been seen as a recession within the industrialised countries has been a period where capitalists have been pitted against each other as the processes of increased centralisation and concentration have expanded. This has resulted in an enhancing of the power of finance capital, bankrolled by petrodollars and Eurodollars. Thai capitalists now face a crisis of structure and accumulation which will be played out in the context of a

> higher degree of centralization and internationalization of capital, a deepening of the capitalist mechanism of unequal development, and the domination of transnational finance capital..., based on ever-closer links between multinational companies and transnational banks...[Andreff, 1984: 58]

Transnational finance capital has had a marked impact on Thailand. As was noted in Table 3.3, the inflow of capital, other than direct foreign investment, has increased rapidly during the 1970s and 1980s. This increased inflow has seen a corresponding increase in foreign debt (see Table 3.4), especially since the mid-1970s when the international capital markets were flushed with funds. By the end of the first quarter of 1985 total external debt had risen to US$13 000 million, of which 61 per cent was public sector debt (*BP*, 27 June 1985: 13). A debt of this magnitude represented, in 1984, more than 36 per cent of GNP and more than 25 per cent of foreign exchange reserves. More importantly, from the viewpoint of debt servicing, over a quarter of the total debt was held as short-term loans and credits. For the first time, the debt-service ratio rose above 20 per cent (Sharpe, 1985: 13), sending shockwaves through business, government and planning circles, as great stock had been laid in maintaining debt below this level. A public debate ensued, much of it concerning the size of the debt and measures that would avoid a 'Philippines problem'—rescheduling of loans, externally enforced austerity programmes and consequently a poor international credit rating. However, while this debate is important, in order to understand the current problems a much wider context must be considered.

Thailand's fiscal and monetary policies have generally been regarded as conservative. After the Second World War the country could afford to be prudent for, as bastions of anti-communism, Thai state managers found themselves receiving considerable US aid and loans. Between 1951 and 1967, Thailand's net economic and military assistance from the US amounted to over US$1000 million (Wilson, 1970: 144). US military spending also buoyed the economy throughout the 1960s and early 1970s as there were thousands of US troops stationed in Thailand, and thousands more arrived on rest and recreation leave (Viksnins, 1973; Boonkong, 1974). Additionally, Thailand had received, by the mid-1960s, more than US$180 million in loans from the World Bank

Table 3.4 Thailand's debt disbursed and outstanding, 1965–83 (US$ millions)

	1965	1970	1975	1980	1981	1982	1983
Debt outstanding and disbursed	405.0	749.2	1 359.6	5 751.6	7 213.9	8 317.7	9 523.6
Private sector	150.0	401.2	736.2	1 751.4	2 098.6	2 296.3	2 658.6
% of total	37.0	53.6	54.1	30.4	29.1	27.6	27.9
Public sector	255.0	348.0	623.3	4 000.2	5 115.3	6 021.4	6 865.0
% of total	63.0	46.4	45.9	69.6	70.9	72.4	72.1
—state enterprises	166.9	136.9	365.9	2 429.6	3 161.8	3 887.4	4 400.4
% of public sector debt	65.4	39.3	58.7	60.7	61.8	64.6	64.1

Source: Prannee & Direk (1985: 1.32).

(Tolley, 1964: 4). While this amount does not seem large, it should be noted that 21 per cent of the funding for the first development plan came from overseas loans, of which the World Bank contributed about a half (Akira, 1985: 4.6–4.7). It was only when US aid and spending began to decrease with the withdrawal from Indochina and then Thailand that the search for external funding quickened. This was especially so as the decline in US spending coincided with a decline in foreign investment and then the first OPEC price rises.

From 1973 there was a clear determination to seek increased capital inflows. In 1974 direct investment increased by almost 140 per cent over 1973, but much of this was due to an oil concession worth 1070 million baht. More important, however, was the more than 200 per cent increase in loans and credits to state enterprises (*Bank of Thailand Bulletin*, various issues). There was also a change in sourcing. Whereas in 1973 public sector debt was mainly held by multilateral agencies (50.4 per cent) and only a fraction by private creditors (11.5 per cent), by 1980 multilateral agencies accounted for just 27.5 per cent and private creditors 44.1 per cent, with the turnaround occurring from 1975 (Virabongse et al., 1983: 146–7), coinciding with the rise in liquidity on the world financial markets.

During the period 1977–79, Thailand experienced an investment boom largely because the government of General Kriangsak Chomanan adopted policies that controlled prices, increased protection, expanded credit and increased state investment. This was primarily funded by loans from private sources raised internationally and resulted in a greatly increased foreign debt. Thus the second round of oil price rises in 1978 saw Thailand in a vulnerable financial position (IBRD, 1983, vol. 1: 14). It was only through continued and expanded borrowing that a severe economic downturn was avoided, albeit temporarily.

It is evident that much of the increased debt has been accumulated by the public sector (see Table 4.4) and that a large percentage of this has been for state enterprises, especially in the energy sector. Indeed, much of the recent debate on debt has been an extended (and often ideologically based) critique of state-enterprise borrowing, in the context of calls for privatisation (Kanitha, 1984; IBRD, 1983, vol. 1). Because the statistics make it clear that state enterprises have been heavy borrowers, a culprit is seen. However, it must be understood that since 1958 state policy has been to promote the private sector with the state providing the economic and social infrastructure (Hewison, 1983: ch. 5; Chesada, 1983: 13, 63). Consequently in the early 1960s when the economic infrastructure was expanded rapidly, public sector debt made up a high proportion of total debt, and state enterprises accounted for a large part of the public sector's borrowings. Without such investments, the boom of the 1960s would not have been so extensive. This pattern has been reproduced in the mid and late 1970s as infrastructural projects were expanded on a large scale.

Following the 1973 oil price increases, which particularly affected electricity generation, state policy was changed to quickly diversify and expand generating capacity through other than oil-fuelled means. In addition, the discovery of substantial reserves of gas in the Gulf of Thailand encouraged state investments to prove and develop these reserves, thus lessening dependence on foreign energy and contributing to further industrial development. Together, the various electricity generating authorities and the petroleum authority account for about 60 per cent of state investment outlays (*Far Eastern Economic Review* (*FEER*), 25 July 1985: 65) and the bulk of debts (Chesada, 1983: 63; IBRD, 1983, vol. 1: 96). Even the World Bank, which has been antipathetic to the promotion of state enterprises (Tetzlaff, 1979: 127), has admitted that the gas discoveries warranted substantial investment and that most borrowing has been for much-needed infrastructure (IBRD, 1983, vol. 1: 42, 96).

The managers of state enterprises also found themselves in a fiscal bind when the government began to restrict subsidies but refused to allow the enterprises to raise their prices and charges. As domestic interest rates have been maintained at higher levels than the international market to prevent capital flight (*Nation*, 12 February 1985: 25), state enterprises were virtually forced to pursue foreign loans (*FEER*, 4 July 1980: 82). Thus, the attacks on state enterprises as the culprits in the debt problem appear misplaced.

While state enterprises are no longer sacred cows, the military has, until recently, remained so, and its role in increasing foreign debt has seldom been questioned, with recent World Bank reports making no mention of this—a strange omission given that the World Bank has admitted the productive nature of many state investments, and the same could not be said of military expenditures.

Following the 1976 coup, which brought the armed forces back to power, military leaders and other right-wing political groups saw communist regimes at Thailand's borders, faced a powerful guerrilla movement, and had seen assistance from the US decline. Thus, beginning in 1976, the armed forces embarked on an ambitious and controversial series of loans for military equipment. The Thanin Kraivixien government drew up a 20 000 baht military spending programme (*BP*, 21 November 1985: 5), and as a result, between 1976 and 1978 at least US$242 million was lent by various transnational banks for arms purchases at rates considerably higher than market rates and over short terms (*Asian Finance*, 15 November 1978: 74). It was only in 1979 that military borrowing was brought under the auspices of general development borrowing programmes, thus giving the government some control over the armed forces' excursions into the world's money markets (Janssen, 1983: 25). Even so, about a quarter of all borrowings on private capital markets has been attributed to military projects (Virabongse et al., 1983: 144–5), and in 1984 defence loans still accounted for a large percentage of direct government borrowings (*Nation*, 11 February 1985: 5). This has placed a heavy burden on the government. The short and medium terms of these loans has, according to one Bank of Thailand official, been the main source of the recent rise in the debt-service ratio (*BP*, 27 June 1985: 13).

Given the generally unproductive nature of military spending, the 1985 decision to purchase advanced F-16 fighter aircraft and equipment from the US at a cost in excess of 9467 million baht caused considerable controversy (*BW*, 21 June 1985: 1). Amid protests from bankers, students, economists and politicians, the contract to purchase was signed at the time that concern over the country's expanding debt was at its height.[5] Military leaders protested about 'unfair' criticism and argued that national defence needed to be strengthened, but they generally took a lower profile following the F-16 debacle (*BP*, 21 November 1985: 5). For some, however, the issue became one not of 'guns or rice' but of 'guns today and rice tomorrow' (*Nation*, 2 July 1985: 5). This was emphasised in the proposed national budget for 1986 which was designated 'no-growth' and allocated 23 per cent of total expenditure to debt servicing and a further 21 per cent to defence and security. By comparison, a paltry 9 per cent was allocated to health and social services combined (*Nation*, 3 July 1985: 19).

While Thailand's debt-service ratio has far exceeded the 20 per cent level and is approaching 30 per cent, Frank and Cline (1970: 104–6) have argued that such figures are misleading. They suggest that debt is not, of itself, a problem, but often the management of the debt is. If this is the case, then a brief examination of Thailand's current account and budget deficits indicates that the Thai economy faces both management and debt problems.

Table 3.5 indicates that neither ISI nor EOI strategies have been conducive to an improvement in the current account or trade balances, with the situation deteriorating over the past twenty years. According to preliminary figures for recent years, these balances saw a slight improvement in 1982 but have deteriorated further since then (*Bank of Thailand Quarterly Bulletin*, 24, 2, 1984: 40, 70–1).

Clearly, imports have been exceeding exports by a considerable margin, with the implication that overseas borrowing is required to acquire the foreign exchange necessary to pay for imports. Despite huge rises in transfers from the masses of Thai labourers working overseas, a 'Buy Thai' campaign and, more significantly, two devaluations of the baht, the impact on trade has been negligible (*Asian Wall*

Table 3.5 Thailand's trade and current account balances, 1960–80 (million baht)

	1960	1970	1980
Merchandise:			
Imports (c.i.f.)	9 498	26 514.5	190 025.3
Exports (f.o.b.)	8 614	14 269.7	132 040.5
Trade balance	−884	−12 244.8	−57 984.8
Net non-factor services	229.2	5 858.0	16 582.5
Balance on goods and services	−654.8	−6 386.8	−41 402.3
Net factor income from abroad	−115.7	178.2	−5 437.6
Net unrequited transfers	770.5	1 011.7	4 275.7
Current account balance	0.8	−5 196.9	−42 564.2
Trade balance/GDP (%)	−1.6	9.0	−8.5
Current account/GDP (%)	0.4	−3.8	−6.2

Source: Abridged from Virabongse et al. (1983: 3)

Street Journal (*AWSJ*), 8 August 1985: 1, 7). In 1985, while there were trade volume increases and a marginal reduction of the trade deficit, there was a worsening of conditions in dollar terms. There are four underlying reasons for this.

First, the proportion of the value of imports accounted for by petroleum products has increased from less than one-tenth in 1965 to almost one-quarter by 1983, and this has offset a decline in the proportion of manufactured imports from more than one-third of all imports in 1965 to less than one-quarter in 1983. Second, while ISI has meant that the proportion of manufactured exports has increased markedly over the period, in 1983 about a half of Thailand's exports are still accounted for by food and beverages (*Bank of Thailand Statistical Bulletin*, various issues), meaning that commodity prices remain extremely important to the economy. Thus the general decline in world prices and demand of many of Thailand's major commodity exports has meant a serious decline in the value of these exports (Kanitha, 1984: 314). In the first six months of 1985 the dollar value of Thailand's exports of maize, rice, tin, rubber and tapioca all fell (despite increases in the volume of exports for the two latter commodities), with only sugar showing both a value and volume increase (*BP*, 20 November 1985: 22). Third, both ISI and EOI strategies demand an increasing technological base for industry, which has meant increased imports of capital goods. The proportion of imports accounted for by machinery remains high, at about a third of the value of all imports (*Bank of*

Thailand Statistical Bulletin, various issues). Fourth, high interest rates on the loans already held have also caused a deterioration in the current account deficit (Virabongse et al., 1983: 1).

Of equal importance has been the government's expanding budget deficits. Since 1960 the government has achieved a budget surplus just once, in 1974, and the size of the deficit has increased significantly (see Table 3.6). To a large extent, the financing of these deficits has been through foreign borrowings (IBRD, 1983, vol. 1: 94).

It is generally agreed that the major cause of the budget deficits is the state's poor revenue structure, and there have been calls for a broadening of the taxation base (Chesada, 1983: 2). The problem is that some 70 per cent of government revenue comes from various taxes and duties which are not expanding at the same rate as the economy as a whole (Twatchai, 1979: 26-8). Economist Krirkkiat Phipatseritham (cited in *Nation*, 2 July 1985: 5) has argued that the deficit has led to short-term solutions such as foreign borrowing, which has meant that the long-term solution of widening the tax base has been ignored.

By late 1986, however, some cautions optimism was returning, as oil price decreases began to have a positive impact in oil-importing Thailand. Prime Minister General Prem Tinsulanonda predicted higher growth and hinted that the government elected in July would adopt more expansionary policies (*AWSJ*, 2 October 1986: 3). But the fundamental problems remain, with commodity prices languishing and many companies continuing to report poor performances (*FEER*, 18 September 1986: 79).

Clearly, the economic crisis of the 1980s calls the direction of Thai economic policy into question. Economic policymaking has seldom been determined in a conflict-free setting. However, during the 1960s and early 1970s, when government was dominated by military regimes and when economic growth was high, opposition could be stifled, with those proposing alternative policies being painted as malcontents or even communists. Nevertheless, even within narrow parameters—capitalist development—there were often disputes over the best growth strategy. For example, the dominance of the EOI strategy over ISI has

Table 3.6 Thailand's budget deficits, 1960-82 (million baht)

1960	-800.1
1965	-1 250.8
1970	-7 352.1
1975	-8 114.8
1980	-18 511.2
1982	-21 368.0

Sources: 1960-75: *Statistical Yearbook* (various issues)
1980-82: Thailand (1984) *Thailand's Budget in Brief*

never been entirely clear in state policy or in business circles, due to competition between various state agencies and between the fractions of capital. It is important to discuss these disputes in order that the political economy of Thai capitalism be understood.

The politics of economic policymaking

Economic policymaking is not carried out in an environment of ideological or political neutrality. Despite the claims to rationality by many economists, the various competing theoretical stances taken by the practitioners of the 'dismal science' attest to its ideological character. It is stating the obvious to assert that economic decisions are based as much on political considerations as they are on 'economic rationality', but this point is often neglected by bourgeois economists.

In the late 1960s and the 1970s the debate over economic policy centred on ISI and EOI strategies, with the Ministry of Industry supporting the former and the Board of Investment the latter (Hewison, 1983: ch. 5). In the 1980s, however, much of the debate has revolved around the measures required to handle the economic crisis. And much of this has had to do with International Monetary Fund (IMF) and World Bank recipes for the economy.[6]

The World Bank and IMF have been closely associated with Thai development policy since the early 1950s, with the first significant international report on the Thai economy being produced by the World Bank mission which visited Thailand in 1957 and 1958 (IBRD, 1959). This report became the basis of Thailand's first development plan, but from that time there has been conflict over the World Bank's suggestions.

This first report caused the Thai government considerable concern, with the Bank of Thailand asking that some parts of it be changed (*Nangsuphim*, 13, 3, 1959: 121, 123). Nevertheless, the Sarit government and its successors were prepared to accept World Bank prescriptions and its aid. Between 1950 and mid-1985 Thailand received US$3704 million in Bank loans and credits (World Bank, 1985d: 168). Most of these were allocated to specific projects based on the Bank's assessment of the state of the economy and the direction it should be taking (Santi, 1981: 21). Basically, this meant that the Thai state retained control over policymaking while accepting Bank advice and money. However, from 1979 this pattern altered.

As the second round of oil price rises began to take effect, the structural problems that had emerged with the 1973 price rises, but which had been neglected due to the ready availability of international loans, were exacerbated. It became clear that a number of highly placed technocrats had decided that the only way to overcome these problems was to adopt a more outward looking economic strategy, promoting EOI, dismantling tariff barriers and opening the country to the world market (Crouch, 1984: 70). Perhaps the first public indication of the extent of the problems faced came in late 1979 when the government, expecting a serious balance of payments shortfall, approached the IMF for emergency credits. Access to these credits was to be conditional upon the government accepting various IMF economic performance criteria including the lifting of luxury imports bans, drastically revised fiscal and monetary policies, a 'realistic' (that is, higher priced) energy policy and a revision of agricultural and industrial policies (Ho, 1979: 94–6). This was the standard package of reforms demanded by the IMF, and it is one that has caused considerable conflict in other countries such as Jamaica, Tanzania and Mexico (Girvan and Bernal, 1982; Pool and Stamos, 1985: 9–14).

While some technocrats such as Phisit Pakkasem, of the Economic Ministers' Council, indicated that it was necessary to accept IMF 'discipline', others such as the then Bangkok Bank president, Boonchu Rojanastien, argued that the government should not '...let the IMF control us. I'm fighting this arrangement', he stated (Ho, 1980a: 40). Indeed, the issue of IMF credits and fiscal discipline became a major part of the political debate over economic management.

Opponents of the Kriangsak government seized upon the conditionality of the proposed IMF credits to emphasise the incompetence of the government in economic matters (Ho, 1980a: 40). In 1979 the government had intended to raise oil, electricity and water charges in an effort to bring them into line with the cost of imported petroleum. However, a 55 per cent increase in electricity prices was met with a hail of protest, especially as inflation was already exceeding 20 per cent. The opposition brought together not only Kriangsak's political opponents, but also right-wing groups, students and some unionists (Nations, 1979: 96–9; Niksch, 1981: 230). In addition, a number of business people, especially industrialists, opposed the government's policies, because while public utility prices had risen substantially the government maintained controlled prices on a large range of goods. ISI manufacturers were especially affected and complained bitterly. When the government raised some of these prices also, a hail of populist protest ensued (*Business in Thailand*, October 1981: 15–18). This opposition played a large role in the early demise of the Kriangsak government in 1980 (Darling, 1980: 186). In the words of one journalist,

> Economic populism...crystallised around the government-authorised price increases, and ran into a head-on clash with cabinet

technocrats determined to stand by the principles of fiscal responsibility and national economic discipline. The technocrats lost. [Nations, 1979: 99]

But they were not defeated.

The World Bank mission of 1980 was to reinforce the technocrats' perception of 'responsibility', 'discipline' and the measures required to restore the economy to high growth levels. This mission listed a number of serious economic problems—balance of trade deficits, inflation, wealth and income disparities, high levels of import protection, an inward-looking industrialisation strategy, stagnation in the agricultural sector, failure to utilise a 'comparative advantage' in cheap labour, and foreign exchange problems (IBRD, 1980: ch. 1; Santi, 1981: 21). The Bank's recipe for overcoming these problems was 'structural adjustment'. In essence, this meant that Thailand's fifth five-year plan was to be one-third financed by the World Bank, if the government agreed to implement specific changes. The basic changes demanded were: increased export orientation, reductions in protection levels, a devaluation, an expansion of the tax base, and lower growth targets so as to reduce imports (Santi, 1981: 22). While admitting that some of its past advice had been wrong-headed, the Bank insisted that Thailand's economic future would be secured if the country opened itself to the world market (Ho, 1981: 40-4).

The policies demanded of the Thai government were in line with a change that was taking place within the World Bank. With the advent of the Reagan administration in the United States, the Bank, which had for a time championed basic needs and employment generation in their programmes, adopted a new orthodoxy which was more in line with the ideological bent of the Reagan administration. The new path to development demanded the acceptance of the 'magic of the marketplace', with a leading role for the private sector and 'adjustments' for 'economic efficiency' (Rowley, 1984: 65). Countries that accepted these prescriptions were to be favoured by the World Bank in its lending policies (Rowley, 1982: 131).

Significantly, these Western, free-market and overtly ideological prescriptions were accepted by General Prem's government, whereas those of the IMF had been rejected only a short time previously. It seems that once in power those who had previously opposed these remedies, most notably Boonchu and the Social Action Party (SAP—*phak kitsangkhom*), were willing to embrace them. This was especially so as the first structural adjustment loans (SALs), while large, left control of economic decision-making largely in the hands of the Thai government. More importantly, Boonchu and his supporters were said to have seen the World Bank as a 'useful and influential ally in their fight to overcome vested interests within Thai business and bureaucratic circles' (Ho, 1981: 40).

It was no coincidence that these Bank proposals coincided with the dreams and plans of some of Thailand's most powerful technocrats, political leaders and business groups. Boonchu's proposal for 'Thailand Incorporated', an efficient, well-oiled and outward-looking economic machine, were congruent with World Bank proposals and emerged at about the same time (Santi, 1981: 23; Ho, 1980b: 40–3). Boonchu and some of his associates had had consultations with the World Bank even before Kriangsak was replaced by Prem, with Boonchu as deputy premier for economic affairs (*FEER*, 23 May 1980: 43). In addition, Amnuay Viravan, who had been a strong supporter of EOI since his time as secretary of the Board of Investment (*Bangkok World*, 2 April 1969: 13), was appointed finance minister. Explaining the World Bank relationship, he stated:

> We have been promoting export-oriented industrialisation for some time—when Boonchu was finance minister four years ago we brought this to the attention of the World Bank's consultative group... This World Bank report... [is] consistent with our belief that this is the way we'll have to chart our industrial development programme. The whole idea is to be able to produce competitively and find markets overseas. And even more important is to channel new investments towards export-oriented industries where we have a comparative advantage, such as labour and natural resources. [*FEER*, 23 May 1980: 46]

The congruence between the fifth plan and the World Bank report is also clear (Santi, 1981: 23).

In spite of the apparent dominance of these 'free-market' views, strong opposition re-emerged. For example, the newspaper *Ban muang* (cited in *BP*, 19 April 1981: 6) reflected a growing concern amongst academics and business people when it stated that if the government was to continue to accept and implement World Bank policies, '... the Thai people would be squeezed to such an extent that they will have no clothes [with which] to cover themselves...'. Further oil and electricity price rises and a dispute over oil supplies brought about a split within the first Prem government. Boonchu and his SAP colleagues wanted total control over economic policy, but this was opposed by the Chart Thai Party which had a strong base of support amongst industrialists who had accumulated their capital under the ISI strategy (Crouch, 1984: 71).[7] Chart Thai won the political fight, and the SAP withdrew from the coalition. This was not to be the end of the battle, however, for the defeat of Boonchu and his associates left the way open for a number of technocrats, who remained in cabinet, to push for more market-oriented, World Bank-type proposals. Indeed, following Bank and IMF advice, the baht was devalued by 8.7 per cent (Niksch, 1982: 191–2, 196).

Economic growth continued apace after the devaluation, and it was only in 1982 that a downturn began. High domestic interest rates and low commodity prices began to have a dampening effect on investment, weakened the current account balance and, together with a 50 per cent shortfall in natural gas production for 1982, meant that the government was again forced to consider the use of its IMF special drawing rights. This time Thailand took its full quota (about US$300 million), and in return the IMF demanded austerity (Suchitra, 1983: 174–5).

The economic situation worsened in 1983 as a balance of payments deficit was recorded and the Bank of Thailand placed restrictions on commercial bank credits for imports. Despite this, as growth rates momentarily rose, imports grew while exports fell. In addition, private sector investment declined by over 13 per cent, while that by the state rose by more than 6 per cent (Suchitra, 1984: 191; *Bangkok Post* (eds), 1983: 15, 33).

All of this occurred as the SALs were being received. The first two SALs were accepted in 1982 and 1983, the first two years of the fifth five-year plan, but the World Bank agreed that structural adjustment had effectively begun in 1979 with the first state enterprise price rises (IBRD, 1983, vol. 1: xv). Other adjustments included the removal of price controls, a further reduction in tariffs, a general review of fiscal policies and the beginnings of industrial projects on the eastern seaboard (IBRD, 1983, vol. 1: 15). The Bank was pleased with Thailand's performance, and when its president, A.W. Clausen, visited Thailand in 1982 he officially handed over the second SAL and praised the eastern seaboard projects (*Business in Thailand*, November 1982: 11–12). Nevertheless, the Bank did suggest that more could have been done to reform state enterprises. However, the government fell behind in its reform programme, mainly due to political opposition to World Bank and IMF adjustment policies which impinged on areas many felt were the rightful domain of the government (*FEER*, 27 September 1984: 109). This became clear in the very public dispute over the further devaluation of the baht.

Both the IMF and World Bank had argued strongly for a 'flexible' foreign exchange policy—that is, they wanted the baht tied to a 'basket' of currencies rather than being effectively tied to the US dollar (*FEER*, 27 September 1984: 109). To do this would have meant an effective devaluation of the baht and, hence, a worsening of the foreign debt problem. When an almost 15 per cent devaluation was announced in November 1984, matters came to a head, with supreme commander of the armed forces General Arthit Kamlang-ek denouncing the devaluation. Military leaders were concerned that the devaluation would damage their foreign purchasing power, and Arthit criticised the government for not consulting with the armed forces prior to taking the decision (*Business in Thailand*, December 1984: 35). A number of other groups supported the Arthit line, including farmers, importers, and the big financial losers, manufacturers still operating under ISI conditions. Indeed, the Chart Thai Party called for parliament to be reconvened so that the devaluation could be debated (*Business in Thailand*, December 1984: 36–9). Nevertheless, the decision stood, the decision being seen as a significant victory for the pro-World Bank policies of finance minister Sommai Hoontrakul (Boonsong & Sherwell, 1985: 14). However, the predicted benefits of the devaluation were slow in coming, and the general economic situation further deteriorated.

Divisions over World Bank and IMF policies being adopted by the Prem government became even clearer in 1985. This was so primarily because the long-avoided recession was beginning to affect increasing numbers of the population. As noted above, reports of rapidly increasing unemployment, large-scale retrenchments and lay-offs, falls in farm incomes, and declining wages and conditions of work began to fill the newspapers. Reflecting the views of those who had opposed the austerity programmes, one news magazine suggested that '. . . it is clear that economic development laws, policies and plans are bound to the financial dictates of transnational institutions such as the World Bank and IMF.' It was further argued that the power of these groups was seen in their demands in areas considered domestic (*Arthit-wiwat*, 9–15 July 1985: 42).

The crisis of the 1980s had had such an impact that bankers, industrialists, bureaucrats and political and military leaders were questioning IMF and World Bank conditionality and austerity programmes. Communications minister and leader of the Prachakon Thai Party, Samak Sundaravej, complained that the World Bank was attempting to dictate policies to him, and he raised doubts concerning future acceptance of Bank loans (and conditions) for a series of projects (*BP*, 28 July 1985: 1, 3). Reflecting this growing concern, one newspaper columnist noted:

> It's not that they don't know that times have changed. It's just that they can't seem to accept it. . . [T]he boys over at the World Bank appear to be having great deal of difficulty in accepting that the good old days are now over—you know, those days when everyone jumped when the World Bank. . . said to jump. . . [P]erhaps not at Tha Chang [Ministry of Finance] where the World Bank's word is still close to law, and perhaps not to Bangkhunprom [Bank of Thailand] which is. . . a World Bank stronghold. . . [But] now, when the World Bank says jump, they're the ones who are likely to be told to go jump instead. [*BP*, 29 July 1985: 15]

It was added that cheaper loans could be raised elsewhere, and without the stringent conditions and loss of national economic decision-making power. Indeed, in 1986 the third SAL was dropped from Thailand's list of priority borrowings, and more emphasis was placed on securing cheaper Japanese loans and credits (*FEER*, 20 February 1986: 9).

The World Bank countered, being drawn openly into the political debate and thus confirming some of the adverse impressions of the Bank's backroom dealings and influence. First, Bank officials publicly disputed the gloomy assessments of the state of the economy, arguing that things would improve. These officials were concerned that criticism of government policy could lead some economic ministers to seek 'quick-fix' solutions rather than adhering to the politically unpopular economic medicine of reductions in state expenditure, 'realistic' exchange rates and keeping inflation low, which the Bank and IMF saw as being necessary for long-term economic health (*BP*, 24 July 1985: 13). Second, the Bank entered the political debate by questioning Samak's statements and even his right to make public comments concerning Bank negotiations with the government (*BP*, 27 July 1985: 1, 20). Third, the Bank reemphasised the need to open the economy and privatise state enterprises, and perhaps surprisingly, given the debate on foreign debt, reaffirmed the importance of international capital flows in development (*BP*, 24 July 1985: 13). At this point, the Bank was clearly siding with those technocrats in the Bank of Thailand and Ministry of Finance who supported Minister Sommai, against the political leaders. This line was continued in the debate over the eastern seaboard industrial developments.

The debate is clearly continuing, but it is also apparent that many are far from convinced that the IMF and World Bank medicine is best for Thailand. This is emphasised by the fact that the allocation of SALs has fallen well behind schedule (*FEER*, 27 September 1984: 109).

Despite the earlier praise for these projects, by mid-1985 the World Bank had been drawn into a conflict which saw free-marketeering technocrats, and especially those at the head of the Ministry of Finance and Bank of Thailand (*BP*, 23 November 1985: 4), arguing that the debt crisis demanded a postponement or cancellation of the scheme. Others, notably the NESDB and the Ministry of Industry, had urged that the project go ahead, reaffirming the original goals of the scheme: to catapult Thailand into an industrial future (*BP*, 23 November 1985: 4; 28 November 1985: 15, 17). The conflict distilled many of the issues separating the competing economic perspectives, such as state involvement, foreign loans, free trade, and import substitution. The World Bank took the opportunity to oppose the scheme, arguing that it would cause a blow-out in foreign debt and questioning its economic viability. This report, put together quickly in order to support the opponents of the scheme, caused considerable adverse comment in the press for its overtly political stance (*BP*, 5 December 1985: 17). The cabinet eventually decided to continue the projects, without major modification, and even though they necessitated considerably overseas borrowing. The decision was a surprise, for the opponents of the project had had a high public profile. However, the proponents of the scheme had been able to lobby the support of Japanese contractors and the Japanese government, and also the support of those ministers more inclined towards economic nationalism, most notably SAP's deputy finance minister Suthee Singhasaneh who openly opposed Sommai. Their opponents fought back, however, and in February 1986 elements of the project were again under threat, especially as local banks were objecting to being 'forced' to participate in the project's capitalisation (*Asiaweek*, 12 January 1986: 73; *FEER*, 13 February 1986: 11; 20 February 1986: 53-4)

These debates are clearly continuing, but it is also apparent that many are far from convinced that the IMF and World Bank formulae are best for Thailand. Bank officials have complained that they find it increasingly difficult to have their projects accepted by the government, claiming that the decision-making process on World Bank projects is 'volatile' (*BP*, 15 December 1985: 7). Meanwhile, there was great pressure on Prem, especially from the SAP, for Sommai to be replaced as finance minister, and the discontent in cabinet eventually led to defections from the SAP and, in part, forced the July 1986 elections (*BP*, 4 December 1985: 1; *Asiaweek*, 12 January 1986: 19; *FEER*, 13 February 1986: 38). In the new cabinet, Sommai was conspicuous by his absence, and even the World Bank could be heard making more conciliatory statements, urging growth rather than restraint (*FEER*, 24 July 1986: 54-5; 18 September 1986: 76-8).

Conclusion

There can be little doubt that the Thai economy has grown at remarkable rates over the past two to three decades. This growth has produced not only a substantial restructuring of the economy but also significant changes in the class structure. Today the capitalist class has emerged as the dominant class, with considerable power in the political sphere.

Since 1960 capitalist development has been advanced markedly through the adoption of an ISI strategy which furthered the interests of industrial and banking capitalists. In more recent times, the emergence of the EOI strategy has further enhanced the position of big manufacturers and their financial backers. The rapid expansion of capitalism saw few major setbacks until the 1980s. The crisis of the

National interests and economic downturn: Thailand 77

1980s, mediated by the World Bank and IMF, has indicated significant divergences in economic policymaking. The clearest and most violent expression of these divergences came in the coup attempts of 1981 and 1985. The 'Young Turks' of the army who perpetrated the 1981 abortive coup stated, *inter alia*,

> In economics, it is... a big mistake for a government to fail to take drastic action to solve problems. The majority of the people are suffering acutely from poverty as the cost of living is skyrocketing. The government was unable ro relieve the people's hardships. The national reserves have been depleted and are now in deficit which harms the country's credit as a whole. The state's indebtedness is worsening and has created a heavy burden for the people. In such a situation, if the same economic line were to be pursued, the majority of people will be in a hopeless situation... [cited in Chai-Anan, 1982: 85]

Taking this populist line further, the 'Young Turks' are said to have drawn up a 'hit-list' of prominent capitalists for elimination (*Prachammit*, 30 May 1981: 10–13). Prem and his supporters, including the ideologically and economically powerful royal family, were able to defeat this coup, but by 1985 the 'Young Turks'' critique of economic policy must have seemed prophetic. The phoenix of populism re-emerged in September 1985 with a further coup attempt, and again economic problems were cited as a justification for the attempted putsch (*Asiaweek*, 20 September 1985: 8–16; *BP*, 10 September 1985).

Less spectacularly, the machinations over economic policy played themselves out within the policymaking bodies where some technocrats favoured the World Bank and IMF market-oriented strategies, while others favoured a more nationally oriented strategy which pushed EOI but maintained and expanded ISI in some areas. This latter group argued that export orientation had opened the economy to the vagaries of the world market, causing problems in areas such as textiles, but they also argued that ISI had not yet run its course, especially in heavy industry and in some areas of light manufacturing (see Virabongse et al., 1983: 20, 98).

This latter argument appears sensible as state economic strategists are making policy on matters that are outside their influence, as Thai capitalists restructure their activities within a rapidly changing international capitalist system. It seems clear that the niche in the system which Thai capitalists were carving out for themselves in the 1960s and 1970s will be maintained, but the conditions for its occupation of this position will be altered. These changed conditions seem to have been largely ignored in the confusion surrounding the economic crisis of the 1980s, where most attention has been given to increased protectionism in the advanced industrialised countries and to the recession. Such attention is warranted, but the assumption that everything will return to 'normal' or to a situation like that of the early 1970s is not entirely justified (Cho, 1985: 65-6).

Recent observers (Cho, 1985; Kenichi, 1985) have noted a trend by some TNCs to return their operations to the advanced industrialised countries. This is due to a number of factors. First, as was noted above, cheap labour became a mirage, as wages increased in one place and the TNC moved to another in search of cheaper wage-labour. Second, technological innovation has vastly increased the productivity of labour in the advanced countries, so that the cheap labour of the Third World is not as attractive as it was. This has even been the case in textiles and electronics, the engines of EOI in many countries (Cho, 1985: 70-5). Third, the major markets remain in the advanced industrialised countries, and production within these areas still carries advantages, especially as protectionism increases. Even some Third World TNCs have moved some of their operations to the advanced industrial countries (Cho, 1985: 72-6). Fourth, real wages have been on the decline in many advanced capitalist countries, and union membership has declined, making the application of wage-labour in these places more attractive for capitalists than a decade ago (Cho, 1985: 76-7). Finally, there is a growing militancy amongst farmers and wage-labourers in the Third World (Broad, 1984; Cho, 1985: 82-3).

All of these trends have had an impact in contemporary Thailand, and it is within this context that Thai capital will reorient its production, and that the state will make its economic policies. In the immediate future, however, the prospects for a sustained economic upturn appear problematic, while the ground for political conflict seems fertile.

Economically, commodity markets seem likely to remain depressed, at least in the short to medium term, and possibly longer, as some economists are now suggesting that the decline is not cyclical but due to chronic structural problems in the world economy (*BP*, 12 December 1985: 19, 21). In addition, increased protectionism and subsidisation in the advanced industrial countries, especially for consumer goods and agricultural commodities, make the future for all Third World countries bleak, especially if the US economy continues to exhibit low growth rates. These prospects make the balance of payments problems more difficult to overcome, although falling oil prices are a bonus. Also, there seems to be no relief on the debt front until the 1990s (Bandid & Narit, 1985).

These economic conditions will mean that there will be more calls for the protection and support of local industry and agriculture (*BP*, 12 November 1985: 16; 25 November 1985: 19). Such a scenario suggests that political conflict could follow. Certainly, the debate over state intervention will continue, and nationalist responses to the economic downturn will be opposed by the IMF and World Bank, and this, in itself, will be opposed. For example, the call has already gone out from Boonchu Rojanastien for Thais to '...refuse to be dragged along by forces beyond our control...[W]e must regain control of our own destiny' (*BP*, 3 December 1985: 3). And as conditions worsen for workers and peasants, they too will be drawn into the political conflict. In previous times conflict precipitated by these groups has left the way open for the military to step in and seize power. The possibility of such a development cannot, despite the movement towards parliamentary forms, be ignored.

S.K. JAYASURIYA

4
The politics of economic policy in the Philippines during the Marcos era

At the end of 1985 the Philippines had the lowest per capita income of all the ASEAN member nations. Indeed, the economy had contracted so rapidly since 1982 that per capita incomes had fallen to the levels of a decade earlier (Table 4.1). Its external debt was nearly equal to gross national product (GNP) and was three times the value of exports. The domestic banking system and other financial institutions were in deep trouble, investment (as a share of GNP) was the lowest for more than two decades, and despite the downfall of Ferdinand Marcos and the accession to power of Mrs Cory Aquino, the country continued to be in the grip of the biggest political and economic crisis since the Second World War.

To many observers this dramatic collapse of the economy, which also destroyed the authoritarian Marcos regime, came as a surprise. After all—if the official figures were to be believed—by many of the conventional indicators, the Philippines had not done too badly during the 1970s. Gross domestic product grew by 5.1 per cent in the 1960s and accelerated during the 1970s to more than 6 per cent. Indeed, its performance in the 1970s was superior to that of oil-importing middle-income countries as a whole. Levels of investment rose during this decade and averaged 30 per cent of GNP in the period 1973–82. Per capita food production grew by more than 20 per cent during the decade, and the country became self-sufficient in rice. Export growth averaged nearly 8 per cent annually compared with only 2.2 per cent in the 1960s. While inflation (over 13 per cent per annum) was considerably higher than during the previous decade (5.8 per cent), this was similar to other lower-middle-income economies as a whole. Social indicators such as life expectancy and literacy, too, were quite high (World Bank, 1983). Despite some insurgency problems (the communist-led New Peoples Army and the Muslim secessionist movement

Philippines during the Marcos era

Table 4.1 Per capita GNP of the Philippines, 1950–85

	Current pesos	1972 pesos
1950	343	806
1955	399	1 006
1960	505	1 101
1965	736	1 244
1970	1 133	1 358
1971	1 310	1 396
1972	1 427	1 427
1973	1 790	1 522
1974	2 430	1 573
1975	2 705	1 622
1976	3 054	1 673
1977	3 454	1 741
1978	3 880	1 810
1979	4 691	1 884
1980	5 486	1 917
1981	6 131	1 939
1982	6 605	1 921
1983	7 284	1 987
1984	10 045	1 644
1985		

Sources: National Economic and Development Authority (NEDA) (1985a) *Philippine Statistical Year Book 1985*
Asian Development Bank (ADB): *Key Economic Indicators* (various issues)
NEDA: *The National Income Accounts of the Philippines 1983–1985 (Advance Estimates as of December 1985)*

in Mindanao), the military-backed Marcos regime appeared to be firmly in control even at the beginning of this decade. Discussions of political changes typically centred on issues of succession in the event of Marcos' death or (more likely) retirement. Martial law had officially ended in January 1981 after more than eight years. But real legislative and executive power remained in the hands of Marcos, who was re-elected in an election six months later (June 1981) in which the biggest problem for the regime was to find an opponent to run against Marcos.

This appearance of general political and economic stability was deceptive, however. Throughout the 1970s fundamental problems were accumulating in the Philippines which would lay the basis for explosive changes in the economic structure and the authoritarian political regime. The developments in the international economy in the early 1980s, expressed in the collapse of commodity prices and the precipitation of a profound crisis in the international financial system centred on the global debt problem, were forcing all the underlying accumulated contradictions in the economy to a head. By the end of 1982, the Philippine economy was already in deep crisis. The country was a powder keg waiting for a spark. This came from the gun of the military assassin who shot dead the opposition leader Benigno Aquino as he stepped down to the tarmac at Manila airport on 21 August 1983.

While the details of the Philippine economic and political history cannot be discussed here, some acquaintance with that history is essential to understanding the more recent developments. When Japanese occupation of the Philippines ended with its reconquest by US forces in 1944–45, the Philippines faced a daunting task of national reconstruction. Its economy was ravaged, and much of its infrastructure had been destroyed or severely damaged. The state machinery was weak, and many of the pre-war political leaders drawn from the traditional Filipino elite were compromised by collaboration with the Japanese occupation forces. A large section of the partisan fighters drawn from the peasantry was under communist leadership. In this situation of a profound economic, political and social crisis, the United States was under enormous pressure, both at home and in the Philippines, to honour its wartime promises and grant independence to the Philippines. Thus, it faced the difficult strategic task of establishing a stable pro-US government which would guarantee continuing US access to Filipino assets—both economic and military.

Thus, it was inevitable that when formal independence was granted in 1946[1] it in no way meant an end to the US role in the Philippines. The rehabilitation of its economy in the immediate post-war years took place under the direct and open supervision of the US.

The post-independence political and economic developments in the Philippines have continued to be conditioned by close links with the US even after the lapsing or changing of many of the more openly 'exploitative' provisions of the treaties agreed to at the time of independence. The recurrent economic crises, the succession of political regimes characterised by corruption, scandal and fraud and the direct threat posed by the revolutionary forces of the communist-led Hukbalahap (Huks) made US intervention and economic and military assistance absolutely essential for the survival of the post-independence regimes until well into the 1950s. During the immediate post-war years, the US had to intervene directly more than once to impose order and some unity on the squabbling politicians and to organise the crushing of the Huk rebellion. From the very beginning of its independent existence the sharpness of class and factional antagonisms brought into sharpest relief the weaknesses of the Filipino elite, who never managed to demonstrate the qualities of strength and leadership needed to inspire and unify the nation to face the challenges of economic development. Lacking economic strength and political will, they had to rely on the state and US patronage for both political and economic power.

The adoption of what later came to be known as the import-substitution industrialisation (ISI) strategy by the Philippines at the beginning of the 1950s was a response to these particular political and economic conditions. Import restrictions had been originally imposed for balance of payments reasons but had been maintained subsequently for protectionist motives. While these had the political attraction of appearing to signal a 'nationalist' orientation, we will argue that, in essence, they were the product of an alliance forged by a weak Filipino elite with major American interests to use the state to extract economic and political power at the expense of the Chinese-Filipino entrepreneurs who had major interests, particularly in trade and commerce. (The resourceful Chinese-Filipino entrepreneurs, however, were often able to find diverse methods of resisting attacks on their economic power.) Thus the Philippines, which had probably the least nationalistic stance in political and economic policies and the closest ties with its ex-colonial power among the newly independent countries of Asia, was one of the earliest to embark on an ISI strategy. And, given the privileged position of US capital within this protectionist system, it generated no opposition in the US.

Exchange and trade controls, many of which were put in place during the balance of payments crisis in 1949, became pervasive by the mid-1950s. Various quantitative controls, particularly quotas and licensing regulations, enabled those who had the levers of the state in their hands to dispense patronage and build up political as well as economic bases of support. Throughout the subsequent three decades and particularly from the late 1950s onwards when problems with the strategy were becoming apparent and its impact on traditional export crop sectors (particularly sugar) were being acutely felt, it generated political opposition. However, it survived in its essentials, and the Philippine manufacturing sector as it emerged into the 1970s was indelibly stamped with the well-known effects of prolonged development within a structure of high protection.

There is no doubt that ISI policies helped the manufacturing sector in the Philippines to grow very rapidly, particularly during its early period in the 1950s. During the 1950s it consistently grew at a faster rate than the economy as a whole and, until 1980, at least kept pace with the rest of the economy (Table 4.2). This growth in manufacturing (and in the industrial sector as a whole) was reflected in the changing structure of the economy. Between 1950 and 1980, the share of manufacturing rose from 8 to 25 per cent and that of industry as a whole rose from 14 to 37 per cent, while the share of agriculture declined from 42 to 23 per cent (Table 4.3).

The initial rapid growth of manufacturing is partly to be attributed to a catching-up process in view of the stagnation and destruction of the war years (Baldwin, 1975). However, the growing economy, too,

Table 4.2 Average annual growth rates (per cent) of GDP in the Philippines, by industrial origin, 1949–85

	1949–53	1953–57	1957–61	1961–70	1970–80	1980–82	1982–85
Agriculture, fishery and forestry	7.7	4.3	4.2	4.3	4.9	3.4	0.0
Industry	8.8	8.1	3.7	6.0	8.4	3.3	−3.7
Manufacturing[a]	14.1	11.1	5.7	6.7	6.9	2.9	−4.3
Services	9.4	0.6	4.6	5.2	5.3	3.4	0.0
GDP[b]	8.6	6.2	4.2	5.1	6.2	3.4	−2.4

Notes: [a] Manufacturing is included in 'industry'
[b] Figures for 1949 to 1961 refer to net domestic product
Sources: Bautista (1980)
NEDA *The National Income Accounts of the Philippines 1983–1985 (Advance Estimates as of December 1985)*
World Bank *World Development Report* (various issues)

Table 4.3 Percentage distribution of gross domestic product in the Philippines, by industrial origin, 1960–85

	1950	1960	1970	1980	1985
Agriculture, fishery and forestry	42	26	28	23	25
Industry	14	28	30	37	32
Manufacturing[a]	8	20	23	25	24
Services	44	46	42	40	43

Note: [a] Manufacturing is included in 'industry'
Sources: NEDA *Philippine Statistical Year Book* (various issues)
NEDA *The National Income Accounts of the Philippines 1983–1985* (Advance Estimates as of December 1985)

provided considerable expansion in demand for a whole range of consumer goods. There was significant growth in many industries including textiles, chemicals, basic metals, machinery and miscellaneous manufactures. By the 1970s the country possessed a substantial industrial base. During this decade it continued to grow quite rapidly. In fact, the share of manufactures in total exports rose remarkably, and by the end of the decade was accounting for about half of the merchandise exports; in 1965 its share had been a mere 6 per cent.

While this performance appears impressive, it must be qualified in several ways. First, by the middle of the 1970s it was becoming clear that most of the older established manufacturing industries were unable to expand beyond the protected home market. Having grown up surrounded by high tariffs—the highest among the ASEAN countries in the mid-1970s—they were inefficient and unable to survive without continuing high subsidies and/or protection and were unable to develop as viable export industries (Bautista & Power, 1979). The most inefficient industries had the highest protection (Tan, 1983). Second, many of the new manufactured exports, which generated the export boom in the 1970s, had very low domestic value added, even though a substantial switch to more labour-intensive manufactures had occurred (Aritt & Hill, 1985). Third, despite the expansion in labour-intensive products, there was a pronounced capital bias in technology which reduced the overall impact on employment. (Total employment in manufacturing has remained virtually stagnant at about 10–12 per cent of total employment since the 1950s (World Bank, 1980).) Fourth, when compared with its ASEAN neighbours—particularly with Thailand, which has many similarities in terms of size of country, population and the like—its performance during the 1970s was poor (Hill & Jayasuriya, 1985). Thus, its average annual growth rate of manufacturing during the decade was only 7 per cent while all other

ASEAN countries had rates of 10 per cent or more; exports (as a percentage of total manufacturing output) were stagnant; the index of real labour productivity was the lowest in ASEAN and, in contrast to all other countries, real wage rates in manufacturing actually declined during the 1970s (Ariff & Hill, 1985), a point to which we will return later.

Agriculture grew steadily during the 1970s, with production growing at an annual rate of 4.9 per cent, up from the 4.3 per cent of the previous decade. While its share in GDP declined, it continued to provide the bulk of employment and a large share of export revenues (National Economic and Development Authority (NEDA), 1985a).

Output growth derived primarily from higher yields of which the changes in the rice sector were the most dramatic. Using high-yielding varieties (HYVs) generated at the International Rice Research Institute (located in the Philippines), the government launched the 'Masagana 99' programme in 1973. The immediate impetus to this effort came from a harvest failure and subsequent rice shortages which threatened to develop into a major political crisis for the newly installed martial law regime. To facilitate adoption of the package of modern inputs and associated practices, the programme provided subsidised credit, inputs and extensive advice. Adoption of the new technology was rapid, and output rose 6 per cent per year between 1973 and 1978 (NEDA, 1985b). In 1977, self-sufficiency in rice was proclaimed. By the end of the decade most of the rice-growing area—both irrigated and rainfed—was sown to high-yielding varieties, and fertiliser use had doubled.

Both maize and coconut output grew throughout the decade, although there was little or no technological change in these crops. Sugar output, after rising rapidly in the mid-1970s, has declined since.

This general growth in agriculture, however, took place in the context of government policies that discriminated against the agricultural sector in general (David, 1983). Despite some subsidies, particularly for rice production, the net effects of government policies were so adverse that agricultural incomes were actually lowered by some 30 per cent (Bautista, 1984). By the end of the decade, few, if any, small farmers were better off. Real wages of agricultural labourers declined substantially from the already quite low levels of the mid-1970s (Coxhead, 1984).

The major external factor adversely affecting the Philippine economy in the post-1972 period was the deterioration in the international (barter) terms of trade. However, the Philippines did experience a very significant favourable change in the terms of trade immediately after the declaration of martial law as prices of its major exports rose to record levels in 1973 and 1974. The rise in export prices more than compensated for the initial effects of the first OPEC oil price rise; the terms of trade in 1974 were 14.5 per cent higher than in 1972 (NEDA, 1983). This favourable exogenous shock assisted the regime to consolidate itself in the crucial early years of martial law.

However, this was short lived. In 1975 the boom ended and the terms of trade moved down sharply, declining by 38 per cent from 1974 to 1977. Despite some improvement in 1978–79, in 1982 it was 49 per cent below the level of 1974 (NEDA, 1983).

Even though Philippine foreign trade, at about a third of GNP, is not particularly high compared with other similar economies, a terms of trade decline of this magnitude nevertheless implied a serious cut in the real income of the country. Adjustment to this situation would have involved painful measures with major political risks.

However, because of a number of factors—which will be discussed in some detail later—the regime was able to avoid such measures principally by resorting to foreign borrowings. Government borrowings were used to finance increasingly large budget deficits (Table 4.4). No real devaluation was implemented. The real effective exchange rate remained almost unchanged between 1972 and 1982 (Pante, 1982; Hill & Jayasuriya, 1985). Both public and private sector investment rose, as did their external debt, with the bulk of the private sector debt being underwritten by government guarantees.

The second oil price shock in 1979 and the subsequent collapse in export commodities—sugar and coconuts were particularly badly hit—worsened the terms of trade while the real interest rates in the

Table 4.4 Budget deficit and public sector debt in the Philippines, 1961–83 (as a percentage of GNP)

Period	Budget deficit	Public sector domestic debt	Public sector foreign debt	Total public sector debt
1961–65	0.97	9.5	1.0	10.5
1966–70	1.18	9.4	2.6	12.0
1971–75	0.6	9.6	3.4	13.0
1976	1.8	9.6	4.5	13.1
1977	1.9	9.7	5.6	15.1
1978	1.2	10.0	6.9	16.9
1979	0.2	8.6	6.2	14.8
1980	1.4	8.3	6.6	14.9
1981	4.0	9.4	9.0	18.4
1982	4.3	11.1	26.3	37.4
1983	1.8	11.5	49.4	61.0
1984	1.5	n.a.	n.a.	n.a.
1985	n.a.	n.a.	n.a.	n.a.

Sources: Asian Development Bank (ADB) Key Indicators of Developing Member Countries of ADB (various issues)
NEDA Philippines Statistical Year Book (various issues).

international capital market were rising. A sharp recession in the economy could be averted only by further increasing borrowings. And this is precisely what the regime proceeded to do. With conditions tightening in the international capital market, recourse had to be made to high-interest short-term borrowings. The impact of rising real interest rates on the debt-service burden started to worsen rapidly, particularly as an increasingly large proportion of debts were on floating interest rates. (According to IMF sources, 41 per cent of the loans were on floating rates in 1982 compared to only 17 per cent in 1976.) Increased export volume compensated to some extent for the decline in terms of trade, but it was completely inadequate to finance the rapid growth of imports.

The debt service, as a ratio of export earnings, nearly doubled between 1980 and 1982, rising from 21 per cent to over 38 per cent. But the worst was yet to come. In 1982 the Latin American debt crisis erupted sending shockwaves throughout the international banking system. Suddenly the Philippines found that the halcyon days of practically unlimited borrowings were over as bankers put up shutters on further lending. The time of reckoning had come for the regime and the economy. Indeed, it was the realisation that this crisis would precipitate major political changes that led to Benigno Aquino's decision to return to the Philippines. Within hours of his assassination the crisis exploded into the open. Certainly, international factors were crucial to the development of the Philippine crisis. However, the pace and pattern of its evolution and its specific characteristics were determined by the nature of the Marcos regime as well as by the particular structural characteristics of the Philippine economy. To understand the nature of the regime, it is necessary to analyse the circumstances in which Marcos established authoritarian rule.

In 1972, the Philippines was in the grip of a profound social and political crisis. This had its proximate roots in the economic crisis that had been precipitated in 1969 by the country's inability to meet its external debt payments (which, in many ways, was a forerunner of the 1983 crisis). Heavy government spending in the election year of 1969 by the first Marcos government had to be financed by both domestic and foreign borrowings, including short-term debt. The budget deficit in 1969 was three times larger than in the previous year and roughly equal to the accumulative deficits between 1961 and 1968; money supply rose by over 20 per cent in the last four months alone (Baldwin, 1975). The balance of payments, which had been steadily deteriorating over the previous period, nosedived, and the country was unable to meet its payment obligations. An emergency mission from the IMF arrived in January 1970, with foreign creditors insisting that a restructuring of debt was conditional on government acceptance of an IMF stabilisation package. The negotiated package included severe restraints on expenditure and a currency devaluation. The peso was floated, and rapidly depreciated by 60 per cent relative to the US dollar by the end of the year. National consumption was slashed with drastic effects on the real wages which suffered a dramatic decline (Lal, 1983).

This crisis, while triggered by large government spending in an election year, had deeper roots. It demonstrated that despite two decades of growth, the economy remained fundamentally weak and vulnerable. It was no accident that none of the administrations, including the first Marcos presidency, had been able to undertake fundamental structural reforms. Two major groups, the agriculture-based oligarchs—mostly in the export crop sectors—and the industrial and mercantilist capitalists dominated the economy. The sugar oligarchs were the most powerful group within the former and traditionally had dominated political and social life. While many of the industrial and mercantilist capitalists originated from or had close ties with the agricultural oligarchs, their economic interests had increasingly come into conflict in the post-independence years. The protectionist regime had enabled industrial capital, often in close collaboration with US capital, to develop into a major force. During the 1950s the overvaluation of the peso, which directly hurt exports, led to periodic conflicts between these groups. For example, those who dealt with export crops had welcomed a devaluation and other liberalisation measures adopted in 1960, whereas major industrial capitalist groups had vehemently opposed them. Throughout the 1960s their conflicts periodically intensified and spilled over into the political arena.

Despite these conflicts, and while the balance of forces shifted at times, successive administrations had strived to establish policies that would reflect a basic compromise between these contending groups. The political institutions and the electoral process provided the framework and the forum in which the conflicting interests attempted to achieve positions of relative strength. The state apparatus and its executive head, the president, were increasingly placed in the position of arbiter between the conflicting interests. Throughout the two and a half decades of independence, the clash and conflict of elite groups and interests had taken place within the (more or less) liberal democratic political institutions (Abueva, 1970) which were the legacy of the Americans. So long as the economic conditions enabled all these groups to thrive, or at least survive, without a fundamental confrontation, this form of political regime could remain. But what was also expressed in the crisis in 1969-70 was that the basic conditions of the continued existence of this alliance were being eroded.

Election expenditure booms had been a feature of Philippine political life, being a necessary instrument for rallying the electorate, through the patronage systems which had deep roots in society (Doranilla, 1985). These relationships had been challenged in the countryside in the post-war period by the revolutionary peasant insurrection led by the communists. Though they were crushed militarily, the root causes of the rebellion remained intact. President Ramon Magsaysay's success in convincing the peasants that real agrarian reform was on the way and the tactical mistakes of the Communist Party leadership (Nemenzo, 1984) combined to reduce the once-mighty Hukbalahap movement to a few isolated bands (Kerkvliet, 1979). However, the countryside remained a potential volcano; the spectre of a resurgent revolutionary movement continued to haunt the Filipino elite.

From the mid-1960s there were signs of increasing radicalisation amongst the masses, reflected initially in growing student militancy. The decline in real wages of the urban workforce (Baldwin, 1975), the continuing high levels of unemployment and underemployment and the lack of any progress in land reforms provided the basis for this. The first Marcos administration was forced to curtail the expansionary policies it followed immediately after it came to power in 1966. Rising inflation and, more importantly, the worsening balance of trade, compelled the government to adopt contractionary policies by mid-1967; the trade account which showed a small surplus in 1965 had slumped to a deficit of US$224 million in 1967 and worsened in 1968.

The dramatic surge in government expenditure which led to the payment crisis of 1969 came in this already-deteriorating situation. The regime could not have survived an electoral challenge if it had adopted policies that slashed the living standards of the mass of the population. Not only were they unacceptable in terms of the inter-elite factional conflicts and electoral battles, but they were also potentially explosive in their possible effects on the very fabric of the existing socio-political system. In 1969, Marcos faced a strong challenge from Sergio Osmena, Jr, and mobilised all the support he could obtain.

With Fernando Lopez, a leading representative of the traditional oligarchy, as his vice-presidential running mate, Marcos won the elections with a substantial majority. Compared with Osmena's extreme pro-US position, Marcos articulated a more nationalist position, suggesting much greater independence from the US both in foreign and domestic policies (Abueva, 1970: 62). This position was given added credibility by the presence of individuals such as Jose W. Diokno in the Nationalista party. As mentioned earlier, a huge spending spree accompanied the successful election compaign. Finally, as Osmena claimed after the elections, he was 'out-gooned, out-gunned and out-gold' (Abueva, 1970: 62).

The economic results of this spending, as described earlier, were not long in coming. With a rapidity that caught even Marcos by surprise, the economy plunged into a deep crisis. During the election Marcos had pledged that he would not devalue the peso. He reiterated this promise in his inaugural address after the election in late December 1969 and again in the 'State of the Nation' address before the congress late in January 1970. But by February the peso was floated, and the IMF austerity package was being put into action. As Tilman (1971: 132) observed, this resulted in an 'abrupt shift from the euphoria of pre-election austerity'. As the government's popularity waned almost overnight, popular opposition began to emerge.

It was this situation that provided the springboard for the massive upsurge of student and youth militancy which brought about the historic mass mobilisation of the 'First Quarter Storm' of 1970 (for a vivid description of these events which conveys the flavour of the times, see Lacaba, 1982). In January, during the 'State of the Nation' address of Marcos, the first demonstrations and the street clashes occurred. With each new rally, confrontation and clash the movement gathered greater momentum, and within weeks it began to encompass sections of the urban working class and the poor.

Faced with this mass militancy the government was unable to stick to its tough stance on austerity measures, and even before the end of the year its money supply targets were in shambles. The international terms of trade continued to worsen in 1971 and again in 1972. Money supply rose 10 per cent in 1971, and inflation was on the upswing. Growing labour unrest, the resurgence of left-wing nationalism and development of a new Maoist-influenced revolutionary communist movement expressed the deep and growing radicalisation of the masses. Important sections of the industrial capitalist class, hurt by the 'stabilisation' policies, projected a more nationalistic stance and attempted to make common cause with the radical popular movements.

These changes were reflected within the Constitutional Convention (whose delegates were elected in 1971) which was in progress in 1972. The delegates began to advance radical nationalistic demands. This radicalisation found an echo even within the Supreme Court which in the famous 'Quasha Decision' ruled that land purchases made by US citizens in the post-war period were illegal and should be transferred to Filipinos. Presidential elections were due in late 1972, and Marcos, serving his second term, was not eligible for re-election. The political scene in the country, so long the exclusive domain of politicians drawn from the elite (or dependent on their support), was being invaded by new and radical forces.

This situation, with the elements of disorder skilfully enhanced and exploited by Marcos, was the setting to the imposition of the martial law regime in 1972. In this, Marcos was able to draw on the support of the military—whose allegiance he had courted during the previous period—as well as diverse groups within society. Important sections of the Filipino capitalist class, in industry, finance and commerce as well as agriculture, and many layers of the middle class—who were looking for a 'saviour' who would impose 'law and order'—saw in the declaration of martial law an end to anarchy and the danger of revolution. Technocrats supported the move in the expectation that a strong government would give them the freedom to pursue 'rational' economic policies. Western powers and international business and financial interests welcomed the establishment of what was expected to be a strong, stable pro-Western government.

The Filipino elite, however, were by no means unanimous in their support for Marcos. The economic crisis and the developing political crisis, in fact, exacerbated the traditional divisions within the capitalist class and the landed oligarchy. In 1971, Marcos had lost the support of Vice-President Lopez who resigned from the National Party. In contrast to Lopez, who was strongly pro-US, some others who defected (including Jose Diokno) adopted left-wing nationalist positions. Benigno Aquino—young, dynamic and from the traditional oligarchy but forging links with the left-wing nationalist movement—emerged as a possible winner in the next presidential elections. Large sections of the traditional elite had begun to mistrust Marcos, whose actions increasingly appeared motivated by the goal of retaining power, even if this meant destroying the existing political framework.

When Marcos destroyed liberal democracy through what was in reality a coup d'etat, it did not mean that he had smashed political opposition in the manner of a Suharto (Lim, 1986). The differences between the Philippines and Indonesian regimes are instructive in this regard. In 1965, Indonesian society was intensely polarised between the communists and their followers, on one side, and the military, supported by Muslims, students and other middle-class sections as well as by the majority of other conservative elements. The military takeover and the subsequent annihilation of the communist forces represented a definitive victory for the former; the contending forces fought out a bloody conflict which resolved the issue of dominance for an entire generation. The Suharto regime emerged as the undisputed power. The martial law regime of Marcos, despite appearances, was quite different.

The declaration of martial law and the Marcos' arrogation of all legislative and executive power, by itself, did not resolve any of the conflicts and contradictions raging in Philippine society. The rules of the game were changed, and the framework within which the conflicts would gain political expression was transformed. Marcos, in fact, leaned on the state bureaucracy and the military but attempted to develop bases of support within other groups that wielded power nationally and regionally. 'Strong and decisive' rhetoric often covered vacillation and hesitancy in action. The regime went to great lengths to establish its constitutional origins and legality even though the fake referenda and the convoluted semantics fooled no one. But it was important for the image it had to project. The military, whose 'Ilocanisation' had begun even before the declaration of martial law with the appointment of relatives and friends from his region, the Ilocos, was his major source of power but was always kept in the background.

Indeed, Marcos attempted to develop a civilian political organisation and the state bureaucracy into a countervailing force while developing factionalism within the military itself (Lim, 1986). Immediately after declaration of martial law private armies of local 'warlords' were eliminated, but subsequently regional power brokers were wooed and coaxed into supporting the regime. Except for those sections of the traditional oligarchy who had become his sworn enemies, in time most of the other factions found representation (if not much power) within the regime.

The essential parameters of the policies pursued by the regime were set, however, by the overriding goal of avoiding a major social confrontation. The regime was fully conscious that, after the first shockwave had passed, martial law would not deter the development of a situation where the forces of the state could face not only student radicals in campuses and groups of peasant rebels in remote mountains but also millions of people taking to the streets in the urban centres. If the economic crises were to continue and deepen, the social cleavages and tensions were bound to precipitate a situation which would compel the political battles to be physically fought out. The task of avoiding such a social crisis was the task to which Marcos brought to bear all his undoubted political skills, with remarkable initial success.

As we have mentioned, the ability to resort to large and sustained external borrowings enabled the Marcos regime to avoid painful austerity measures in the mid-1970s which would have entailed major political risks. This particular 'strategy' was welcomed in many quarters at the time, without much scrutiny as to how the borrowed funds were used. This was the period when the strategy of reliance on external borrowings to embark on a path of economic development which could generate high rates of growth was very much in fashion. Constant references to the 'Brazilian miracle' were heard.

In the Philippines, perhaps more than anywhere else in developing Asia, this strategy was given fervent intellectual support by an influential body of technocrats and academics (mostly economists) who had been trained in the most prestigious American universities. They had developed competence and faith in the economic theories and models in fashion in US academic circles. The most 'brilliant and dynamic' of these were drawn into the administration and were placed in high-ranking positions. Geraldo Sicat, Cesar Visata, Jaime Laya and such like were people whose professionalism, integrity and technical competence were considered beyond question.

Previously, these technocrats had often found that they were powerless to implement many of the policies that they believed in. The multitude of lobby groups, and inefficiency and corruption in the state institutions and the bureaucracy, were seen as major impediments to effective policy implementation. Martial law appeared to change this situation; the technocrats expected that they could now proceed to act on their theories.

This was most welcome to the international financial institutions. The IMF in particular had been involved in influencing policy since the 1950s. The major decontrol measures of 1960–62, for example, were a result of IMF intervention (Payer, 1974; Baldwin, 1975). However, it exercised little day-to-day control on policymaking and only managed to exercise significant influence in times of payments crises, as demonstrated in 1970. Further, its influence was generally confined to macro-economic policies with little impact on other spheres. Now, with like-thinking technocrats in charge of economic policymaking, the international financial institutions felt that they could rest secure in the knowledge that economic management was in good hands. Freed from the shackles of 'unnecessary' political pressures, appropriate changes to economic policies could now be made.

From the enthusiasm with which the regime opted for foreign borrowings in the mid-1970s, it may appear that the development strategies of the technocrats (and the IMF and World Bank) were accepted and followed by the regime. Certainly, when the regime's own goals and objectives coincided with the policy prescriptions of the technocrats, as was the case with foreign borrowings, there was no problem. But in general the actual course of policy debate, formulation and, most crucially, implementation during the decade of martial law demonstrated clearly that the regime was no mere puppet of 'US imperialism, multinationals and the IMF/World Bank conglomerate'.

This is not to deny that, in the final analysis, the regime could not have lasted long without the support and assistance of the US and international financial institutions. However, the actual practice of the regime in policymaking and implementation was the product of the complex interplay of many—often conflicting—forces and pressures. This was demonstrated most clearly over the issue of economic 'liberalisation', particularly in relation to trade liberalisation. But before we move on to that topic it is useful to examine the role and importance of foreign capital investment in the Philippines.

The role and significance of foreign direct investment in the Philippines has been the subject of much controversy (Lindsey & Valencia, 1982). According to much popular nationalist rhetoric, the Philippines has long been economically and politically dominated by foreign capital through various multinational corporations (see, for example, Constantino, 1979). Developments during the 1970s brought this issue into sharper focus; we can see the particular relationship between foreign and domestic capital in the Philippines more concretely in the specific economic and political context and assess it in a more objective fashion.

Historically, foreign investment (dominated in this century by US capital) has been of great significance both quantitatively and qualitatively (Inamura, 1978; Lindsey & Valencia, 1982). Its role and importance tended to decline through the 1950s and 1960s (Golay, 1983). During these years when a 'Filipinisation' policy was in operation—constrained, however, by the legal provisions granting US citizens equal rights and, more importantly, by the requirements of the political alliance with the US—the inflow of new capital from abroad was small, though some reinvestment of profit probably took place. A significant proportion of investment funds were raised in the Philippines itself (Villegas, 1982). There were significant shifts in the sectoral composition of investment, with capital moving into areas that gave the greatest opportunities for exploiting the potential home market. By the early 1970s 'the accumulated share of foreign (largely United States) control of assets in the Philippines economy has remained relatively large—probably in excess of one-third of the total assets of organised industry. United States direct investment, as well as direct investment generally, has traditionally been directed mainly towards primary product exports and manufacturing for the protected domestic Philippine market.' (ILO, 1974: 299) In 1977, local sales were 83 per cent of total sales of US-majority-owned foreign affiliates, according to the US Department of Commerce (1981). The shift of US investment into manufacturing during the post-independence period is also shown by the fact that while two-fifths of US direct investment firms were engaged in manufacturing for the domestic market (and a further one-fifth was involved in commerce—export/import and internal distribution—in 1970), direct investment in manufacturing in the late colonial period ranged from a mere one-sixteenth to one-twentieth of total direct investment (Golay, 1983). While some disinvestment took place during the 1960s (particularly in anticipation of the expiry of the Laurel—Langley agreement in 1974) and the flow of direct investment into import-substituting industries slowed down after the 1962 peso devaluation, clearly US capital was firmly entrenched.

This demonstrates the most significant difference between ISI policies followed by the Philippines in contrast with those of various nationalist regimes during the 1950s and 1960s; the protective barriers were *not* an instrument for the exclusion of foreign capital but a framework within which national capital could forge an alliance with dominant foreign capital for joint exploitation of a lucrative protected market. Of course, this does not imply that some indigenous entrepreneurs were not able to develop and expand their operations or that there were no conflicts between domestic and foreign interests.[2] But when international financial institutions moved to pressure the Marcos regime for the removal of protectionism, they were certainly not articulating the direct and immediate interests of the then dominant US investors in the Philippines.

The declaration of martial law was welcomed by foreign investors, but this did not lead to a major inflow of new investment capital into the Philippines. Certainly, the level of inflows increased substantially over the previous decade. However, while precise quantification is difficult because of data inadequacies, the absolute levels appear quite small. Bello, Kinley and Elinson (1982), on the basis of IMF and World Bank data, state that between 1973 and 1979 net inflows were only US$87 million. According to the Organisation for Economic Cooperation and Development (OECD), between 1977 and 1981 total private equity capital inflows were below US$200 million (Hill & Jayasuriya, 1985). In the aggregate, they were a small fraction of total investment in the country. In comparative terms, these were well below the levels of inflows into neighbouring ASEAN countries such as Thailand, Indonesia and Singapore.

The net capital inflow figures, however, understate the level of domestic investments undertaken by foreigners. Foreign firms, sometimes with Filipino partners, actually raised the bulk of their investment capital in the *domestic* capital market—a practice already established in the previous period (Lindsey & Valencia, 1982; Villegas, 1982). In a study of the Bataan Export Processing Zone, Warr (1984) found that more than 90 per cent of the total capital invested by the firms, of which 95 per cent was borrowed, was raised domestically.

Since the regime did relax many of the regulations inhibiting foreign investment and, in fact, improved the incentives for such investment, including measures such as the creation of export processing zones and granting of tax holidays, it appears somewhat surprising that net inflows did not increase significantly. But the reluctance to bring new capital into the Philippines was strong and due to many factors. These included the perception by foreign investors of the underlying potential for radical political changes in the Philippines despite the apparent stability of the Marcos regime, the system of bureaucratic controls and regulations which were often changed and managed to benefit individuals and firms with close ties to Marcos, as well as the growing militancy and organisation among the workforce. Joint ventures with

Filipino capitalists, particularly where they had the right political links, were arrangements that became increasingly popular (Tsuda, 1978; Lindsey & Valencia, 1982). Raising capital in the domestic market enabled foreign investors to minimise risks and benefit from subsidised interest rates and other concessions granted to foreign investors. Furthermore, close links with the Marcos cronies helped to ensure that the rules and regulations would be appropriately bent or changed to their advantage. For some Filipino firms, the joint ventures were an efficient arrangement to link up with foreign capital and obtain access to technology and markets. However, for many, this was a mechanism for parasitic exploitation of their positions of political power through their ties to Marcos.

The joint ventures had a further attraction for many Filipinos. They were useful not only for amassing wealth in the Philippines but also because they created a convenient mechanism for moving assets overseas. Indeed, the level of illegal capital outflows from the mid-1970s to 1982 (i.e. before the Aquino assassination) was greatly in excess of capital inflows through direct foreign investment. Estimates of capital flight between 1974 and 1983 range from US$4.2 billion (Table 4.5) to US$5.9 billion (*Business Day*, 19 February 1985), but it is likely that even these are underestimates as they do not fully incorporate

Table 4.5   Estimated capital flight from the Philippines 1974–84 (in US$ billion)

	Cumulated change in gross external debt since 1973[a]	Cumulated change in external assets since 1973[b]	Cumulated current account since 1973[c]	Cumulated trade balance since 1973[c]	Cumulated implicit capital outflow since 1973[d]
1974	1.0	0.6	0.2	0.4	0.2
1975	2.1	0.5	1.1	1.6	0.5
1976	3.6	0.4	2.2	2.8	1.0
1977	5.2	0.2	3.1	3.6	2.0
1983	21.3	0.7	16.4	15.9	4.2

Notes: [a] Includes accumulated direct investment inflows. While these inflows are not usually considered part of a country's external debt, they are included here because direct investment inflows do help to finance private capital outflows. Cumulated direct investment flows from 1973 through 1982 amounted to US$1.62 billion.
[b] Total reserves less gold plus commercial bank assets.
[c] Deficit equals +
[d] Cumulated implicit capital outflow since 1973 equals the change in gross external debt since 1973 minus the change in external assets since 1973 minus the current account balance since 1973.

Source: *Business Day*, 2 February 1985 (Data from 1974 to 1982: International Finance Discussion paper no. 227, *Business Day* calculations for 1983).

transfers through methods such as underinvoicing of exports and transfer pricing. The perception that the peso was an overvalued currency would have created incentives for such transfers in any case, but the more important factor was probably the belief held by many who amassed fortunes during Marcos' rule that they should prepare for life overseas in the event of a change in the regime. The close personal and cultural links with the United States, which upper- and even middle-class Filipinos have, encouraged the transfer of assets particularly to the US, which was often seen as a second home.

The protectionist trade regime of the country had come under intermittent attack from both domestic and foreign sources. During the two major crises of the 1960s—which resulted in the devaluations of 1962 and 1970—the emphasis, however, was more directly on liberalisation of the capital market to remove exchange controls.[3] Nevertheless, throughout the 1960s there was growing pressure for changes in the trade regime. Clearly, the country was unable to meet its import bills without expanding exports. But the home-market-oriented industry which had grown under protectionist barriers did not have much incentive to expand exports. Further, while the protectionist system benefited those foreign investors already entrenched within the home market, it restricted market access to newcomers who wanted to exploit the opportunities available in the Philippines.

This is not the place to go into a discussion of the economic, political and ideological factors which guided the shift of international funding agencies (such as the World Bank) from their earlier advocacy of ISI to export-oriented industrialisation (EOI) as the recipe for economic development in less-developed countries by the beginning of the 1970s. However, even before the World Bank adopted this policy in relation to the Philippines, support for this shift came from the group of technocrats at the National Economic Council (later National Economic Development Authority (NEDA)), largely from a pool of US-trained economists (many of whom held academic positions at the prestigious University of the Philippines at the Diliman campus). Drawing on a body of research that analysed the effects of protectionism in the Philippines, they launched a sustained campaign for a policy stance which would move the country towards more 'liberal' economic policies (see Power & Sicat, 1971; Sicat, 1972). These technocrats, according to one of their own group, 'became the *de facto* political representatives of export producers, especially those of non-traditional labour-intensive manufactured products' who at the time were 'a very small class of industrial entrepreneurs' (Bautista, 1984).

However, the political power of the local beneficiaries of the ISI strategy was such that they were able to resist any major incursions into their privileges. Some sections were also willing to use nationalist rhetoric to enhance their bargaining power and resist any attacks by linking up with mass movements which became increasingly more radical and willing to espouse 'nationalist' slogans in the immediate period before martial law was imposed. During the first few years of martial law, despite these expectations and the lip service paid to the EOI development strategy, no real action was taken to dismantle the protectionist regime.

Both the local technocrats and the international financial agencies, in particular the World Bank, seem to have confidently expected that the martial law regime would dismantle the ISI policy structure and adopt an EOI strategy. The positive attitude towards foreign capital and the steps taken to reassure foreign investors were interpreted as a welcome sign of this expected new policy stance. Not much was done to remove protectionism, but export-oriented industries were supported through the setting up of export processing zones (EPZs) (of which the one at Bataan was the most important) as well as through special incentives given under the Export Incentive Act of 1970. The EPZs were enclaves within the protectionist economy and, as mentioned earlier, constituted a net drain on the economy due to the implicit and explicit subsidies given to investors.[4]

The policies of the government in relation to a switch towards EOI were inherently contradictory, as it attempted to raise incentives for exports within a market economy without a fundamental breakup of the protectionist system. An International Labour Organisation (ILO) mission in 1973 recommended the phasing out of the counter-incentives given to enterprises registered with the Bureau of Investments in order to offset the biases of the protectionist system in a selective manner. This recommendation was not even seriously considered (Bautista, 1984). By the late 1970s it was clear that, despite the cosmetic changes made to appease the international funding agencies and financiers, no basic shift in strategy had actually occurred. In 1980, Philippine industries had an average rate of effective protection of more than 70 per cent (Bautista, 1981); this had not declined from the levels in the mid-1960s (Power & Sicat, 1971).

By the late 1970s, the regime was under increasing pressure from the World Bank and the IMF to undertake serious steps to dismantle protectionism. It was also more vulnerable to such pressure, as its reliance on external financing to meet budget and balance of payments deficits had risen markedly. In 1979, the government agreed to undertake a major tariff reform programme which would substantially reduce the average level of protection. The World Bank, in one of the first loans of its kind, extended a structural adjustment loan (SAL) which was to be coordinated with an IMF extended fund facility.

However, almost at the same time, the government proclaimed a plan to develop eleven major industrial projects, largely in the field of heavy industry which had a strong import-substitution flavour. They included aluminium and copper smelters, an integrated steel mill, diesel-engine manufacturing and a petrochemical complex. The stated objective was to develop an efficient industrial base for downstream user industries, which are natural-resource users. They were all declared to be 'export-oriented' and were to be joint ventures with foreign investors. The World Bank opposed the projects as being of doubtful economic viability, and the government found it very difficult to raise foreign finance. Finally it was forced to shelve the projects.

Preparations were made to implement tariff reform in a number of phases, which would have halved the average rate of protection from the pre-reform level (Bautista, 1981). The tariff reforms were to be accompanied by the selected rehabilitation of a number of selected industries.

The preparations for implementing even the first phases of the tariff reform brought out opposition within and without the Marcos government. Significant elements of the business community, including some multinationals who benefited from protectionism, were opposed to them, and the opposition was reflected even within Marcos' own party. When the political and economic crisis erupted in 1983 few, if any, significant dents had been made in the protection structure, and the reforms were effectively shelved until Mrs Aquino's accession to power.

In contrast to the stubborn resistance shown towards trade liberalisation, the regime showed greater readiness to accept foreign banking activities in the country. This was not accidental; it was a reflection of the regime's dependence on foreign finance capital, a dependence that grew over time. An offshore banking system was established by presidential decree in 1976 which enabled certain financial institutions to operate outside the regulatory framework of banks operating 'within' the country. By the beginning of the 1980s major foreign banks (of whom the most important were US banks) were well represented in the Philippines. In 1981, Citibank was the major private commercial bank in terms of its assets (exceeded only by the government-owned Philippine National Bank) and dominated the foreign exchange market. Foreign banks were permitted to engage in many areas of economic activity including ownership of equity of domestic financial institutions. The major 'investment houses' in the country had tie-ups with foreign banks which also owned equity in most major commercial banks (Villegas, 1984). In practice, foreign banks were able to get around restrictions such as those on lending in domestic currency.

Financial reforms proposed by the International Monetary Fund and the World Bank (IMF/WB, 1979) were accepted by the government in 1980 and aimed at the 'rationalisation' of the financial institutions. Interest rates were deregulated gradually from 1980 onwards, and by the end of 1982 all interest rate ceilings were removed. This led to a considerable rise in real interest rates, particularly in 1981. Restrictions on the scope of financial institutional activities were relaxed, and the objective was to move towards a few large, strong banks. But, with the onset of the 1983 balance of payments crisis, these reforms actually made the financial system more vulnerable to the pressures emanating from that crisis (Remolona & Lamberte, 1985).

Exchange controls remained in place throughout the Marcos period. Such controls were selectively administered, however, and failed to control capital flight, not least because the leading culprits were the Marcos family and their close cronies. But pressures to completely liberalise the capital market and 'adjust' the exchange rate (i.e. devalue) substantially were resisted; the political effects of large devaluations, such as in 1970, had not been forgotten by the regime.

While debates and discussions on the strategy of economic development were going on in the higher echelons of the political and technocratic apparatus, with an occasional technical input from academia, significant changes were occurring in the cities and the countryside among people who were totally excluded from participation in these policy formulation processes.

Rural Philippines has long been plagued by the chasm between large landed elites and tenant farmers and is unique in this respect in Southeast Asia. The peasants have long demanded land reform, and in the past they had provided a fertile soil for revolutionary movements. However, little had been achieved by the time martial law was declared. Indeed, by the beginning of the 1970s, the tenant farmers of Central Luzon had once again begun to move towards a revolutionary solution to the problem of agrarian reform by developing bases of support for the New Peoples Army (NPA).

At the time martial law was declared, the NPA, although a growing force, was nevertheless not a major threat to the central government in Manila. However, Marcos was sufficiently perceptive to realise that, given favourable conditions, it could become a major threat; hence one of the first acts of the martial law regime was to declare a land reform. The 'New Society' promised to deliver justice and land to the land-hungry farmers so that they did not need to look to the Communist Party of the Philippines (CPP) for land.

As with much else in the Marcos era, the gap between word and deed was to prove large. The regime did not want to alienate its supporters within the landowners, the rural rich and the conservatives within the military and bureaucracy. The 1972 decree excluded coconut and sugar lands as well as those devoted to fruit and root crops; the land reform was to cover only rice and maize farmers whose landowners owned more than 7 hectares. This meant that 60 per cent of tenant farmers and over 85 per cent of the total agricultural labour force would not be entitled to land. After a decade only a small fraction of even those who were entitled had actually been issued Certificates of Land Transfer; at this rate, by the year 2000 only 42 per cent of the target group would receive the certificates. Because amortisation payments start after the certificates are issued, the majority of farmers would not be able to even start marking payments, let alone own the land in their lifetimes (Ledesma, 1982).

While the actual pace and scope of the programme was severely limited, its proclamation and early implementation in the centres of agrarian unrest in Luzon did have an important political impact. It brought the regime an important political gain in the short term; the momentum of growth of the NPA-CPP was arrested, and a potentially serious threat to the entrenchment of the regime was neutralised.

A growth of large plantations devoted to export crops occurred during the 1970s, except for the sugar sector, yet most agricultural activities were carried out on smallholdings. There has been much debate about the 'mode of production' in agriculture in the Philippines and the degree to which it is capitalist in character (see, for example, Ofreno, 1980; Rivera et al., 1982; Adriano & Adriano, 1983). While subsistence production remains undoubtedly significant and elements of feudal tenurial relationships continue, it is undeniable that the agricultural producers have been drawn into the wider market economy in no uncertain fashion and are directly and deeply affected by both national and international market forces. During the 1970s, these tendencies strengthened further as commercialisation and monetisation of rural production deepened, with even small-scale producers increasing the use of marketed inputs of varying kinds—including wage labour.

From the mid-1970s, the conditions of the small farmers and landless labourers began to deteriorate. The benefits of 'green revolution' technology were confined to land-owning farmers in the irrigated areas. But as real rice prices declined (a 45 per cent drop between 1972 and 1982 (Hill & Jayasuriya, 1985)) and subsidies were removed, even the land-owning small farmers found that their conditions were no better than before. Declining world prices, exacerbated by the crony monopolies, devastated the farmers and farm workers in the coconut and sugar industries. As mentioned earlier, real agricultural wages fell. Starvation was a real threat in the major sugar areas by the early 1980s (McCoy, 1985).

Elsewhere, such as in Mindanao, the operations of the foreign international companies operating large plantations (banana, oil palm, pineapple) led to evictions of farmers and tribal people from traditional lands; sometimes the evictions were effected by resorting to the use of armed goons. The many rural development projects funded by international donors made little impact on the deteriorating conditions of the rural population (Bello, Kinley and Elinson, 1982).

This situation provided the conditions for revitalisation and expansion of the NPA–CPP insurgency which by the early 1980s was the most rapidly expanding communist movement in Asia. It also moved to forge links with the Muslim secessionist movement led by the Moro National Liberation Front (MNLF). By the end of the 1970s, the NPA-CPP, while unable to mount an immediate challenge for power, became a formidable political and military presence in most of the provinces. Furthermore, they were extending their political influence throughout the country, including the urban centres where youth and trade union militancy was rising and the middle classes were beginning to seek a political alternative to continued Marcos rule. A communist takeover of the Philippines could no longer be dismissed as an improbability. This was becoming evident not only to the regime itself, which found itself incapable of achieving a military solution through the destruction of the NPA-CPP. Even more importantly, this was increasingly recognised by sections within the Filipino elite and the military and by foreign supporters of the regime, notably the United States.

In this situation, the growing radicalisation in the urban centres (where a third of the population lived) was of great political concern. For nearly three years after the declaration of martial law, the urban working class had been quiescent. The arrests of trade union activists, the proclamation of laws making most strikes illegal and the general atmosphere of repression and intimidation had permitted a rapid erosion of real wages and working conditions.

However, a major confrontation with the urban working class was foreshadowed in a strike in 1975 by some 500 workers at the La Tondena distillery in Manila, who successfully defied government attempts to break up the strike and who mobilised significant support from among the wider population. In the subsequent period, working-class resistance spread when more radical unions were organised as alternatives to the tame 'official' unions. By the end of the decade militant unionism had spread even to the export processing zones, forcing even the 'official' union leaders to adopt a tough stance at wage negotiations in response to the threat posed by the rival, more radical leadership. In 1980, when the left-leaning militant Kilusan Mayo Uno (KMU, or the May 1st Movement) was launched as a rival trade union federation, it was already established as a significant force within the urban working class, particularly in Manila.

This revival of militant trade unionism, openly campaigning on a platform of radical political and economic demands and widely thought to have at least informal links with the NPA–CPP (which were operating through a front organisation: the National Democratic Front (NDF)), compelled the government to grant significant wage increases by 1980. While this drew criticism from employer groups, the political imperatives left little room for manoeuvre. Certainly, the escalation of working-class activities in open defiance of the government was one factor that pushed the regime to 'lift' martial law in 1981. By restoring the right to strike—even though with limitations—the regime was attempting to avert an open confrontation in the cities. It was hoping that its loyal supporters in the official unions would be able to retain some credibility and act as a moderating influence. At all costs, the regime wanted to avoid a situation where communist influence could become dominant within the urban working class. Thus, Marcos found himself pushed to compromise with a resurgent labour movement at a time when the oil price rise of 1979 and the collapse of the sugar and coconut prices in 1980–81 had eroded the economic basis for any improvement in the real wages and living standards of the workforce.

State intervention and 'crony capitalism'

Despite the influence of the technocrats, the World Bank, the IMF and various international financial institutions, state intervention in the economy actually increased greatly during the martial law period. In an analysis of the economic crisis, a group of academic economists stated: '...the main characteristic distinguishing the Marcos years from other periods in our economic history has been the trend towards the concentration of power in the hands of the government, and the use of government functions to dispense economic privileges to some small factions in the private sector' (De Dios et al., 1984: p. 10) By the end of the 1970s, all major areas of economic activity including product and financial markets were subjected to the pervasive influence of state intervention in one form or another.

The expansion of the government sector in the economy during the Marcos period was most directly reflected in the share of the government in total national expenditure, which at the end of the 1970s was 50 per cent higher than during the pre-Marcos period of the 1960s. While government expenditure increased both absolutely and relatively, its composition changed. The share of education, health and other social services was drastically reduced. On the other hand, the shares of public administration and military expenditure grew.[5]

Large budget deficits (financed by foreign borrowing) were incurred as a result of capital expenditures. Most of these, in fact, were unproductive and wasteful, going into the construction of imposing 'glamour' buildings and projects. (These latter-day pyramids nevertheless provided lucrative contracts for the cronies of Marcos; in this regard, the Philippines was similar to Indonesia (Robison, 1986).)

During 1981–83, when many of the crony firms went bankrupt, the bulk of state capital expenditures were in fact used to 'bail out' those firms and to meet the deficits of large nonfinancial public corporations (De Dios et al., 1984). In other words, the bulk of foreign borrowings created little or no new wealth for the country; rather, directly or indirectly they were used to build up and maintain the wealth of the Marcos family and their cronies.

The building up of fortunes by the Marcos family and their close friends and relatives was not a new activity. Soon after declaration of martial law, Marcos had moved to expropriate for himself and friends the assets of his political enemies from the traditional oligarchic families. The 'takeover' of the assets of the family of his ex-vice presidential colleague and later bitter enemy, Fernando Lopez, was followed by the rapid and systematic extension of institutions and methods designed to enable Marcos and his cronies to carry out organised plunder of the entire economy.

Sugar and coconut sectors, which generated a major proportion of the export revenues of the country, were subjected to monopolies which had a stranglehold on those industries. In sugar, the monopoly was headed by Roberto Benedicto; in coconut, Eduardo Cojuanco and Juan Ponce Enrile were in charge. The sugar monopoly was ostensibly a government monopoly; the coconut monopoly, on the other hand, was supposed to be a cooperative organisation of the country's coconut farmers. Accounts of these organisations were closed to public scrutiny. Sugar producers were forced to sell all their sugar through the monopoly, the National Sugar Trading Corporation (NASUTRA). Through these mechanisms, producers were deprived of between 11.6 to 14.4 billion pesos between 1974 and 1983 (De Dios, 1984), and most of this wealth went to Benedicto and his mentors. In a similar fashion, coconut farmers were forced to pay a levy which was deposited interest free in a bank controlled by the Cojuanco—Enrile group. The levy was supposed to fund rehabilitation of the industry and assist farming families but, in fact, was a tax collected by the cronies. As is now well known, the numerous other government interventions—for example, into sugar milling and the award of contracts to favoured Japanese contractors—were in reality channels through which national wealth (including public sector foreign borrowings) were 'redistributed' to the cronies and their head in Malacanang Palace.

The situation was similar in other sectors. Rodolfo Cuenca built up the Construction and Development Corporation of the Philippines into one of the largest firms in the country, involved initially in construction and later branching into real estate, hotels, etc. Eighty per cent of the construction work was done on government contract (Bello, Kinley & Elinson, 1982). Other prominent cronies included Dewey Dee, Herminio Disini and Ricardio Silverio who all excelled in using their palace connections to amass huge fortunes.

These fortunes were built not only with state patronage and support but also with close links to foreign financial and commercial ventures. Major multinational firms forged close links with them and benefited from the many lucrative deals and favours that they could obtain through their access to the seat of political power (see Bello, Kinley & Elinson, 1982, and references cited therein). Funds flowed into their coffers from the state banks as well as foreign banks, who knew that they were the 'chosen elite' among the Filipinos.

The link between the extension of state intervention in the financial markets and the growth of crony capitalism was close. The Central Bank ceased to be an independent institution in any sense, and its policies in relation to the commercial banking sector were directly influenced by the needs of crony capitalists. But the government also extended its influence directly through the state-owned banks—the Philippine National Bank, the Development Bank of the Philippines and other state financial institutions that had taken on the role of commercial banks in practice. Further, some commercial banks were so closely tied to the government through the crony link that they came to be called 'political banks' (Patrick & Moreno, 1981). The state financial institutions were heavily dependent on Central Bank credit for their funds and, in addition, became major foreign borrowers as well. By the early 1980s the combined assets of the government financial institutions and the 'political banks' were over half of the total assets of the entire commercial banking system and reflected a massive growth in concentration in the financial system (De Dios, 1984).

These financial institutions were the source of funds for the commercial empires that were being built by the cronies. Literally billions of dollars were lent to the major crony firms by these banks. Major sections of the Philippine capitalist class, which had supported Marcos as the saviour of the country from communism and anarchy, now found that their very survival was at stake. In the 'New Democracy', only the cronies could flourish.

The proliferation and dominance of crony capitalism was a product of the particular class and factional interests that the Marcos regime represented. While a few individuals from the pre-1972 landed oligarchy remained within the regime, it became increasingly clear as the 1970s drew to an end that it was directly representing only a tiny group who, however, had managed to become enormously wealthy through state patronage. By and large, these were people whose origins were to be found not in the traditional elite but in the 'petit bourgeois'. As Nemenzo (1985: 50) argued, the regime could be best described as 'Bonapartist':

> It achieved 'relative autonomy' from the ruling class with the support of the army and pliable mass organisation. The circumstances which allowed Marcos to assume total power were remarkably similar to what created the opportunity for Louis Bonaparte to pose as the saviour of France: intense contradictions in the ruling class and a mighty challenge from below, resulting in the paralysis of the old state machine.

The behaviour of Marcos and the cronies certainly bears resemblance to that of Louis Bonaparte and his close supporters, described so well by Karl Marx (1975: 178). They, too, lost no time in using the state to amass personal fortunes.

As long as the international bankers were willing to lend, this system seemed capable of going on for ever. However, when the second oil price shock in 1979 and the collapse of export prices was followed by the emergence of the *international* debt crisis, the situation changed in dramatic fashion.

The first tremors of the impending crisis hit the Philippines when in early 1981 one of the leading cronies, 'industrialist' Dewey Dee, fled the country owing nearly a hundred million dollars in debt. Suddenly, international lenders awakened to the sobering fact that their loans could be in danger of not being repaid. Sources of new credit began to dry up rapidly while short-term debts were recalled. Many of the cronies who had built their empires on credit faced immediate bankruptcy. But such bankruptcy could not take place in isolation. The very scale of their operations and the extent of the involvement of financial institutions in these companies ensured that the entire financial system would be caught up in the impending collapse. A major crisis shook the entire system. Approximately 2.1 billion pesos were withdrawn from non-bank financial institutions alone in the first half of 1981, and only massive Central Bank support averted insolvency. (Furthermore, the situation was aggravated by the fact that many of the major public corporations, too, had become a chronic drain on funds, to a large extent because of wasteful government expenditure and corruption.)

The government reacted to the crisis by rushing to the rescue with 'bail-out' operations which included direct financial assistance as well as conversion of loans of state financial institutions into equity in the affected companies. But they were equity in firms totally bankrupt and, hence, worthless. In fact, a massive collapse of fictitious capital had occurred. Since much of this was foreign debt, the country now was in debt with no corresponding assets. (The prudent cronies, who had shifted some of the capital overseas and converted it into foreign assets, of course did not suffer much.) At the end of 1981 and certainly by mid-1982, the Philippines had become both a contributor to, and an integral part of, the global debt crisis.

The development of crony capitalism in the Philippines (with the Marcos group utilising its control over the state to continually widen its economic base) was until the end of the 1970s tolerated but not welcomed by the international financiers or by foreign multinationals. Some individual foreign corporations and firms were able to successfully exploit the system, but the ideal of an economy with no restrictions on trade and capital movements was in conflict with the realities of the Philippines scene. Certainly, it is misleading to describe the developments during the 1970s as being orchestrated by international capital and dutifully implemented by a totally subservient regime. It is also difficult to agree with the proposition that 'The main substance of the changes during the martial-law regime is the re-orientation of the national economy from its colonial structure into an industrial neo-colony' (Magallona, 1982: 75–6). In fact, this was a period which saw conflicting tendencies in operation, where the needs and interests of various groups of foreign and domestic capital often came into conflict with those of the crony capitalists around Marcos. The political risks inherent in an open confrontation with the Marcos regime resulted in an uneasy compromise; further, there was hope that pressure could be effectively applied to push the regime to undertake the reforms, though the process was rather slower than desired.

But in 1981 the World Bank and the IMF demonstrated a sharp change in attitude. A much greater aggressiveness was seen in their stance. Elements of the structural adjustment package were more vigorously pushed, and Prime Minister Cesar Virata, also in charge of finances, showed a much higher political profile in support of the reform package.

The reasons for this change in attitude are to be found in changed international circumstances. The second oil price rise and the collapse of commodity prices had exposed the underlying fragility of the Philippine economy at the same time that its political weaknesses were also becoming apparent. The viability of the Philippines economy, as one that could generate the export surpluses to repay its debts, was becoming very important to the entire international financial system. The overwhelming exposure of international capital in the Philippines was not in direct foreign investment but in the billions that had been lent to the government and private firms. The need to restructure the economy to ensure that the Philippines did not precipitate a crisis with global repercussions meant that reforms could not be postponed any longer. Too much was at stake for them to continue with compromises with the Marcos regime.

The wheel had come full circle for the regime. In the mid-1970s, it had been able to entrench itself and avoid politically risky measures by using the credit then readily available from international banks. At the time they had been desperately seeking outlets for the large petrodollar deposits and were aggressively promoting credit to Third World countries (Makin, 1984). For a period, real interest rates were negative. The Philippines, with its newly established pro-Western authoritarian regime, appeared a most attractive creditor. Secondly, and for the same reasons, foreign aid and concessional loans from institutions such as the World Bank increased rapidly.

According to sources cited by Bello, Kinley and Elinson (1982), bank assistance rose from a meagre US$326 million during 1950-72 to more than US$2.6 billion between 1973 and 1981).[6] Now, these debts placed the government in a most vulnerable position and made it the subject of intense pressure.

The changed stance of the IMF and the World Bank precipitated political conflict within the government. Virata came under fire from sections within Marcos' own party for his 'subservience' to the IMF and the World Bank. The coconut levy was removed in September 1981 but was reinstated later under pressure from Enrile and Cojuanco. The bailouts of bankrupt crony firms were opposed by the IMF, but Marcos, reluctant to antagonise his close cronies, went ahead with them and partly as a consequence also expanded money supply well beyond the IMF recommendation. The conflict between Marcos (and his cronies) and the IMF-World Bank policies became intense.

Sensing this conflict and responding to the political crisis within the government, major sections of the capitalist class, which had been badly hurt by crony capitalism, came out into the open to denounce the regime's support for such cronyism. Jaime Ongpin, head of the Benguet Mining Corporation (and brother of the minister of industry) directly challenged the government on the bail out issue. The growing dissatisfaction within the business community was also expressed in the more vocal opposition that came from the influential Makati Business Group which was formed in 1981 and headed by Enrique Zobel of the Ayala Corporation. The participation of the liberal opposition in the highly successful election boycott of 1981 was a reflection of these developments. The Catholic Church, headed by Cardinal Sin, began to shift to a more directly oppositional stance, a position partly influenced by the growing radicalisation of the lower orders of the clergy and the need to avoid a split in its own ranks. After a decade of martial law, the regime found that it was being alienated from those very forces, nationally and internationally, which had enabled it to stay in power. Throughout 1982, the regime was under pressure from diverse forces, inside and outside, but was unable to undertake any decisive moves.

In 1972, Marcos could declare martial law and establish his authoritarian rule precisely because the conservative forces, both local and international, saw in him a man capable of resolving the chronic social and political crisis by taking decisive action. In 1982, it was dawning on both supporters and opponents that Marcos himself was now part of the crisis. A decade after martial law was imposed, all the unresolved issues and conflicts of 1972 were once again on the agenda. Extending the analogy with Louis Bonaparte and paraphrasing Marx (1975: 178), it was clear after Aquino's murder that Marcos had reached the point where he 'throws the entire bourgeois economy into confusion, violates everything that seemed inviolable in the [past], makes some tolerant of revolution, others desirous of revolution, and produces actual anarchy in the name of order, while at the same time stripping its halo from the entire state machine, profanes it and makes it at once loathsome and ridiculous'. The ailing old dictator with his fake medals and stolen wealth had come to the end of the road.

Post-Marcos

The political crisis which opened up with the murder of Benigno Aquino paved the way for the accession to power of his widow, Mrs Corazon Aquino, in February 1986. A popular uprising and a split in the military forced Marcos out and set the stage for a new era in Philippine politics.

The new government inherited an economy in ruins. Massive capital flight after the Aquino assassination had exposed the fact that the Philippines was unable to meet its international debt. Several rounds of debt rescheduling had averted an open package which brought inflation down by late 1985 but saw the economy contract sharply (for a discussion of developments in 1983–84, see Philippine Institute of Development Studies (1985)). However, Marcos in his last election in February 1986 once again indulged in huge expenditures which saw money supply surge well beyond the IMF guidelines and emptied what was left in the government coffers.

The new regime was a coalition of all the forces, except the communists and their close supporters, who had opposed Marcos. By their last-minute defection, Defence Minister Juan Ponce Enrile and Armed Forces Chief, General Fidel Ramos, had brought the military into the post-Marcos government. The Catholic Church, which under Cardinal Jaime Sin exerted great influence in the political developments leading to Mrs Aquino's victory, played a crucial role in uniting big sections of the business community which had been hurt by crony capitalism, remnants of the pre-martial law oligarchy and middle-class liberal democratic forces to form a broad-based coalition. With Mrs Aquino's successful projection of an image of being above factional or class divisions, in the early euphoric post-Marcos days the regime appeared capable of unifying the entire nation in the difficult times ahead.

The fundamental economic and political problems of the Philippines, however, do not permit much room for a lengthy period of bonhomie where consensus and compromise can flourish. The crisis cannot be wished away; it demands rapid and ruthless solutions.

Thus, it is no surprise that sharp differences over the major economic and political issues have come into the open within the Aquino government. On the economic front, these differences have crystallised around the policies towards repayment of the international debt and the attitude to the IMF–World Bank economic reforms and stabilisation policies.

On the debt issue some have advocated that there should be, if not a complete repudiation, at least a selective repudiation of those debts where the loan was transacted under circumstances that implicated the creditors.[7] Despite substantial support within the cabinet and, apparently, much popular support, Mrs Aquino rejected this position and sided with the new Finance Minister Jaime Ongpin and (Marcos-appointed) Central Bank governor Jose Fernandez. But the issue remains divisive. Minister of National Development and academic economist Solita 'Winnie' Monsod, who supported the concept of selective debt repudiation, has called for debt repayments to be conditional on the achievement of a trade surplus. These positions, which strain relations with the IMF and the international banking community, are opposed by the more conservative elements.

But the fact remains that, in the absence of a large capital inflow for investment purposes, significant repayments can be achieved only at the expense of economic growth and by imposing further severe reductions in living standards and real wages.[8]

A further issue of contention has been the trade liberalisation measures. The implementation of these measures is a key condition of an IMF agreement and, despite the objections of a majority of the cabinet (*FEER*, 25 September 1986), substantial reductions in protection for domestic industry have already been achieved. These are strongly opposed by the domestic industrialists; Jose Concepcion, the Minister of Trade and Industry, has argued that trade restrictions, whose removal is demanded by the IMF, are absolutely essential in the short term for the survival of many domestic industries (*FEER*, 28 August 1986). The removal of protection has been strongly supported by Mrs Mansod and her academic colleagues at the School of

Economics, University of the Philippines, who, as we know, have a long record of support for trade liberalisation.

Also related to these issues of economic policy, but with a more directly political character, the government attitude to wages and industrial relations has further aggravated tensions. Trade unions, utilising the new democratic freedoms, have campaigned to arrest the decline in real wages and have become increasingly more militant and assertive. Labour Minister Augusto Sanchez, a former human rights lawyer, is accused by conservatives within the government of being too soft on the unions, particularly on the KMU, which has grown from 100 000 in 1980 to 600 000 in 1986 and has become the dominant power in the union movement (*FEER*, 28 August 1986). It is led by members of the Partido ng Bayan, which also includes the founder of the Communist Party, Jose Maria Sison.

The economic picture is even bleaker in the countryside. The major export crops, sugar and coconut, have not experienced any improvement in international prices, and medium-term prospects are for continued depressed prices. While the monopolies have been removed, low prices have not permitted a real improvement. Indeed, the sugar industry was expected to contract even more sharply in the 1986/87 crop year. The issue of a serious land reform sharpens all the tensions and contradictions within the government.

The Philippines cannot expect major favourable changes from international economic developments. A sustained international economic recovery, leading to an expansion of international trade and growth in demand for exports from less-developed countries, is not in sight. Thus, the painful repercussions of stringent austerity measures flowing from an IMF stabilisation package together with the immediate effects of reforms in the trade regime on a manufacturing sector (which had developed under protection for three decades or more) are bound to strain the political fabric to its limits. The tensions and the conflicts within the regime as well as outside it are bound to sharpen in future. The economic weakness of the country and the political choice of the regime to collaborate with the IMF and other international financial organisations as well as Western powers, particularly the US, has enabled far-reaching changes to be made in aspects of the economy like the trade regime. However, the continuation of the policy package will inevitably usher in a situation that will make it difficult for the unity of the present coalition to be maintained. The present 'differences of opinion' will be transformed into different political programmes. What lies ahead is a period of turbulence and political turmoil where the issues and conflicts that were posed but not resolved during the Marcos era will imperatively demand resolution.

October 1986

JOMO KWAME SUNDARAM

5
Economic crisis and policy response in Malaysia

This chapter examines the domestic dimensions of the Malaysian economic crisis in the first half of the 1980s and the government's policy responses to it. It begins with a brief review of post-colonial economic development policy, paying particular attention to industrialisation. Different aspects of the current crisis are then explored in turn, including growth and deflation, the balance of payments, the fiscal crisis and the debt problem. Various new economic policies which have emerged in the last half-decade—during the period of Mahathir's premiership—are then reviewed, with special attention to the Industrial Master Plan and the Fifth Malaysia Plan, both released in early 1986. Finally, the chapter looks at the forces and interests that have contributed to recent policies and the current predicament, before touching on some prospects for the future.

Economic policy after independence

On 31 August 1957, formal political authority was officially handed over by the British to the local elite represented by the Alliance Party led by Tunku Abdul Rahman. The changes that have occurred since then, especially rapid economic growth, have been quite impressive: the annual growth rate of the gross domestic product (GDP) in peninsular Malaysia rose, on average, by 5.8 per cent during 1957–70 (Rao, 1976); and the GDP for the whole of Malaysia—including Sabah and Sarawak—rose by 7.8 per cent per year, on average, between 1971 and 1980 (Malaysia, 1981).

After independence in 1957, and especially during the 1960s, the Malaysian economy successfully diversified from the twin pillars of the colonial economy, rubber and tin. Besides developing import-substituting industries primarily under the auspices of British-owned agency houses, the plantation agencies increasingly began to switch from rubber to oil palm. The government moved not only to diversify agriculture (e.g. with the introduction of oil palm, tobacco, cocoa, etc.) but also to industrialise, including the establishment of industries based on local primary resources. Rural development efforts affecting the peasantry contrasted with British colonial neglect. Initially, such efforts were aimed at consolidating the yeoman peasantry, but since the early 1980s more attention has been given to the development of capitalist agriculture—i.e. large farms involving more modern management methods—for export markets.

Meanwhile, rice production rose from the late 1960s with the completion of major irrigation schemes for double-cropping. In the early 1970s petroleum production, off the east coast of peninsular Malaysia, began almost providentially as oil prices soared. Agricultural diversification continued, with cocoa now promising some new hope for the future.

Emphasis in industrial development policy shifted from import-substitution industrialisation (ISI) in the late 1950s to the mid-1960s, to export-oriented industrialisation (EOI) since the late 1960s. Since the early 1980s massive public investments have gone into selected heavy industries, while natural gas production has come on stream, offering yet another new engine for the future growth of the Malaysian economy.

However, Malaysian economic development, considered praiseworthy in some regards, has not only maintained but probably even widened the income gaps within each major ethnic group in peninsular Malaysia, especially among the Malays. Inter-ethnic tensions have also increased. Among the important reasons for this are the common Malay misperception that the Chinese community controls the country's economy and the equally erroneous non-Malay belief that the Malays as a whole control the government. In fact, only small elites from each of the two major ethnic groups enjoy such power. Nevertheless, both these beliefs have influenced the thinking and consciousness of the majority of Malaysians.

Despite the impressive growth performance, largely attributable to good luck as well as favourable external conditions, it is increasingly evident that the sources of export-led growth in the Malaysian economy are not reliable. In fact, the very success of export-led growth, dominated by foreign investment in the past, his discouraged serious efforts to develop a more balanced and better integrated national economic structure. As will be seen, Malaysia's highly open economy has been extremely vulnerable to external economic conditions, especially in the OECD economies, and the dictates of foreign capital. In so far as current development strategy and economic policy do not attempt to fundamentally change the Malaysian economic structure, it will be impossible to seek a solution to the economic problems at the root of the present crisis. It has also become clear that the Malaysian economic situation will not necessarily improve with recovery in the OECD economies. There appears to be no long-term solution to the problem of dependent vulnerability on the Malaysian economic horizon.

From import-substitution industrialisation (ISI) to export-oriented industrialisation (EOI)

British economic policies shaped industrial development in colonial Malaya. By emphasising export-oriented raw material production and favouring British-manufactured imports during the colonial era, local industry was largely confined to the processing of raw materials for export and the production of a limited range of items for local consumption.

In contrast, the post-colonial Malayan government has actively sought to promote industrialisation. While early efforts in this direction were sometimes erratic and haphazard, a clearly discernible thrust was made towards ISI, with state intervention limited to auxiliary support facilities and provision of protective tariffs and other incentives. This was consistent with the Alliance government's 1955 election commitment—based on the 1954 World Bank mission's recommendations—to encourage local industrial capital, attract foreign capital, offer new tax and other incentives, provide industrial-estate facilities and infrastructural development. The rationale for the strategy adopted was to encourage foreign manufacturers to set up production, assembly and packaging plants in the country to supply goods that had previously been imported. To promote import-substituting industries, the government directly and indirectly subsidised the establishment of new factories and protected the domestic market.

However, by the mid-1960s the inherent contradictions of the Malaysian ISI strategy were becoming clear. The Raja Mohar committee was established to recommend measures to accelerate industrial growth. It proposed several measures, including diversification into new industries. The committee's proposals led to the 1968 Investment Incentives Act 'to encourage the expansion of export in manufactures' (quoted in Lo Sum Yee, 1972: 89). Hence, this legislation signalled the strategic switch from ISI to EOI. Meanwhile, the Federal Industrial

Development Authority, established in 1965, began in 1967 to attract and develop export-oriented industries. The labour laws were also amended to minimise industrial relations problems in the largely labour-intensive export-oriented industries.

In general, industrialisation was not unresponsive to government policies. After independence, industrial growth proceeded rapidly from its modest beginnings, with manufacturing output rising at an average annual rate of 17.4 per cent between 1959 and 1968. Manufacturing's share of the gross national product (GNP) rose from 8.5 per cent in 1960 to 12.7 per cent in 1968, while employment in the manufacturing sector rose from 135 700 or 6.4 per cent of the labour force in 1957 to 214 800 or 9.1 per cent in the fiscal year 1967/68. However, the sector's labour-absorptive capacity had been found to be comparatively low. For instance, the number of workers employed per million ringgit (M$million) of final demand for this sector was found to be about a third of that for the agricultural sector. With the growth of big industry outpacing small-scale enterprise, and capital-intensive industries expanding much faster than labour-intensive ones, employment creation suffered.

While the annual growth rate of the manufacturing sector did not rise significantly between 1959 and 1968, the growth rate of real output of officially encouraged 'pioneer' industries actually dropped quite dramatically. While it is not possible to conclusively explain this tendency with available information, it probably reflects the inherent limits of ISI in a small, open capitalist economy. The 'small domestic market' constraint on such an industrial strategy not only reflects the economy's small population and the relatively low average income level, but also, more importantly, its skewed income (and hence expenditure) distribution pattern coupled with the basic external orientation of both production and consumption in the national economy. The absence of a commitment to a more self-reliant and equitable development strategy to transform this economic structure (with its pattern of effective demand) ultimately renders expanded industrial production for mass-consumption needs almost impossible.

Confronted with the limits of import substitution, the switch to an EOI strategy was necessary to give fresh impetus to industrial growth. This new emphasis was subsequently spurred by the policies embodied in the Second Malaysia Plan, 1971–75, which heralded the beginning of the so-called New Economic Policy (NEP) and, among other things, a commitment to an open industrialising capitalist economy.

By the early 1970s, government efforts to attract and encourage export-oriented industries were in full swing. Various new measures, notably the establishment of 'free trade zones', were introduced to facilitate Malaysia's integration into the merging new international division of labour, with transnational enterprises relocating various production assembly and testing processes in secure foreign locations offering reduced wage and other costs.

Two main types of export-oriented industries developed. Resource-based industries involved the increased processing of older (e.g. rubber, tin) and newer (e.g. palm oil, timber) primary commodities for export. While considerable scope for expansion existed in this area from a technical point of view, it was also severely constrained by existing tariff structures as well as freight and other related rates, determined by transnational cartels, which continue to favour the export of less-processed raw materials.

Non-resource-based export industries have had far more impressive growth and employment-generation records. Many involve the relocation of certain labour-intensive processes in stable, low-wage environments, such as those offered by Malaysian free trade zones. The most spectacular example of this has been the electronic semiconductor industry. While the employment-generating consequences of the location of such industries in Malaysia can hardly be denied, such industrial diversification has actually further integrated Malaysia into the world capitalist economy, albeit on different terms, in the context of the new international division of labour.

To sum up, import-substitution in Malaysia has generally involved the domestic assembly, packaging and final processing of finished goods (previously imported from abroad) by domestic labour using machines and material still largely imported from abroad. The employment-generating capacity of such industrialisation has been limited by the typically capital-intensive foreign technology utilised, the weak linkages of the industries concerned with the rest of the national economy, and also the small domestic market available because of the limited and skewed purchasing capacity of the population. Being relatively capital-intensive, such employers have generally been more able to afford conceding real wage increases to labour because their wage bills account for a relatively small proportion of production costs.

In contrast, the success of export-oriented industrialisation has been contingent on the government's ability to attract foreign investors seeking to lower production, especially labour costs, to be more competitive in the international market. Precisely because of their use of labour-intensive production techniques, these industries tend to generate more employment (in a direct sense) but are also therefore more sensitive to changes in wage costs. Also, many such industries have been characterised as 'footloose', i.e. more easily capable of relocating elsewhere if sufficiently attracted to do so.

Growth in the 1980s

Economic growth trends in the first half of the 1980s suggest that the Malaysian economy may have entered an ominous new phase. The average GDP growth rate (in constant 1978 prices) during 1981–85 was 5.8 per cent per annum, with the annual growth dropping from 7.6 per cent in 1984 to 2.8 per cent in 1985. However, in current price terms, this actually involved a decline from a growth rate of 13.9 per cent in 1984 to 1.5 per cent in 1985! In constant 1978 prices, exports (of goods and non-factor services) rose from M$22.6 billion in 1980 to M$33.2 billion in 1985, i.e. from 52 to 60 per cent of the GNP in 1978 prices, but declined from 59 to 58 per cent of the GNP in current price terms. In the meantime, imports rose from M$23.9 billion in 1980 to M$31.3 billion in 1985 in constant 1978 prices, i.e. they rose from 55 to 56 per cent of the GNP in 1978 price terms, but declined from 56 to 53 per cent in current price terms (Malaysia, 1986a: 46, Table 2.2).

In constant 1978 prices, private investment grew by an average of only 1.8 per cent per annum during 1981–85—well short of the Fourth Malaysia Plan (4MP) target of 10.7 per cent annually in real terms! In fact, real private investment actually fell by 8.0 per cent in 1985, after growing by 10.6 per cent the year before (Malaysia, 1986a: 46, Table 2.2). Private consumption trends followed general growth trends, to average 3.6 per cent during 1981–85, instead of the 4MP target of 5.4 per cent.

In contrast, public investment grew by an average of 12.5 per cent annually during 1981–85—more than three times the 4MP target of 3.7 per cent in real terms. In fact, public investment grew by 41.5 per cent in 1981 before being trimmed to 20.7 per cent in 1982, 10.2 per cent in 1983 and −4.4 per cent in 1984. Public consumption experienced a similar trend, dropping from 13.3 per cent growth in 1981 to 8.7 per cent in 1982, 4.6 per cent in 1983 and −4.9 per cent in 1984. As with public investment, the level of public consumption did not change much in 1985, averaging 4.1 per cent during 1981–85, i.e. short of the 5.5 per cent 4MP target.

Tertiary sector growth, averaging 7.9 per cent per annum (in 1978 price terms), exceeded the 4MP target of 7.7 per cent largely due to the 9.8 per cent average annual growth of government services (23.8 per cent in 1981 alone) and the 7.0 per cent growth in commerce, hotels and restaurants. Meanwhile, primary sector growth, of 4.2 per cent per annum, fell short of the 4MP target of 4.8 per cent. The secondary sector achieved only 5.5 per cent, instead of the 7.2 per cent target. Manufacturing growth at an average of 4.9 per cent per annum fell short of the targeted 6.0 per cent, while construction growth of 8.1 per cent also fell short of the 11.6 per cent target. Between 1980 and 1985,

Policy response in Malaysia

the primary sector's share of GDP declined from 32 per cent to 30 per cent, while the secondary sector's share stayed at 24 per cent, and the tertiary sector's share rose from 39 to 44 per cent. In the meantime, manufacturing's share of GDP also stayed at 19 per cent.

Exports

As we can see from Table 5.1, the current value of Malaysian commodity exports grew from M$28.2 billion in 1980 to M$38.6 billion in 1984, before falling to M$38.1 billion in 1985. Negative growth in 1981 and 1985 offset impressive expansion in 1983 and 1984 for an average growth of 6.2 per cent for 1981–85, rather short of the 4MP target of 8.5 per cent per annum. A breakdown of the various aspects of export performance can also be found in Table 5.1. Perhaps the major point to note is the degree to which net petroleum exports became the number one primary commodity earner for Malaysia in the 1980s, with the more traditional exports of rubber and palm oil in a secondary role.

Of gross commodity exports in 1980, petroleum (23%) led, followed by manufactures (22%), rubber (16%), sawlogs (8%), palm oil (8%), tin (8%) and sawn timber (4%). By 1985, however, the order had changed as follows: manufactures (32%), petroleum (23%), palm oil (10%), rubber (7%), sawlogs (7%), liquefied natural gas (LNG) (6%), tin (4%) and sawn timber (2%).

During the same period, agriculture's share of exports declined from 26.3 per cent in 1980 to 19.3 per cent in 1985, while export volume rose 24 per cent; export prices dropped 20 per cent to maintain total agricultural export value almost constant (see Table 5.2). Similarly, forestry's share dropped from 13.5 per cent in 1980 to 9.7 per cent in 1985, as export volume rose 10 per cent, while export prices dropped 12 per cent, to reduce forestry's total export value by almost 3 per cent. Mining's share dropped from 33.3 per cent in 1980 to 28.1 per cent in 1985 (excluding LNG, which accounted for another 6.1 per cent), with export volume rising 21 per cent and prices dropping 6 per cent, to raise mining's total export value by 14 per cent. Meanwhile, manufacture's share of exports rose from 22.2 per cent in 1980 to 32.1 per cent in 1985, with export value rising 95 per cent during 1981–85. Gross exports rose by 35 per cent over the period, and by 38 per cent during 1982–84 alone (Malaysia, 1986a: 49, Table 2.4).

While the move towards manufactured exports was welcome, in that it meant that the Malaysian economy was not so totally vulnerable to the world trend of declining commodity prices, it also plunged Malaysia into increasingly cutthroat competition with other manufacturing exporters. Along with these other manufacturing exporters it also had

Table 5.1 Malaysia: commodity exports, 1980–85, in M$ (ringgit) billions (and average annual growth rate)

Commodity	1980	1981	1982	1983	1984	1985	1981	1982	1983	1984	1985	1981–85	Fourth Plan
Crude petroleum													
Volume ('000 tonnes)	11 226.9	10 143.2	11 973.9	14 224.0	16 497.4	17 025.0	−9.7	18.0	18.8	16.0	3.2	8.7	8.3
Unit value ($/tonne)	597.6	682.4	642.6	553.4	529.6	526.9	14.2	−5.8	−13.9	−4.3	−0.5	−2.5	−2.5
Value ($ million)	6709.1	6921.4	7694.2	7871.0	8737.4	8970.0	3.2	11.2	2.3	11.0	2.7	6.0	5.5
Palm oil													
Volume ('000 tonnes)	2136.2	2361.1	2700.0	2912.9	2959.4	3188.0	10.5	14.4	7.9	1.6	7.7	8.3	9.4
Unit value ($/tonne)	1177.5	1154.2	983.7	1022.0	1531.1	1237.0	−2.0	−14.8	3.9	49.8	−19.2	1.0	−0.3
Value ($ million)	2515.3	2725.2	2656.1	2976.9	4531.1	3944.0	8.3	−2.5	12.1	52.2	−13.0	9.4	9.0
Rubber													
Volume ('000 tonnes)	1525.7	1485.3	1378.1	1563.0	1590.6	1495.0	−2.6	−7.2	13.4	1.8	−6.0	−0.4	1.0
Unit value (cts/kg)	302.7	250.0	192.7	234.4	230.8	191.6	−17.4	−22.9	21.6	−1.5	−17.0	−8.7	−0.5
Value ($ million)	4618.0	3713.1	2655.1	3663.6	3671.5	2864.0	−19.6	−28.5	38.0	0.2	−22.0	−9.1	0.4

Sawlogs										
Volume ('000 cu. m)	15 117.0	15 866.1	19 270.0	18 657.9	16 877.6	18 781.0	5.0	21.5	−3.2	−9.5	11.3	4.4	2.7
Unit value ($/cu. m)	173.1	155.9	175.3	149.7	165.3	142.0	−9.9	12.4	−14.6	10.4	−14.1	−3.9	0.6
Value ($ million)	2 616.2	2 472.8	3 378.2	2 792.2	2 790.0	2 667.0	−5.5	36.6	−17.3	−0.1	−4.4	0.4	3.3
LNG										
Volume ('000 tonnes)				1 830.0	3 700.0	4 500.0				102.2	21.6		
Unit value ($/tonne)				454.3	479.6	515.3				5.6	7.4		
Value ($ million)				831.3	1 774.7	2 319.0				113.5	30.7		
Tin										
Volume ('000 tonnes)	69.5	66.4	48.6	57.1	39.6	54.5	−4.5	−26.8	17.5	−30.6	37.6	−4.7	−6.0
Unit value ($/tonne)	36 049.0	32 182.0	30 543.0	30 070.0	29 351.0	29 240.0	−10.7	−5.1	−1.5	−2.4	−0.4	−4.1	−3.3
Value ($ million)	2 505.3	2 138.1	1 483.9	1 718.2	1 162.3	1 595.0	−14.7	−30.6	15.8	−32.4	37.2	−8.6	−9.1
Sawn timber										
Volume ('000 cu. m)	2 999.9	2 691.3	2 942.1	3 288.8	2 700.4	2 577.0	−10.3	9.3	11.8	−17.9	−4.6	−3.0	1.5
Unit value ($/cu. m)	392.8	360.6	351.8	371.2	368.1	395.8	−8.2	−2.4	5.5	−0.8	7.5	0.2	1.6
Value ($ million)	1 178.3	970.4	1 034.9	1 220.7	993.9	1 020.0	−17.6	6.6	18.0	−18.6	2.6	−2.8	3.1
Manufactures										
Value $ million	6 269.8	6 328.3	7 398.5	9 501.8	12 148.5	12 229.0	0.9	16.9	28.4	27.9	0.7	14.3	19.1
Total gross commodity exports										
Value $ million	28 171.6	27 109.4	28 108.2	32 771.2	38 646.9	38 094.0	−3.8	3.7	16.6	17.9	−1.4	6.2	8.5

Sources: Malaysia (1986a) *The Fifth Malaysia Plan*, pp. 47–8, Table 1.3
Department of Statistics, Malaysia: *Preliminary Figures of External Trade*, 1980, 1981, 1982, 1983, and 1984.

Table 5.2 Malaysia: gross export index by sector, 1980–85 (1980 = 100)

Sector	1980	1985	Average annual growth rate (%) 1981–85	Fourth Plan
Agriculture[a]				
Volume index	100.0	124.0	4.4	4.6
Unit value index	100.0	79.9	−4.4	−0.5
Value index	100.0	99.2	−0.2	4.1
Share of total (%)	26.3	19.3	—	—
Forestry[b]				
Volume index	100.0	110.2	2.0	2.4
Unit value index	100.0	88.1	−2.5	0.9
Value index	100.0	97.2	−0.6	3.3
Share of total (%)	13.5	9.7	—	—
Mining[c]				
Volume index	100.0	120.8	3.9	5.0
Unit value index	100.0	94.4	−1.1	−2.7
Value index	100.0	114.0	2.7	2.3
Share of total (%)	33.3	28.1	—	—
LNG				
Value index (1983=100)	—	279.0	67.0[d]	—
Share of total (%)	—	6.1	—	—
Manufactures				
Value index	100.0	195.0	14.3	19.1
Share of total (%)	22.2	32.1	—	—
Other exports				
Value index	100.0	138.0	6.7	4.5
Share of total (%)	4.7	4.7	—	—
Gross exports				
Value index	100.0	135.2	6.2	8.5

Notes: [a] Comprises rubber, palm oil, pepper and cocoa
[b] Comprises sawlogs and sawn timber
[c] Comprises crude petroleum, tin and copper
[d] Refers to growth rate for 1984–85
Source: Malaysia, 1986a: p. 49, Table 2.4

to cope with growing protectionism in the advanced industrial countries and to demonstrate that it had the infrastructure, skills, organisation and stability sought by large-scale international investors.

Balance of payments

The merchandise account of Malaysia's balance of payments has obviously been influenced by the performance of its exports. In 1980, the last year of the primary commodities boom of the late 1970s,

Malaysia recorded a healthy surplus of M$5.2 billion in its merchandise account. In the next two years, Malaysia recorded negative balance on its merchandise account as export value fell, while imports continued to increase. By 1983, the merchandise account recovered for five main reasons despite the decline of the prices of petroleum (by 13.9 per cent in 1983, though this was offset by an increase in production) and sawlogs (by 14.6 per cent): (i) Imports grew less (by 3 per cent in 1983, compared to 19 per cent in 1981 and 9 per cent in 1982). (ii) The rubber price increased (by 21.6 per cent in 1983). (iii) LNG production and exports came on stream (worth M$0.8 billion). (iv) Tin exports picked up (by 17.5 per cent). (v) Manufactured exports grew (by 28.4 per cent). The trade surplus continued to grow to M$6.9 billion in 1984 and M$8.6 billion in 1985.

In contrast, however, performance of the services account has been discouraging. While the previous growth in freight and insurance payments abroad has been curbed since the early 1980s and has actually come down after 1982, investment income flows abroad (mainly returns on foreign investments and debt-servicing payments) have been growing at an alarming pace. They rose from M$1.8 billion in 1980 and 1981, to M$2.7 billion in 1982, M$4.2 billion in 1983, M$5.2 billion in 1984 and M$5.7 billion in 1985.

As a consequence, the current account deficit grew from M$0.6 billion in 1980 to M$5.6 billion in 1981, M$2.7 billion in 1982, M$4.2 billion in 1983, M$5.2 billion in 1984 and M$5.7 billion in 1985. The current account deficit has by and large been offset by capital flows from abroad except for a few years in the early 1980s (1981–83). Foreign corporate investments—the traditional source of capital inflows—rose from M$2.0 billion in 1980 to M$3.3 billion in 1982, before falling off to M$1.9 billion in 1985, totalling M$13 billion during the Fourth Malaysia Plan period (1981–85). In comparison, official foreign borrowing brought in about M$22 billion over the same period. Federal government borrowings rose from M$0.3 billion in 1980 to M$2.9 billion in 1981 and M$4.6 billion in 1982, before declining to M$3.8 billion in 1983, M$3.2 billion in 1984 and M$1.1 billion in 1985. Even as such loans began to decline after 1982, loans for non-financial public enterprises (NFPEs)—previously known as off-budget agencies (OBAs)—began to increase dramatically, from M$0.7 billion in 1982 to M$2.0 billion in both 1983 and 1984, before coming down to M$1.5 billion in 1985.

Though the economy's productive capacity, and hence ability to repay, are supposed to be greatly increased by capital investments, capital inflows in the form of either foreign investments or foreign loans have not really provided a fundamental solution to the balance of payments problem. Such capital inflows eventually involve even larger outflows abroad, mainly in the form of investment income payments abroad, whether returns to investors or loan-servicing (repayments plus interest). There would only be a net gain to the Malaysian economy if the growth of increase in production due to such inflows actually substantially exceeds the outflows attributable to these inflows, as well as the related costs or expenditure. The overall growth record as well as the performance of government development expenditure and the OBAs or NFPEs since the early 1980s would suggest that no significant overall gains can be expected from the foreign borrowing spree of the early 1980s. In other words, the Malaysian economy has become extremely dependent on foreign investment and foreign loans to provide the capital flows to offset the adverse current accounts balance.

Fiscal crisis and the growth of public debt

Between 1979 and 1981 the Malaysian government relied heavily on deficit budgets to sustain high growth in the face of adverse international economic trends. This sudden jump in public expenditure was due to the government's counter-cyclical policy to offset the depressive effects of the global economic downturn by increasing government spending. It was argued by Malaysian policymakers at that time that the economic conditions in 1980–81 were 'cyclical' in nature and hence quite temporary. Alternative views and suggestions that the downturn had important 'structural' roots—that could not be overcome merely by boosting public spending—were rejected as alarmist views of 'prophets of doom' who had always been exaggerating slight weaknesses in otherwise-sound Malaysian economic policy.

This budgetary deficit grew slowly but steadily in the early and mid-1960s, though never exceeding M$600 million in any particular year, before actually declining in the late 1960s. With the New Economic Policy, the deficit jumped by 120 per cent from M$476 million in 1970 to M$1.0 billion in 1971, rising fairly rapidly thereafter—except during 1973—until the annual deficit jumped again by 90 per cent from M$3.7 billion in 1979 to M$7.0 billion in 1980. In 1980, total expenditure rose by 47 per cent (compared to 1979), with development expenditure alone jumping by 76 per cent. In 1981, development expenditure was raised a further 52 per cent to M$11.1 billion, with the budget deficit rising to M$11.0 billion. Hence, in these two years (1980–81) alone, development expenditure rose 168 per cent, while the budget deficit rose by 199 per cent! With total federal government expenditure allocations stabilising around M$29 billion after the 1982 revision, development expenditure has been steadily trimmed, as operating expenditure continued to rise with government revenue. The net effect has been the reduction of the size of the annual budget deficit after 1982, at least until 1985.

The deficit in the consolidated public sector accounts (including the federal government, state governments and statutory bodies) has been even greater than the federal government deficit alone; it has also grown more rapidly, more than tripling in two years—from M$3.5 billion in 1979 to M$12.1 billion in 1981—with the deficit–GNP ratio jumping from 7.9 per cent in 1979 to 21.7 per cent in 1981. The 1981 consolidated public sector deficit to GNP ratio was one of the highest in the world, which had a 1980 average of 3.3 per cent according to the International Monetary Fund. With the consolidated public sector deficit declining since 1982, this ratio has declined correspondingly.

Malaysia's debt problem is relatively recent in origin, having grown out of the fiscal and balance of payments problems of the early 1980s. As a result of the decline in most Malaysian primary commodity prices since the turn of the decade, and declining prospects for export-oriented industries due to growing protectionism in the OECD economies, the two main engines of Malaysian export-led growth in the 1970s ran into serious trouble. This has, in turn, adversely affected Malaysia's balance of payments position, particularly the current account. Also Malaysia's counter-cyclic budgetary strategy during 1980–82, and the continued growth of off-budget public expenditure (for the NFPEs) for several years after that have required financing. Malaysia's previous high credit rating, due to its impressive growth record and other factors (e.g. its status as a net oil-exporting economy), enabled it to accumulate a huge external debt—in addition to its growing domestic debt—over a relatively short period in the early 1980s.

The government's austerity campaign, announced in mid-1982, spelt an end to the previous counter-cyclical budgetary policy. In the next two years, the government trimmed development expenditure drastically, from the originally announced budgetary allocation of M$14.6 billion for 1982 to M$8.0 billion for 1984. However, continued government-guaranteed borrowings by the OBAs–NFPEs not subject to the usual budgetary constraints sustained the rapid growth in the public debt, especially the foreign borrowings, over the next couple of years.

The total outstanding Malaysian public debt, *inclusive* of federal government-guaranteed loans, rose quite steadily from M$11.9 billion in 1975 to M$26.5 billion in 1980, before jumping to M$34.2 billion in 1981 and M$46.2 billion in 1982, largely due to the accelerated increase in government foreign market loans. It continued to increase rapidly to M$57.8 billion in 1983, before beginning to slow down to M$66.7 billion in 1984 and M$72.4 billion in 1985.

Table 5.3 Composition of outstanding public debt (inclusive of federal government-guaranteed loans), 1975–85, in M$ million (and as percentages)

	1975		1976			1977			1978		
	Amount	% of total debt	Amount	% of total debt	Annual Increase	Amount	% of total debt	Annual Increase	% Increase	Amount	% of total debt	Annual Increase	% Increase

	Amount	% of total debt	Amount	% of total debt	Annual Increase	Amount	% of total debt	Annual Increase	% Increase	Amount	% of total debt	Annual Increase	% Increase
Total domestic debt	3927	75	10573	71	1646	12709	73	2436	20	14074	72	1365	11
Total external debt	3013	25	4312	29	1299	4740	27	428	10	5439	28	699	15
Total public debt	11940	100	14885	100	2945	17449	100	2564	17	19513	100	2064	12

	1979				1980				1981			
	Amount	% of total debt	Annual Increase	% Increase	Amount	% of total debt	Annual Increase	% Increase	Amount	% of total debt	Annual Increase	% Increase
Total domestic debt	16744	72	2670	19	19206	72	2462	15	22929	67	3723	19
Total external debt	6636	28	1197	22	7264	28	628	9	11231	33	3967	55
Total public debt	23380	100	3867	20	26470	100	3090	13	34170	100	7700	29

	1982				1983				1984				1985			
	Amount	% of total debt	Annual Increase	% Increase	Amount	% of total debt	Annual Increase	% Increase	Amount	% of total debt	Annual Increase	% Increase	Amount	% of total debt	Annual Increase	% Increase
Total domestic debt	29305	63	5376	28	34612	60	5307	18	38773	58	4161	12	41510	57	2737	7
Total external debt	16873	37	6642	50	23215	40	6342	38	27952	42	4737	20	30918	43	2966	11
Total public debt	46178	100	12008	39	57827	100	11649	25	66725	100	8898	15	72426	100	5703	9

Source: Calculated from Government of Malaysia *Financial Statements 1984*, Table 1

Net public sector domestic borrowings rose from M$2.3 billion in 1980 to M$5.9 billion in 1982 and M$3.7 billion in 1985, while public sector external borrowings jumped from M$0.3 billion in 1980 to M$3.4 billion in 1981, and M$4.9 billion in 1982 before slowing down to M$4.6 billion in 1983, M$3.1 billion in 1984 and M$0.9 billion in 1985.

As we can see from Table 5.3, which disaggregates the total outstanding public debt by source—i.e. domestic or foreign—the domestic debt rose fairly steadily both before and after 1980. The dramatic growth in the public debt after 1980 was largely due to very much increased foreign borrowings from 1981, which decelerated only gradually after that. The total outstanding public external debt jumped by 55 per cent between 1980 and 1981, compared to only 9 per cent in the previous year. Subsequently, such foreign borrowing grew by 50 per cent (1981-82), 38 per cent (1982-83), 20 per cent (1983-84) and 11 per cent (1984-85) respectively.

In the meantime, the domestic debt proportion of the total outstanding public debt vacillated slightly in the late 1970s declining only slightly from 75 per cent in 1975 to 72 per cent in 1980. However, with the tremendous growth of foreign borrowings after 1980, this proportion fell dramatically to 67 per cent in 1981, 63 per cent in 1982, and 60 per cent in 1983, before declining more slowly to 58 per cent in 1984 and 57 per cent in 1985. In other words, the foreign debt component of total public debt rose slowly from 25 per cent in 1975 to 27 per cent in 1985.

The significance of the growth of Malaysia's external debt in the early 1980s can be seen in Table 5.4. As a proportion of the gross national product (GNP), the federal government debt has grown from 10 per cent in 1980 to 28 per cent in 1983 and 30 per cent in 1985, while the total public sector debt (including federal government-guaranteed loans) rose from 21 per cent in 1980 to 41 per cent in 1985. Taking private sector debt into consideration, the total Malaysian debt as a proportion of the GNP rose from 28 per cent in 1981 to 49 per cent in 1983 and 56 per cent in 1985. Private sector debt in Malaysia is significant not only in itself but also because much of it involves borrowings by government-owned or controlled private sector companies.

Malaysian government policymakers have prided themselves on the fact that, as a proportion of Malaysia's total exports, public external debt servicing has remained low, at only 6 per cent in 1983, according to Table 5.5. While relevant, this ratio can be misleading because Malaysia is a very open economy exporting a high proportion (about 60 per cent) of what it produces. In fact, in relation to the GNP, the size of Malaysia's external debt is a matter of great concern. According to the

Table 5.4 Malaysia: outstanding external debt, 1980–85, in M$ million (and as percentages of GNP)

Year	Federal government debt	Government-guaranteed debt	Public sector debt	Private sector debt	Total debt	Federal debt as % of GNP	Public sector debt as % of GNP	Total debt as % of GNP
1980	4 847					10		
1981	8 278	3 071	11 349	4 019	15 368	15	21	28
1982	13 158	3 715	16 873	7 410	24 283	23	29	42
1983	17 728	5 487	23 215	8 600	31 815	28	36	49
1984	20 848	7 105	27 953	9 665	37 618	28	38	51
1985	21 594	8 605	30 199	10 040	40 239	30	41	56

Source: For 1981–85: Bank Negara *Annual Report*, 1983, 1984 and 1985
Note: These figures include drawings from the IMF facility in federal government debt and are thus higher than Ministry of Finance figures.

Table 5.5 Malaysia's external debt compared to other countries, 1983

	Total debt US$ billion	As % of GNP	Public debt US$ billion	As % of GNP	Public debt as % of exports	Service as % of GNP
Malaysia	13.6	49	10.7	39	6	3.5
Brazil	79.6	40	58.1	29	29	3.5
Mexico			66.7	49	36	7.3
South Korea	23.1	31	21.5	29	13	3.4
All developing countries	598	36	495	30	19	3.9

Sources: Khor Kok Peng, 1987: p. 12, Table 5
Total debt for Malaysia: Bank Negara *Annual Report 1984*
All other data: World Bank (1985d) *World Debt Tables 1984/85*

World Debt Tables (see Table 5.5), in 1983 Malaysia's total external debt was 49 per cent of its GNP, compared to the developing country average of 36 per cent. Malaysia's public external debt was 39 per cent of its GNP, compared to the developing country average of 30 per cent, while public external debt servicing came to 35 per cent of the GNP, a little below the developing country average of 39 per cent. However, according to Malaysian central bank figures (Table 5.4), Malaysia's public external debt rose from 36 per cent of the GNP in 1983 to 38 per cent in 1984 and 41 per cent in 1985! In the meantime, Malaysia's total external debt rose from 49 per cent of the GNP in 1983 to 51 per cent in 1984 and 56 per cent in 1985. The apparently paradoxical situation in 1983 of a relatively high debt ratio to GNP is easily explained. Debt repayments on loans incurred during the early 1980s borrowing spree were not yet due in 1983. The situation has already begun to look quite different in subsequent years as some of the new borrowings from the early 1980s become due.

In essence, this means that the option of resorting to foreign loans to alleviate fiscal and balance of payments problems induced by declining commodity prices has already been extensively exercised, and there is little scope to explore this avenue further without creating a crisis in debt servicing.

Debt servicing

Total debt servicing has, somewhat inevitably, continued to grow, from M$2.6 billion in 1980 to M$6.0 billion in 1984, before doubling to an estimated M$11.9 billion in 1985. Predictably, domestic debt servicing

Policy response in Malaysia

has risen fairly steadily from M$2.0 billion in 1980 to M$4.5 billion in 1985. While government foreign debt servicing rose a little faster, from M$0.6 billion in 1980 to M$2.7 billion in 1984, it jumped to M$7.5 billion in 1985.

Federal government loan repayments rose from M$0.4 billion in 1975 to M$1.1 billion in 1980 and vacillated during 1980–84, before soaring to an estimated M$6.4 billion in 1985, mainly for early foreign loan prepayments to take advantage of lower interest rates, by refinancing earlier loans taken at higher interest rates. Federal government interest payments, on the other hand, have risen more steadily, reflecting the growing size of the debt, interest rates, including fluctuations, and the increasing proportion of foreign, especially market loans.

Not surprisingly, therefore, the fastest growing item in federal government operating expenditure has been debt servicing. As a proportion of operating expenditure, federal government debt servicing rose from 19 per cent in 1980 to 30 per cent in 1984, before jumping to 56 per cent in 1985! (Ministry of Finance, 1985–86, Statistical Appendix 4.5, 4.6). The proportion of federal government foreign debt servicing alone rose from 4 per cent in 1980 to 13 per cent in 1984, before jumping to 37 per cent in 1985! Meanwhile, debt servicing as a proportion of federal revenue actually declined slightly from 21.0 per cent in 1975 to 18.5 per cent in 1980, before soaring to an estimated 39 per cent in 1985, with little prospect of declining again, for reasons we shall examine later.

In 1975, new borrowings of M$2.1 billion significantly exceeded debt servicing of M$1.1 billion by 97 per cent. By 1980, after a few more years of moderate debt expansion, debt servicing of M$2.6 billion had caught up with new borrowing of M$2.6 billion. The tremendous growth of debt in the early 1980s pushed new borrowings well ahead of debt servicing during the years 1981–83, but by 1984 the chickens had begun to come home to roost, as debt servicing almost caught up; by 1985, debt servicing was almost three times the value of new borrowings.

Malaysian external debt-servicing payments rose from M$2.3 billion in 1981 to M$3.7 billion in 1983 and M$6.3 billion in 1985. Interest payments abroad grew steadily with the growth of the external debt, being offset only slightly by the lowering of interest rates in the early 1980s. Total interest payments abroad rose from M$1.2 billion in 1981 to M$3.5 billion in 1984.

Clearly then, the accelerated increase in external debt servicing has been primarily due to the increase in debt repayments or loan amortisation after 1983. Total external debt repayment rose from M$1.1 billion in 1981 to M$1.5 billion in 1983 and M$2.8 billion in

1985. Public external debt amortisation rose gradually from M$0.4 billion in 1981 to M$0.7 billion in 1983, M$0.9 billion in 1984 and M$1.3 billion in 1985. Most of this was accounted for by federal government loan repayments, which rose from M$0.2 billion in 1981 to M$0.5 billion in 1983, M$0.7 billion in 1984 and M$0.9 billion in 1985. Loan repayments also accelerated during 1984–85 because the Malaysian government chose to amortise its fixed-interest-rates loans incurred during the inital phase of the borrowing spree in the early 1980s when higher interest rates prevailed.

The gross external debt service ratio has been rising rapidly—with the growth of foreign borrowings, and especially loan repayments—from 7.1 per cent in 1981 to 9.7 per cent in 1983 and 14 per cent in 1985. The public sector external debt service ratio alone has grown from 3.8 per cent in 1981 to 6.0 per cent in 1983 and 9.0 per cent in 1985. This has largely been due to the rise of the federal government external debt service ratio from 2.6 per cent in 1981 to 4.6 per cent in 1983 and 7.0 per cent in 1985. As explained earlier, actual debt-service ratios have appeared so much higher during 1984 and 1985 as the Malaysian government made prepayments.

Table 5.6 presents World Bank projections for Malaysian public sector external debt servicing for 1984–91 based on outstanding loans

Table 5.6 Malaysia's public sector external debt, projections for debt servicing, 1982–91

	In US$ million			In M$ million		
Year	Total debt service	Principal	Interest	Total debt service	Principal	Interest
1982	794	257	537	1 841	596	1 245
1983	955	286	669	2 238	669	1 565
1984	1 344	371	973	3 261	900	2 361
1985	1 570	566	1 004	3 878	1 398	2 480
1986	1 858	871	986	4 589	2 151	2 435
1987	1 917	994	923	4 735	2 455	2 280
1988	2 347	1 518	829	5 797	3 749	2 048
1989	2 101	1 402	699	5 189	3 463	1 727
1990	1 844	1 270	574	4 555	3 137	1 418
1991	1 641	1 173	467	4 053	2 897	1 153

Notes: 1 1982, 1983 are actual data; 1984–91 are projections.
2 Exchange rate: 1982, US$1 = M$2.3185; 1983, US$1 = M$2.3387; 1984, US$1 = M$2.4263; 1985–91, US$1 = M$2.47 (May 1985 rate).
3 The projections are based only on outstanding loans as of 1983. If additional loans taken after 1983 are taken into account, debt servicing would be considerably higher.

Source: World Bank (1985d) *World Debt Tables 1984/85*, reproduced from Khor Kok Peng, 1987: p. 9, Table 4.

as of 1983. If new loans of M$7.2 billion in 1984, M$4.4 billion in 1985 and more thereafter are taken into account, these debt-servicing projections would be much higher. Hence, based only on the outstanding public sector external debt of M$23.3 billion as of 1983, debt servicing was expected to rise to M$5.8 billion in 1988, before falling off after that.

However, this is not likely to happen because the public sector's external debt continues to grow, albeit not as rapidly as in the early 1980s. Perhaps even more important, we have to recognise that debts—like drugs—are addictive. The more one borrows, the more one needs to borrow.

It should be clear that most countries—including Malaysia—cannot seriously expect to borrow their way out of economic difficulties. If anything, such borrowing usually tends to worsen, rather than relieve the problems. Hence, it now should be apparent that what was perceived as a solution to an apparently temporary problem in the early 1980s has actually turned out to be a virtually permanent affliction on the Malaysian economy—namely debt addiction.

Policy initatives

In early 1981, Dr Mahathir Mohamad took over as prime minister of Malaysia and president of the United Malays National Organisation (UMNO). Mahathir's accession to national leadership coincided with the unfolding of various developments associated with the present crisis, most notably the balance of payments and fiscal problems, which have resulted in an accelerated foreign debt expansion. Further increased public spending in the early 1980s was not only counter-cyclical in intent, but also attempted to make up for the shortfall in private investment.

Under Mahathir's leadership, however, the continued expansion of government spending and the financing of non-financial public enterprises or off-budget agencies have had an added significance. More than any previous prime minister of Malaysia, Mahathir has a definite vision of what he would like Malaysia to be, namely a newly industrialising country (NIC) under Malay capitalist entrepreneurial dominance. In this sense at least, Mahathir is a sort of economic nationalist, albeit a bourgeois one. Though inspired by the Japanese economic miracle, his real model for emulation is probably Park Chung Hee's South Korea. Yet, to be fair, Mahathir's development strategy is not merely imitative. Incoherent and faulty as they may be, the various economic development policies introduced in recent years nevertheless represent a serious effort—in circumstances not of his own choosing —to transform Malaysia into a newly industrialising country with a particular ethnic bias, attributable to Mahathir's perspective on Malaysia's ethnic and political heritage. Mahathir's economic policies may appear somewhat incoherent but they are circumscribed by the New Economic Policy especially its wealth restructuring considerations. They also contain some ideas espoused in his controversial *Malay Dilemma* (written in the aftermath of May 1969) and reflect the interests of the influential businessmen who are said to surround him. For better or worse, Mahathir should be credited with the major policy innovations of the past half decade, which have been variously characterised as anti-labour, authoritarian, nationalist and capitalist. These 'attributes' were also important ingredients in South Korea's industrialisation under the late General Park.

Mahathir's essentially modernising–industrialising, or NIC vision is captured in his exhortation to 'Look East', specifically to Japan and South Korea. While many Malaysians believe that of the four East Asian NICs, only South Korea was explicitly identified because it is not Chinese (unlike Taiwan, Hong Kong and Singapore), the very special features of the Hong Kong and Singapore economies also disqualify them as candidates for emulation. Hence, the real choice involves only Taiwan and South Korea. The choice of Taiwan is, of course, also complicated by diplomatic considerations besides the ethnic factor, and many would argue that Taiwan's industrialisation—managed by a refugee Guomindang government—has been somewhat less impressive than South Korea's.

Central to any NIC vision, of course, is the question of industrialisation strategy. NIC development strategies have generally involved export-led industrialisation—pursued by Malaysia since the late 1960s. Hence, it is not export-led industrialisation, but rather Mahathir's much-espoused commitment to develop heavy industries that has distinguished his leadership. This commitment to heavy industrialisation has involved expensive investments as well as burdensome protectionist measures. As a result, there has been less capital for other uses, and foreign borrowings have mounted while product prices have risen. There are, of course, also those opposed to heavy industries in principle, either because of the high capital intensity and low employment-generating capacity of such industries or else because they believe that 'small is beautiful'.

Others believe that it is desirable to support carefully selected heavy industries to achieve a more balanced, integrated and coherent national economy and industrial sector. They note, however, that most of the heavy industries chosen by the Malaysian government for development face stiff competition internationally due to existing excess global production capacity, and they require heavy protectionism with little likelihood of longer-term viability. Examples are steel, cement, petrochemicals, shipbuilding and repairs. The question for them then is not *whether* to develop heavy industries, but rather *which ones* and under what conditions.

For decades, one of the Malaysian government's main arguments in favour of foreign investment has been the desirability of technology transfer. However, this argument is faulty even in conception. It is inconceivable that transnational corporations—reliant on technological superiority to ensure profitability—will voluntarily surrender their technological edge, especially to potential competitors. This does not mean that no technology transfer can ever take place. Rather, such a transfer is planned to maximise profitability, not lose it. Hence, it would be naive to expect that such technology transfer can eventually develop an internationally competitive technological capacity.

In their study of electronics and electrical firms in Malaysia in 1980, Cheong and Lim (1981) found that the transnationals retained research and development activities with the parent firm in the home country and controlled equipment and parts supply, key personnel and marketing. Activities in Malaysia mainly involved assembly, processing and testing, requiring little skill and training, which were in any case generally irrelevant to most other industrial activities. Owing to weak linkages with the rest of the economy, other industries hardly benefited from technology diffusion.

Another Mahathir policy related to industrialisation is the population target of 70 million for the year 2100. It is argued that such a large population would be desirable to provide a sufficient domestic market for Malaysia's enhanced industrial capacity, especially for the heavy industries. However, except for certain basic consumption needs and amenities (e.g. food, clothing, shelter), a larger population does not generate a correspondingly larger market in itself. In fact, a market is basically determined by effective demand, which would, in turn, be defined by the level and distribution of income and hence consumption or purchasing capacity. Therefore, to get beyond production of basic needs, the crucial factors are raising per capita income levels and ensuring more equitable distribution rather than raising population numbers.

The final draft of Malaysia's National Agricultural Policy (NAP), announced in early 1984, is said to have been personally authored by the prime minister himself. The NAP emphasises efforts to increase peasant incomes by raising productivity, introducing crop variation and improving agricultural management practices. It has reduced the previous emphasis on food self-sufficiency and instead recommends export-oriented cash crops. Mini-estates are proposed to overcome problems of uneconomic farm sizes and abandoned farm land, which would favour landowners over those without land of their own. Land reform measures to overcome land hunger, limit land rents and provide land to the tiller are ignored in the NAP. Even the cooperative movement is de-emphasised, while small-scale capitalist agricultural management practices are expected to resolve the main problems associated with peasant agriculture.

The role of the Malaysian government in economic development, defined primarily by the New Economic Policy since the 1970s, has come under critical scrutiny since Mahathir's accession to power. He advanced the 'Malaysia Incorporated' slogan—with its corporatist overtones—in an effort to improve relations between the government and the private sector, and more importantly, to try to get the government to play its traditional role of serving private capitalist interests. As is well known, the term 'Malaysia Inc.' is adapted from the pejorative term 'Japan Inc.' which emerged in the industrial West in the 1960s as it first faced stiff competition from the more strongly state-backed Japanese business interests. The background to Malaysia's problems relating to government private sector relations, however, is quite different. While the Malaysia Inc. slogan has tried to remind government officers of the typical role of government under capitalism, the campaign has not really addressed the specifically Malaysian problems underlying government–private sector relations.

Mahathir's privatisation policy is actually somewhat Western in inspiration, with Thatcher's Britain and Reagan's America setting global trends. Although the generally lacklustre performance of the Malaysian public sector, including most statutory bodies and government-owned companies, cannot be denied, the question is whether such inefficiencies are characteristic of the public sector and cannot be overcome other than through privatisation. If, however, the generally poor record of Malaysian public enterprises is primarily due to the nature, interests and abilities of those in power, rather than to public ownership *per se*, then privatisation cannot overcome the problem for which it is touted as a panacea. Though privatisation may improve enterprise efficiency in order to increase profits for the private owners concerned, such change will not necessarily benefit the public or consumers in every aspect. Since major targets for privatisation have been public monopolies, privatisation will in effect hand over their monopolistic powers to private interests likely to use them to maximise profits. The privatisation of public services tends to place the burden on those who can ill afford the higher prices of privatised services. Needless to say, private interests will only be interests in potentially profitable activities and enterprises. This will mean that the government will be stuck with the unprofitable and less profitable activities,

Policy response in Malaysia 137

which will only worsen the already-poor public sector performance. Public sector inefficiencies and other related problems certainly need to be overcome, but privatisation will primarily enrich the few with the strong political connections to secure such profitable opportunities, while the people's interests become increasingly vulnerable to private capitalists' power and interests.

The authoritarian and anti-labour policies considered necessary for capitalist, especially industrial, development have been quite pronounced since the start of this decade. After the tightening up of the labour laws in 1980 in the aftermath of the 1978–79 industrial action taken by employees of Malaysian Airline System, industrial relations machinery and labour policies have continued to change, largely at the expense of labour. Continued capitalist expansion has led to increased wage employment, although membership of trade unions actually declined in the early 1980s. In the meantime, the official unemployment rate has risen from 5.7 per cent in 1980 to 7.6 per cent in 1985, and is expected to reach 10.1 per cent in 1990. The increasingly widespread use of poorly paid and badly treated immigrant contract labour, especially in plantation agriculture, land development schemes and construction, as well as government and management endorsement of the more easily controlled in-house unions, have also helped to further weaken the bargaining position of labour in the 1980s. At the same time, the government's promotion of supposedly Japanese work ethics and other related campaigns (such as quality control circles) were intended to boost labour productivity at minimal cost and in a manner subservient to management. The penalties for those who step out of line have been sufficiently severe to discourage labour militancy.

The Industrial Master Plan

The publication of the draft Industrial Master Plan (IMP) in early 1986 has also opened up new issues. While the export-led industrialisation strategy remains, the IMP envisages rationalisation, or cutting down protection on import-substituting industries, many of which currently enjoy handsome profits behind high tariff walls, despite considerable inefficiency. The IMP also seeks to boost and diversify manufactured exports as well as cut down drastically on their high import content by dramatically changing the entire industrial incentive system.

The publication of the Industrial Master Plan by the Malaysian Industrial Development Authority in early 1986 was the first master plan of its kind in Malaysian history. Unfortunately, only fifteen of the twenty-two reports have been released. Hence, crucial relevant information is unavailable for scrutiny.

The IMP documents that have been made public include a combination of sober—even somewhat critical—analysis of Malaysia's industrial heritage and current problems, on the one hand, and what has best been described as 'enlightened wishful thinking' regarding industrial policy proposals, on the other. The IMP offers a useful analysis of the structural problems associated with Malaysia's manufacturing sector, but then goes on to propose policies ostensibly meant to improve Malaysian industry but without getting at the root of most of the structural problems it identifies.

Malaysian manufacturing's structural problems

The IMP points out that despite, or rather because of, its growth and development records, Malaysia has been a relative latecomer in terms of industrialisation. The IMP attributes Malaysia's 'delayed industrialisation' to the success of its primary commodity exports. Malaysia apparently lagged behind because successful primary exports expansion financed its import needs, thus weakening the imperative to industrialise. The availability of more profitable alternative investment opportunities in primary production also discouraged industrial investments. The IMP suggests that, as a result, 'industry will develop only after income levels and investment rates have risen as a consequence of the growth of primary production' (Malaysia, 1986b: vol. 1, 11). The IMP also acknowledges that Malaysia's industrial structure is characterised by imbalance. It contends that the manufacturing sector is narrowly based on a few labour-intensive and resource-based industries. Despite the official emphasis on export-oriented industries, since the late 1960s, manufactured exports account for less than 20 per cent of total manufacturing output. These industries produce low-skill, labour-intensive exports, requiring simple final-assembly activities. Meanwhile the relative share of resource-based products has also declined, accounting for only 19.7 per cent of all manufactured exports in 1983 (Malaysia, 1986b: vol. 1, 13). Concerning heavy industries, the IMP correctly argues that the debate should not be whether to develop heavy industries, but rather which heavy industries to develop. The IMP recognises that most of the heavy industries developed so far will have to deal with existing gluts on the world market, including steel, cement, petrochemicals, shipbuilding and repairing.

Like many previous analysts, the IMP agrees that the import-substituting manufacturing sector in Malaysia has been excessively protected. It has been estimated that the effective rate of protection for the entire sector rose from 25 per cent in 1962, to 50 per cent in 1966 and 70 per cent in 1972 (Edwards, 1975). For example, the rise in import duty per bicycle in 1978 from M$18 to M$60 pushed up the

Policy response in Malaysia

retail price of the cheapest bicycle from M$80 to M$140 (Khor, 1983a: 17).

The 'infant industry' argument should not be used to justify such protection because it has primarily been given to foreign firms which have readily been granted tariff protection 'almost without exception' (Edwards, 1975). Large profits, and possibly inefficiency as well, have been protected by such policies at the expense of consumer welfare. Thus, by substituting the import of parts, plant and equipment, for finished products, these transnationals have secured highly profitable monopolies.

The IMP also recognises that export-oriented manufacturing is heavily dominated by two types of industries, namely electronics and electrical products, plus textiles and garments, which accounted for M$6.4 billion or 65 per cent (i.e. almost two-thirds) of a total of M$9.8 billion worth of manufacturing exports in 1983, of which semiconductor assembly alone accounted for 41 per cent. In February 1984, 128 539 or 39 per cent of the 331 228 industrial workers were accounted for by these two types of industry (Khor, 1983a: 25).

While acknowledging the impressive growth of the electronics industry, the IMP recognises the limited and lopsided nature of its development to date:

> Structurally, it has a heavy dependence on production of components accounting for 80 to 85 per cent of the industry's total output; and within this sector, semiconductor assembly and testing activities have predominated, contributing 83 to 92 per cent of total component output. The consumer and industrial electronics which normally account for more than 55 to 70 per cent of total output in other NICs and advanced countries, only contribute 15 to 20 per cent in Malaysia. This lopsided structure makes the Malaysian electronics industry very precarious, particularly because components manufacturing is limited to relatively simple assembly and testing activities based on imported materials, and is dominated by foreign transnational corporations whose main motivations to operate in Malaysia are low wages and attractive tax incentives available in the country. The side effect of this extreme structural skewness is the lack of linkages within the industry, especially between the companies in FTZs [free trade zones] and non-FTZs. [Malaysia, 1986b: vol. 1, 49]

The IMP also acknowledges 'extremely weak inter-industry linkages' (vol. 1, 11). Unfortunately, the report discussing this has not been made public. This problem has been highlighted by others over the years (e.g. Thoburn, 1973; Edwards, 1975). From their survey of thirty-two electronic and electrical products factories, Cheong and Lim (1981) found that only a quarter obtained some simple parts—not requiring any advanced technology—from local firms, while the remaining three-quarters imported all their requirements. The IMP (vol. 1, 69) itself acknowledges that in 1982 only 6.5 per cent of the raw materials used in the free trade zones (FTZs) were from local sources outside the FTZ. In 1981, according to the IMP (vol. 1, 31), the ratio of imports to output for non-resource-based industries was 93 per cent! Lim Chin Choo (1979) found that, during 1973–79, total exports from Malaysian FTZs were M$4020 million, compared to total imports of M$3990 million, yielding a net export surplus of only M$30 million, before taking profit repatriation, royalties and other fee payments into account!

Foreign domination

While claiming that foreign investment has made a positive contribution in manufacturing growth, the IMP acknowledges that 'heavy' and 'sustained' dependency on foreign investment in some important industries' 'key areas' of technology, marketing, management and components supply, jeopardises the development of an indigenous industrial base (Malaysia, 1986b: vol. 1, 13). The plan also acknowledges that the manufacturing sector is dominated by large, often foreign-controlled firms.

However, the IMP documents do not mention the massive outflow of economic surplus in various forms as a consequence of foreign ownership and control of the manufacturing sector. According to the 1981 *Industrial Survey* (Department of Statistics, 1981), foreign-controlled companies accounted for only 513 (or about 2.5%) of the 20 429 manufacturing firms in 1981, M$3.0 billion (or 29%) of the sector's fixed assets worth M$10.4 billion, and M$15.3 billion (or 40%) of its total revenue of M$38.7 billion. According to the 1983 *Financial Survey of Limited Companies* (Department of Statistics, 1983), covering limited companies with annual revenue of at least M$5 million, 193, or more than one-fifth of the 873 firms in the manufacturing sector were foreign-controlled. They accounted for 40 per cent of equity share capital, 47 per cent of shareholder funds, 63 per cent of gross profit and 65 per cent of net profit; they also accounted for M$642 million, or 94 per cent of investment income accruing to non-residents (Khor, 1983a: Tables 1 and 2). Although local firms accounted for only 35 per cent of net profit, they accounted for 51 per cent of the increase in net fixed assets in 1981, reflecting the greater tendency for local firms to reinvest locally compared to foreign firms. In fact, taking investment income outflows into account, on a net foreign investment of M$747 million the investment income to non-residents was $680 million and net capital inflow was only M$65 million.

Policy response in Malaysia 141

As the IMP acknowledges, the Malaysian manufacturing sector's technological dependence is excessive. Such dependence has resulted in the outflow of royalty payments, fees and other charges to the parent transnational, ostensibly in connection with technology transfer. As any transnational corporations actually prefer to have joint ventures with local firms, especially in industry and the services, such outflows have increased in significance compared to simple profit repatriation. It has been found that most joint ventures with local majority holdings were actually controlled by the foreign partner, especially in technology-related matters (Abdul Razak, 1984).

Royalty payments have been conservatively estimated at 2 per cent of sales revenue—which would have amounted to M$196 million in 1978 for foreign firms alone, i.e. equivalent to 46 per cent of their after-tax profits (Khor, 1983b: 211).

Though there is no detailed study of the extent and significance of transfer pricing in Malaysia, Khor (1983b: 215) has estimated that if export prices were undervalued by 10 per cent and imports were overvalued by 10 per cent in 1978, actual pre-tax profits would have been M$1460 million, or 115 per cent higher, than the M$680 million reported. Lall (1978: 179) found evidence of transfer pricing practices in the pricing of completely knocked down (CKD) automotive packs imported for assembly in Malaysia. Such packs were often priced higher than completely built up units of the same vehicle. And when locally made components were substituted, the CKD pack prices did not go down correspondingly by the value of the components.

IMP solutions

The IMP identifies five major problems that have adversely affected Malaysian industrialisation:

1 Technology dependence and lack of indigenous industrial technology capacity
2 Shortage of engineers and technicians
3 Deficiencies in the current industrial incentive systems including:
 * ad hoc and excessive domestic market protection
 * large firm, capital-intensive bias due to pioneer status incentive
 * neglect of small industry problems and requirements
 * rigidity and inflexibility of existing incentive system
 * biases in export incentives
 * little incentives for technological development
 * some major incentives not automatically available
4 Lack of private sector initiative
5 Constraints imposed by New Economic Policy (NEP) restructuring.

While the IMP acknowledges the incapability of Malaysia's industrial entrepreneurs (especially in terms of technology and organisation) and the problems arising from the kind of state intervention that has taken place, it makes fairly predictable proposals focusing on technology, manpower and incentives.

By ignoring the reasons for the skewed character of the existing Malaysian market structure—largely attributable to the inequitable distribution of wealth and power, and hence income, and therefore purchasing power and the pattern of effective demand, as well as modern transnational corporate ideological influences (especially through advertising)—the IMP planners are left with little choice but to advocate yet more of the same, namely export-led industrialisation.

In the process, they make unrealistic, but crucial assumptions—e.g. an impossibly rosy average GDP growth rate of 6.4 per cent yearly over the next decade—and wishfully set arbitrary ten-year targets—e.g. a billion ringgit worth of tyre exports and another billion ringgit worth of industrial electrical equipment in 1995, from zero and M$87 million ringgit in 1981 respectively.

Perhaps the most welcome IMP proposal is reduction of excessive protectionism, which has inequitably 'protected' high profits and inefficiency among the mainly foreign-dominated import-substituting industries, at the expense of Malaysian consumers.

It is widely acknowledged that achievement of the IMP goals will depend very much on progress in the first couple of years. Yet, it is also acknowledged that such progress depends very heavily on restoration of investment confidence, partly through reform of the relevant bureaucracy, legislation and policies, which will be difficult to achieve in the immediate future, especially in view of the entrenched vested interests and prevailing attitudes among the policymakers involved.

The Fifth Malaysia Plan

Economic planning in an open capitalist economy is necessarily of limited and dubious significance. Planning in a capitalist economy, even one with a large, dominant public sector, is primarily indicative in nature, i.e. can only suggest desired targets, because of the crucial independent role of the private sector. Furthermore, the vulnerability of Malaysia's very open economy to the uncertainties of external economic conditions makes planning doubly hazardous in the Malaysian context.

One might legitimately argue that economic planning acquired a greater significance in Malaysia in the 1970s as capitalist-type state intervention grew in the wake of implementation of the New Economic

Policy response in Malaysia

Policy. However, since the early 1980s, for various reasons, the rhetoric, ideology and even policies of 'deregulation', 'Malaysia Inc.' and 'privatisation' have slowly but surely begun to roll back the earlier growth of the public sector and state intervention.

The publication of the Fifth Malaysia Plan (5MP) in March 1986 not only reiterates official commitment to Mahathir's economic philosophy and policies in general (also found in the Mid-Term Review of the Fourth Malaysia Plan, published in early 1984), but also proposes a renewed and expanded role for the private sector in particular. One might legitimately argue that Malaysian state planners and policymakers have little alternative to banking on the private sector within the existing economic framework, especially after the nearly disastrous consequences of accelerated deficit spending and foreign borrowing in the early 1980s. The revival of anti-Keynesian free-market and laissez-faire philosophies and policies in the West (such as monetarism and supply-side economics) and the growing vulnerability of Malaysian economic policy to external pressures (as a consequence of increased indebtedness and other related problems) have also contributed to this trend.

The result, not surprisingly, is greater recourse to wishful thinking, especially as far as the envisaged role of the private sector is concerned. This, of course, raises serious doubts about the credibility of the plan as a whole, particularly with regard to its internal consistency, especially since so much of it is premised on achieving ambitious private investment targets, which are clearly beyond the control of government Furthermore, given the experience with previous five-year plans, particularly in terms of private sector target achievement, increasing doubts have surfaced about Malaysian economic planning even as a limited indicative exercise.

In fact, private investment actually dropped between 1984 and 1985 by 10.9 per cent in nominal terms—from M$13.3 billion in 1984 to M$11.9 billion in 1985—or by 8.1 per cent in constant 1978 prices, from M$10.4 billion in 1984 to M$9.6 billion in 1986 (Malaysia, 1986a: 46, Table 2.2). Perhaps more significantly, private investment as a percentage of the GNP has been declining every year during the past half-decade, from 20.6 per cent in 1981, to 16.3 per cent in 1985 (Malaysia, 1986a: 56, Table 2.8). Corporate investment in 1985 was estimated at M$1.9 billion, 12.5 per cent lower than in 1984 (Bank Negara, 1986: 186). While public investment growth is envisaged to remain constant between 1985 and 1990 new private investment is expected to grow by more than half, from M$11.9 billion in 1985 to M$18.0 billion in 1990.

The government envisages attracting more private, especially foreign investment by providing more attractive incentives and cutting down existing bureaucratic and regulating impediments, there is little reason to believe that this will somehow miraculously bring in massive new investments after similar efforts failed to do so in the first half of this decade and also in light of recent foreign investment trends internationally.

Malaysia's exports are expected to grow by an average of 3.2 per cent per annum (4.8 per cent in 1978 prices) during 1986–90, compared to 6.9 per cent (8.0 per cent in 1978 prices) during 1981–85. Meanwhile, imports are expected to grow by 3.7 per cent (2.2 per cent in 1978 prices) during 1986–90, compared to 6.0 per cent (8.0 per cent in 1978 prices) during 1981–85.

While the depreciation of the ringgit since September, 1985, has discouraged some imports, past trends suggest a higher propensity to import and a greater inelasticity in Malaysia's demand for imports than the 5MP seems to take account of. After all, as the GDP grew by an average of 5.8 per cent during 1981–85, imports grew by an average of 5.5 per cent per annum (in constant 1978 prices).

Doubtful growth projections

The Fifth Malaysia Plan envisages an average annual GDP growth rate of 5.0 per cent for 1986–90, compared to 5.8 per cent during 1981–85, while GNP growth is expected to average 5.1 per cent during 1986–90, compared to 4.9 per cent achieved in the previous half-decade (all in constant 1978 prices).

In current price terms, however, the GNP actually fell in 1985 by 2.7 per cent, according to Bank Negara (by 2.1 per cent, according to the 5MP). This is largely attributable to the 5.6 per cent deterioration in Malaysia's international terms of trade during 1985. With the international terms of trade expected, by Bank Negara, to decline by a further 15.5 per cent in 1986, GNP in nominal terms was expected to drop by another 5.7 per cent in 1986. More ominously, per capita GNP in current prices fell by 4.9 per cent in 1985 and was expected to drop by another 7.9 per cent during 1986.

The 5MP, however, is more optimistic about the international terms of trade, expecting it to decline by 13.9 per cent over five years between 1985 and 1990, in contrast to Bank Negara's forecasted decline of 15.5 per cent during 1986 alone. In 1985, M$2.3 billion was lost in commodity earnings due to price changes. Primary commodities income losses were expected to rise to M$7.3 billion in 1986, according to Bank Negara (1986: 3, Table 1.3), of which crude petroleum would account for M$2.9 billion, palm oil for M$2.1 billion, LNG for M$1.1 billion and tin for M$0.7 billion.

The increase in private investment envisaged by the 5MP is almost stupendous. From an average growth rate of 2.7 per cent per annum (1.8 per cent in constant 1978 prices) during 1981-85, it is projected to jump to 8.6 per cent per annum (7.0 per cent in 1978 prices) during 1986-90. How this is going to be achieved, in view of recent trends, is surely one of the most crucial questions about the feasibility of the 5MP.

While the GDP is expected to grow by 5.0 per cent during 1986-90, imports are almost miraculously expected to grow by only 2.2 per cent (in constant 1978 prices)!

It should be emphasised that we are not prophets of doom, pessimistically rejecting well-founded grounds for optimism in planning projections. The point rather is that national economic planning in an open capitalist economy like Malaysia's is necessarily a very speculative affair involving a great deal of wishful thinking. Realistically, long-term planning in such a context cannot be meaningful. But even short-term projections should be realistic and consistent to be meaningful. As things stand this would appear not to be the case. The 5MP projections raise serious doubts about the plan's internal consistency, especially with regard to its analysis of private investment.

Concluding remarks: predicament and prospect

Economic policymaking changed drastically in the aftermath of the race riots and the 'palace coup' of 13 May 1969. While government policy before the New Economic Policy was generally considered to be basically *laissez faire* in approach, and responsive to, as well as supportive of, both foreign and (predominantly Chinese) domestic private sector interests, the 1970s was characterised by growing state intervention, primarily in favour of the nascent Malay bourgeoisie. While such intervention generally did not threaten capitalism *per se*, particular capitalist interests—usually Chinese or foreign—have been threatened at various times. Seen against this background then, the policies of the 1980s suggest the beginning of a swing away from the excesses of 1970s type interventionism, e.g. through privatisation, 'Malaysia Inc.', deregulation and 'NEP concessions'.

The past half-decade has also highlighted the limits of state interventionism in the context of Malaysian capitalism. Though the Malaysian export engine has run into deteriorating commodity markets and protectionist barriers, the growth strategy continues to be export-led as policymakers will not undertake redistributive measures that can substantially expand the domestic market. In the early 1980s, deflationary pressures were fought off by massive increases in public development expenditure. To compensate for the deterioration in the balance of payments and to finance the growing budgetary deficits, the government rapidly increased the public debt, especially foreign borrowings, in the early 1980s. Even after government development expenditure was reined in around mid-1982, government-guaranteed foreign borrowing continued to grow rapidly until 1984, especially to finance investments in government-owned and controlled non-financial public enterprises, also known as off-budget agencies.

It has been very tempting to relate various government policy initiatives during the past half-decade to specific business interests associated with leading politicians. In fact, it is openly acknowledged that business interests now influence politics more than ever before in recent Malaysian history. For instance, at the last general assembly of the United Malays National Organisation (UMNO), the dominant partner in the ruling coalition, over half the delegate were businessmen. Daim Zainuddin, UMNO treasurer and finance minister since mid 1984, is a very close associate of the prime minister who had no previous cabinet or government experience, but had developed a considerable reputation as a successful businessman. In August 1986, Tan Koon Swan resigned as president of the Malaysian Chinese Association (MCA), ranked second only to UMNO in the ruling coalition, after being convicted in Singapore for business malpractice. He had been elected MCA president by about four-fifths of the delegates in November 1985 after rising to prominence over the past decade as a Chinese business leader. In mid-1986, Samy Vellu, the president of the Malaysian Indian Congress (MIC), also defended the close relationship between politics and business. Many leading government politicians have openly acknowledged the growing influence of 'money politics', corruption as well as other consequences and manifestations of the increasing convergence of business and political power. Many observers would agree that such recent wealth in Malasyia is political, rather than entrepreneurial in origin. And undoubtedly, many businessmen-politicians and politically well-connected businessmen have secured business advantages from most of the recent economic policy initiatives.

Yet, it would be attractively simplistic, but more importantly, erroneously misleading to explain away recent policies as simply reflecting the interests of the politically influential beneficiaries concerned. While such interests have undoubtedly tended to dominate the actual implementation of the policies concerned, there have been at least two other major influences deserving of attention.

Firstly, the massive increase in foreign borrowings in the early 1980s and the great expectations of massive direct foreign investment, especially to revive currently flagging economic fortunes, have rendered the Malaysian economy and related policymaking far more vulnerable to foreign economic policy influence, especially by multilateral agencies, such as the IMF and the World Bank, which can strongly affect Malaysia's international credit and investment rating. Many recent deflationary and deregulatory policies, as well as other policies, such as privatisation, continued export-led growth (especially industrialisation), and greater encouragement of foreign investment, should be seen in this light.

Secondly, while working from the premise that the Malaysian state is capitalist in nature, it is important to appreciate some of its particular characteristics, especially those explaining the limited autonomy of the state manifest in some important government policies. Rooted in Malaysian class formation from the colonial period with its complex ethnic manifestations (Jomo, 1986), the strategic shift from Malay dominance to Malay domination after 1969—e.g. as reflected by implementation of the NEP—explains various economic policies in the 1970s which did not necessarily foster the interests of the major blocs of capital. Yet, while Malay domination provided the impetus for a growing role for the state, the momentum of state interventionism was also encouraged by the enhanced powers of bureaucrats, politicians and politically well-connected businessmen. Yet ironically, the apparent retreat, in the 1980s under Mahathir, from the heavy-handed state interventionism of the 1970s has been possible precisely because the enhanced powers of the state after 1969 increased and facilitated the growing concentration of powers in the hands of the executive under Mahathir's leadership. In these circumstances then, Mahathir seems committed to accelerated capitalist growth and industrialisation in Malaysia under temporary foreign auspices while paving the way for eventual domination by private Bumiputra capital.

Prospects

The circumstances and outlook for the Malaysian economy at the time of writing (i.e. in the second half of 1986) are generally considered bleak. Owing to the open nature of the Malaysian economy, it has been past practice to predict an economic upturn following recovery of the OECD economies, especially the US, allowing for some lag time, of course. The failure of the recent upturn in the OECD economies to bring about such a recovery in Malaysia has been ominous, to say the least. It has become almost fashionable to take this as a sign that the current recession is not cyclical but structural in nature. However, perhaps even more disturbing is the proposition that OECD economic recovery must henceforth necessarily be at the expense of the South, especially in terms of keeping commodity prices low. Thus, it is envisaged that while labour surpluses keep wages down, the oversupply of commodities will keep their prices low. Almost all Malaysia's relatively diversified primary commodity exports have suffered depressed prices, at least since early 1986. Continued low prices will certainly continue to take an inflationary toll on economic growth and adversely affect Malaysia's merchandise account and hence its overall balance of payments. And while OECD economic recovery has not revived the primary commodity exporting economies of the South, it is unclear what measures will. The likelihood of organising producer cartels in the present difficult economic times is remote, let alone their chance of success in view of the massive supply overhangs for many commodities.

The prospects for domestic engines of growth are not much better, not least because most of them rely on export markets. And as far as most of the primary commodities are concerned, the major problems are not on the supply-side. However, for continued economic expansion, Malaysia needs continued investments. Private investments from abroad are supposed to sustain capital inflows, previously provided by foreign borrowings in the early 1980s. For ethnic and political reasons as well, it appears that the Malaysian government is favouring foreign investment, rather than the still predominantly Chinese domestic investment. If successful, this strategy will further enhance foreign capital's dominance of Malaysian industry and subordinate the state and Malay capital to it. However, in view of recent international investment opportunities and trends, as well as the still over-regulated domestic environment (apparently made necessary by ethnic political considerations), it is unlikely that the massive foreign investments desired will be forthcoming, at least in the amounts desired. The government might then be tempted either to resort to foreign borrowings once again or to open up the oil tap some more, especially if the petroleum price picks up again. Needless to say, neither of these options really offer sustainable, long-term solutions to the fundamental problems of the Malaysian economy, but then, the time horizons, and more importantly, the interests of policymakers cannot be relied upon to find such solutions.

GARRY RODAN

6
The rise and fall of Singapore's 'Second Industrial Revolution'

Of all the economies of Southeast Asia, Singapore's has been most completely incorporated into the structure of the new international division of labour (NIDL). The explanation for this lies in the peculiar and historically specific circumstances of Singapore's social structure in the 1960s. These account for both the inclination of the ruling People's Action Party (PAP) to consider an export-oriented industrialisation (EOI) strategy under the aegis of international capital, as well as the capacity to implement such a strategy. In particular, the degree of relative political autonomy from both capital and labour, which the PAP came to enjoy, had placed economic policy formation in Singapore in a somewhat different context from that of neighbouring economies.

The exact socio-historical juncture that afforded the PAP such an atypical degree of manoeuvrability in economic policy will be outlined below. For now, it need only be recognised that at the time of the failed political merger with Malaysia in 1965, which thereby undermined the economic basis of Singapore's import-substitution industrialisation (ISI) strategy, the PAP was insulated from direct political control by either capital or labour. Furthermore, by this time the PAP had secured its political pre-eminence, due in no small part to the merging of state power with party interests to quell opposition and institutionalise PAP dominance. This pre-eminence was fundamental to the Singapore state's generation of the social, political and economic prerequisites for successful EOI. The decimation of the left-wing independent labour movement by the state was the principal, but not exclusive, such prerequisite.

The PAP's destruction of the labour movement was, of course, intended to ensure low wages and a tame labour force, thereby rendering Singapore a competitive export base for manufacturing by international capital. Intervention at the economic level also contributed to a conducive investment climate for export production. The state instigated and coordinated substantial physical and social infrastructural development in support of the new strategy. It also provided a host of concessions and subsidies which favoured specific forms of production. Moreover, it provided a degree of overall synthesis and accessibility to the factors of production which earned Singapore a reputation for an efficient and supportive bureaucracy.

As is well documented, the PAP's EOI strategy achieved dramatic and remarkable results. Because of the massive inflow of international capital, Singapore's high and potentially chronic unemployment was quickly transformed. Before too long, the rapid pace of industrial growth was actually threatened by labour shortages. Throughout the 1970s, near double-digit economic growth rates were averaged as the volume and quality of manufacturing investment grew. Singapore was the shining example of the successful EOI economy. The model promised even bigger things when the PAP embarked on its so-called 'Second Industrial Revolution' in 1979.

The aim of the 'Second Industrial Revolution' was to elevate Singapore's technological status in the hierarchy of the new international division of labour. On the one hand, the state actively discouraged low-value-added, labour-intensive production by raising labour costs to employers. On the other hand, simultaneously the state improved the quality of social and physical infrastructure and ensured low establishment and operational costs for more-sophisticated, higher-value-added production. In effect, the PAP set out to test the limits of mobility open to newly industrialising countries (NICs) in the NIDL through concerted state efforts to shape comparative advantage.

What we see below is that, after some initial limited success, the strategy failed to generate the pace or extent of industrial restructuring anticipated by the PAP. The advent of the global recession thus found Singapore's economy in a precarious position. Singapore found itself too costly a production site to fall back on less-sophisticated production to maintain economic growth and employment. As a result, in 1985 Singapore suffered negative economic growth for the first time in its history. Not coincidentally, the PAP's electoral fortunes suffered in the same year.

Acknowledging the seriousness of the problem, the PAP has subsequently reversed key components of the 'Second Industrial Revolution'. Special focus is being given to reducing labour costs in the endeavour to regain competitiveness in areas other than higher-value-added production. Efforts to promote more-sophisticated manufacturing production have not been abandoned, but it is implicitly recognised that this cannot be the sole or even primary basis of industry if growth and employment are to be maintained. However, as will be explained below, whichever way the PAP turns in attempting to resolve the economic contradictions confronting it, domestic political problems are likely to result. The political economy of Singapore seems set for new turbulence. The predicament of the Singapore economy as a result of the experience of the 'Second Industrial Revolution' has important implications for our understanding of the EOI model and the mechanics of the NIDL.

Background to the 'Second Industrial Revolution'

The colonial period

Historically, Singapore was incorporated into the British colonial umbrella in 1819 to counter Dutch access to and control over Oriental trade. Singapore offered considerable strategic advantages in the contest for commercial superiority. Thus, from the outset the British intended the island to perform quite specific economic functions. However, for Singapore to fulfil the entrepot trading role designed for it, the British had to attract experienced and knowledgeable merchants operating in the region so that links could be established with the various producers and merchants in the archipelago and beyond. At the time of colonisation, Singapore's population was both tiny and without such expertise. Due in no small way to the free-port status of the island, the requisite Malayan and Chinese traders were successfully attracted.

By the 1920s it was possible to delineate a clear and complementary structure of ownership and control in the Singapore economy. European investments controlled primary production and the trade associated with it (through the large agency houses), whilst the local predominantly Chinese merchants operated an intrinsic network of small-scale collection, distribution and retailing (Buchanan, 1972: 33). Though there were also direct productive investments by local Chinese in the tin and rubber industries, these activities too were largely circumscribed by European capital (Puthucheary, 1960: 82).

Following the severe slump of the Great Depression, the perils of the heavy dependence of Chinese capital on Western business interests prompted some traders to explore both secondary industries and banking (Turnbull, 1982: 139). For some time, however, Singapore's trading role predominated and remained linked to the dynamism and logic of British colonialism and capitalism. Opportunities for capital accumulation by the domestic bourgeoisie perpetuated the basic structure imposed by the British. As a result, the industrial bourgeoisie was conspicuous only by its economic weakness right up until self-government in 1959.

In spite of the susceptibility of the trade-oriented Singapore economy to fluctuating commodity prices, it was not until after the Second World War that serious consideration was given to diversifying the island's economic base. Singapore's now more stable and fast-growing population coincided with growing economic nationalism in the region.[1] This threatened to slow the rate of economic growth at precisely the point when rapid employment generation would be required. Theoretically, there were considerable possibilities for the expansion of Singapore's manufacturing sector. The sector was primarily geared to meeting the limited needs of the domestic market and was largely a complement to Singapore's entrepot role up until this point.

The first serious re-examination of the structure of the Singapore economy was embodied in a report compiled in 1955 by the International Bank for Reconstruction and Development (IBRD). It pointed to industrialisation as the panacea for the increasing pressure to generate employment, with the creation of a national market for Singapore and Malaysia as the appropriate context for it. However, the preoccupation with colonial disengagement by authorities meant that little action was taken on the report. Despite official inaction, the establishment and emergence of the PAP in this period was to prove fundamental to the promotion of industrialisation. This party came to office in 1959 with a strong commitment to the development of an ISI strategy as the basis for the resolution of unemployment and improvement of living standards. The make-up of the PAP and the class structure of Singapore society was to significantly influence the capacity to effect this strategy and other subsequent attempts to promote Singapore's industrialisation.

People's Action Party and the early industrial policy

One of the consequences of close integration of the domestic bourgeoisie with the interests of British capital was that it did not share or comprehend the post-Second World War nationalist sentiment of the Singapore masses. This contributed to the radicalisation of the masses which was fuelled and harnessed by the left-wing labour movement. Thus, for middle-class aspirants to power in a post-colonial Singapore, exploitation of the left's considerable popularity and organisational strength was a political necessity. Equally though, to minimise the repression of its movement by colonial authorities in the build-up to self-government, the left itself had a political need for an alliance with a force more acceptable to Britain. Such a force presented itself in a group of middle-class professionals led by the English-educated Lee Kuan Yew. This marriage of convenience gave rise to the formation of the PAP in 1954. For the time being, the left was content with the appearance of moderate control of the party. Nevertheless, a struggle for control of the executive between the two factions after colonial disengagement was inevitable.

In the subsequent struggle of the early 1960s Lee's faction prevailed, due largely to its astute and ruthless exploitation of executive power to frustrate the left's constitutional challenge. This led in 1963 to the left forming its own party, the Barisan Sosialis (BS). The split meant that, apart from being insulated from the direct political control or influence of capital, the PAP was now no longer constrained by the left-wing labour movement. This position was played up by the PAP which now claimed to derive its legitimacy on the basis that it was capable of representing the national interest without answering to any particular interest group or class. The new political latitude was to prove paramount in the future industrialisation of Singapore.

Ironically, the issue that precipitated the final parting of ways concerned political merger with Malaysia, something to which the left was committed in principle, but not whilst it opened the way for their persecution by a right-wing federal government. This, of course, was one of the attractions of merger for Lee. There was also an economic basis to merger, however, for it was expected to lead to the establishment of a Malaysian Common Market. Indeed, access to this market was the premise upon which Singapore's ISI strategy rested. For a variety of political reasons, merger proved untenable and in 1965 Singapore separated from the Federation of Malaysia. Lee's vision of industrial expansion through access to a common market consequently had little prospect of fruition. Though domestic opportunities for ISI were far from exhausted, the sort of economic growth required to arrest unemployment could not be satisfied without a much more substantial market. The situation also posed political challenges for the PAP since much of its credibility had been invested in merger. This placed even more onus on a satisfactory and prompt resolution to the economic dilemma.

The export-oriented industrialisation (EOI) strategy

The PAP's relative political autonomy from capital and labour was to assume special significance in the reconsideration of economic strategy. It became increasingly obvious in the post-1965 period that the option offering the most rapid private led industrialisation rested on export orientation. However, following the examples of Hong Kong and Taiwan would necessitate seriously considering labour costs and competitiveness. At the same time, the decision to adopt an EOI strategy through the attraction of international capital would work against the interests of the domestic industrial bourgeoisie. It lacked the capital and expertise to partake to any significant extent in such a strategy. Fortunately for the PAP though, not only had it already seriously undermined the independent labour movement through exercise of state power, but it also had little need to worry about the domestic industrial bourgeoisie. The ISI strategy had not really got off the ground so the industrial bourgeoisie remained economically and politically weak—certainly in no position to frustrate the shift in strategy.

Following separation, the PAP stepped up measures to control labour. Already, through the government-sponsored National Trades Union Congress (NTUC), the party had members in key administrative positions. This influence was exploited to promote a sense of special responsibility for the labour movement to make sacrifices to avert economic crises. The notion of unions acting as pressure groups was dispelled by PAP officials who, instead, viewed unions as instruments of the government's social and economic management. Towards this systematic elimination of effective independent unions and institutionalised control over labour, the PAP stepped up its direct representation of cadres in the NTUC.

Having successfully institutionalised labour control, the PAP ushered in draconian labour legislation in 1965 to enhance the attractiveness of Singapore's labour to international capital. Through the Employment Act (1968) and the Industrial Relations Act (1969), employees' wages and benefits were reduced, working hours were increased, and the bargaining powers of unions severely curtailed. Strikes over economic claims could now also be deemed political, in so much as they constituted a threat to Singapore's national interest. These changes were introduced without protest from the NTUC.

Clearly the 1968 legislation seriously undermined the capacity for collective bargaining between employer and employee. Moreover, when inflationary pressures in the 1970s threatened to bring instability to industrial relations, the government took more direct control over wage levels. In 1972 it formed the National Wages Council through which, effectively, it dictated wage guidelines to employers.

In addition to the successful taming of labour, reflected in the fact that 1969 was free of industrial stoppages, the PAP introduced a number of economic initiatives in support of its EOI strategy. In particular, the Economic Development Board, a statutory body established in 1961, came to assume increased significance in centralising and coordinating relations between government and capital on proposed investments. In 1968 the government also established the Jurong Town Corporation to relieve the Economic Development Board of responsibility for the development of industrial estates, in which infrastructural facilities (apart from technical training) were centralised and provided at low cost to private companies. These were rapidly expanded following the shift to an EOI strategy and formed an important part of the overall effort to enhance Singapore's competitiveness. Singapore was the first Southeast Asian country to develop industrial estates.

Amongst other initiatives to foster EOI, in 1968 the PAP established a public limited trading company, International Trading Company (INTRACO), to help develop overseas markets for Singapore-made products and to find cheaper sources of raw materials for local industries through bulk buying. In 1969 a 100%-government-equity public limited company, Neptune Orient Lines, was established to expedite foreign trade and ensure lower freight charges for Singapore-manufactured goods. Yet another initiative was the creation in 1968 of the Development Bank of Singapore, a public company with majority government equity, to provide finance for industry at below market rates and to stimulate investments through equity participation. The government's direct participation in the finance sector also extended to the Central Provident Fund (CPF) and the Post Office Savings Bank, through which it appropriated the major share of domestic savings. This appropriation was important to the government's ability to provide the social and physical infrastructure required by the strategy. Finally, generous tax concessions were offered to companies investing in export-oriented manufacturing activities.

In short, the PAP state assumed a leading hand in ensuring the social, political and economic prerequisites for EOI. Moreover, it did this in such a way as to significantly influence the allocation of factors of production. It contributed to Singapore's comparative advantage as an export base for low-skill, labour-intensive manufacturing production.

The EOI strategy achieved remarkable and rapid success. Foreign investment in gross fixed assets in the manufacturing sector increased from S$157 million in 1965 to S$995 million in 1970 and S$3054 million by 1974. Meanwhile, the value of direct exports by industry rose from S$349 million in 1965 to S$1523 million in 1970 and S$7812 million by 1974. As a consequence, Singapore's unemployment rate steadily dropped from 8.7 per cent in 1965 to 3.9 per cent in 1974 (see Table 6.1).

So successful was the industrial programme in meeting the pressing objective of providing employment that before long the PAP began to promote capital- and skill-intensive investments. Under the 1970 Economic Expansion Incentives (Amendment) Act, special incentives were introduced for this purpose. Finance Minister Hon Sui Sen's 1973 budget speech also outlined a ten-point programme to attract preferred investments, including a S$100 million Capital Assistance Scheme.

Table 6.1 Selected economic indicators, Singapore, 1965–75

Year	Cumulative foreign investment S$ million	Domestic industrial exports S$ million	Unemployment rate %
1965	157	349.2	8.7
1966	239	404.9	8.7
1967	303	208.2	8.1
1968	454	659.5	7.3
1969	600	1 265.3	6.7
1970	995	1 523.0	6.0
1971	1 575	1 954.7	4.8
1972	2 283	2 641.7	4.7
1973	2 659	4 269.8	4.5
1974	3 054	7 811.9	3.9
1975	3 380	7 200.7	4.6
1976	3 739	9 575.9	4.5
1977	4 145	10 969.4	3.9
1978	5 242	12 632.7	3.6

Sources: Economic Development Board, Singapore *Annual Report* (various years)
Department of Statistics, Singapore *Yearbook of Statistics Singapore* (various years)

This provided up to half of the required equity for the establishment of specialist support firms. These measures had been adopted following indications from capital that it was prepared to exploit Singapore's relatively sheltered labour force by engaging in processes other than simply assembly.

Before the PAP was able to put its new policies to the test, the 1974–75 recession forced the government on the defensive. The pronounced external orientation of the manufacturing sector rendered it particularly vulnerable. Heavy job losses ensued as exports dropped and investments slowed. An intimated 17 000 people or 2 per cent of the total workforce were retrenched between mid-1974 and mid-1975; 12 000 or 71 per cent of these occurred in the manufacturing sector (*New Nation*, 24 January 1975). Total unemployment thus rose to 4.6 per cent in 1975 (see Table 6.1).

The government responded to these new circumstances with an all-out effort to attract investment regardless of its degree of technological sophistication. Through the lowering of labour costs, compared with those of its competitors, it was hoped that Singapore would attract a greater share of the limited new investment over the next few years. Thus, through the National Wages Council, wages were held down, a policy maintained up until 1979.

Severe as the 1974–75 recession was for Singapore, its effects were short-lived. After having dropped by 8 per cent in 1975, domestic industrial exports rose by 33 per cent in 1976 and a further 15 per cent for both the next two years. Similarly, investment growth by international capital quickly recovered, increasing by S$1862 million from 1975 to 1978. As a result, by the end of 1978 Singapore's official unemployment rate had fallen to just 3.6 per cent—the lowest at any time since self-government (see Table 6.1).

Ironically, by late 1978 the most serious constraint on economic expansion was a shortage of labour rather than insufficient investment. By this time, jobs were being created at an average rate of about 40 000 per year, while the workforce was expanding at an average of about 30 000–32 000 per year (McCue, 1978). Labour shortages had particularly threatened planned expansions and upgradings in Singapore's important electronics industry. One answer to the problem would have been to further increase Singapore's already considerable intake of guest labour. However, by now the PAP took the view that the reserve of unskilled, cheap foreign labour had acted as a disincentive for the low-value-added, labour-intensive industries, such as textile, leather and wood-based industries, to improve productivity. It wanted these industries to increase productivity and release some of their labour to other areas of the economy. In short, by the late 1970s the PAP considered that labour-intensive and more-skilled and capital-intensive production were beginning to contradict each other's expansion.

The PAP was also concerned about the possible political consequences of an expanding dependence upon guest labour. This concern was heightened by the necessity to now rely on workers from beyond Malaysia to such countries as India, Bangladesh, Sri Lanka, Thailand and the Philippines. It feared a repeat of the social problems experienced in European countries with high intakes of workers from different cultures. Amongst other considerations, the PAP was keen to retain a disciplined workforce, and therefore preferred domestic workers who by now appreciated the special role of the NTUC.

In addition to the above pressures for a nationalisation of labour in favour of higher-value added production, Singapore's policymakers were also aware of the growing list of lower-waged regional competitors in the export of low-skill, labour-intensive manufactures. Furthermore, the government recognised that sooner or later Singapore would be stripped of 'developed country' status by the World Bank and, therefore, lose its GATT Generalised System of Preferences (GSP) trade advantages in various labour-intensive products.

By the end of the 1970s then, the PAP had need to re-examine the finer details of its EOI strategy to secure its longer-term competitiveness within the new international division of labour. The substantial increases in both the quantity and quality of international investment in

Singapore in 1978 gave the PAP confidence to adopt an aggressive approach to the problem.[2]

The 'Second Industrial Revolution'

Government policy

Throughout 1979, and subsequently, a range of policies were adopted by the government intended to hasten Singapore's transition to a qualitatively new phase of industrial sophistication. The 'Second Industrial Revolution' was expected to ensure Singapore's graduation in the hierarchy of the new international division of labour, taking it out of direct competition with lower-wage countries. Singapore was to be 'developed into a modern industrial economy based on science, technology, skills and knowledge' (Goh Chok Tong, 1981: 2). Primarily this was to be realised through the manufacturing sector which, it was envisaged, would raise its share of gross domestic product (GDP) from 22 per cent in 1979 to 31 per cent by 1990. At the same time, though, Singapore was to become a 'financial supermarket', a regional centre for sophisticated financial services.

Singapore's leaders had a clear idea of the sorts of industries and processes appropriate to this new phase. Amongst others, these included: computers, computer peripheral equipment and software development; machine tools and machinery; automotive and aerospace components; speciality chemicals and pharmaceuticals; electronic instrumentation; precision engineering equipment; optical instruments and equipment; medical and surgical apparatus and instruments; and advanced electronic components, including wafer diffusion.

The PAP's strategy to promote a rapid shift in the direction of higher-value-added production comprised four major components: the 'corrective' wage policy; expansion and improvement of social and physical infrastructure; introduction of various selective fiscal and tax concessions and incentives; and changes to the institutional control of organised labour.

Certainly the most significant feature of the PAP's new strategy was its 'corrective' wage policy. The previous policy of holding down wage levels was considered responsible for artificially propping up inefficient industries. By 'correcting' wage costs to reflect the true market value of labour, labour could now be released to priority industries. Thus, through the National Wages Council, substantial wage cost increases were introduced between 1979 and 1981. Total recommended increases were between 54 and 58 per cent, of which 12 per cent comprised increased contributions to the Central Provident Fund or contributions

Singapore's 'Second Industrial Revolution'

to the newly established Skills Development Fund. Without any apology, the PAP tried to force lower-value-added, labour-intensive industries to upgrade operations or close operations in Singapore altogether. It remained fundamentally important that Singapore offer *lower* labour costs, the lure for higher-value-added investments, but not the *lowest* labour costs per se.

In conjunction with the higher wages policy, the PAP energetically and imaginatively boosted the provision and standard of infrastructure. Thus, whilst placing pressure on firms engaged in lower-value-added production on the one hand, on the other it made sure that there was adequate technical and capital opportunity for investment in more skilled production. Top priority was given to increasing the output of engineers. A number of new Joint Industrial Training Centres were also established in sophisticated technological processes.[3] Costs of such centres were shared by the Singapore government and the participating company or foreign government. At the same time, the Jurong Town Corporation embarked on a new ten-year plan (1980–90) to improve the quality and supply of industrial buildings, land and supporting infrastructure. This involved the creation of special facilities and several priority estate projects to facilitate the government's preferred industries.[4] Progress towards the Jurong Town Corporation's objectives and increases in required expenditure have been rapid since 1979. Its development expenditure increased from S$127 million in 1978/79 to S$435 million in 1982/83, an increase of 243 per cent (Jurong Town Corporation, *Annual Report 1979/80*: 65, *Annual Report 1982/83*:3).

Through the introduction of a range of tax incentives and financial assistance schemes since 1979, the PAP ensured that, wherever possible, firms with the capacity or inclination to invest in higher-value-added products and processes were actively encouraged to do so. Not only did it exercise the exemption of 40 per cent company tax for periods of up to ten years to attract preferred investments, a provision already available, it also offered substantial long-term, fixed-rate concessional loans, in certain cases interest-free loans for up to ten years.[5] Liberal tax deductions were introduced for research and development (R & D) expenditure, and liberalised and accelerated depreciation allowances for machinery, plant and buildings, including special deductions for automated equipment. Schemes were also introduced to provide easy and ample finance for R & D purposes, and the Capital Assistance Scheme had its initial 1975 budget of $100 million raised to $300 million in 1981 (Economic Development Board, *Annual Report, 1981/82*: 34). Funds were also made available through the Training Grant Scheme to defray the costs of training to employers. In the electronics industry, for example, between 30 and 90 per cent of such costs were subsidised for special projects (Economic Development Board, *Annual Report 1983/84*: 55).

In addition to the three forms of economic intervention cited above, the PAP also employed direct government investments to stimulate and influence market developments. In this respect it used its holding companies to initiate favoured investments and also established a Singapore Technology Corporation as a means of promoting more indigenous technological progress.[6] The most important project in which it directly involved itself, however, was the S$2 billion petrochemical complex at Palau Ayer Marbau which was intended to epitomise Singapore's new industrial sophistication.[7]

Understandably, the government's economic initiatives involved considerable cost, especially those pertaining to social and physical infrastructure. Outlays through the Development Fund thus rose from S$1890 million in 1977/78 to S$5155 million in 1981/82 (Department of Statistics, Singapore, *Year 1983/84*: 209). However, the government's access to domestic savings, notably through the Central Provident Fund, indirectly underwrote the financial capacity of the state to meet such commitments.

Although the 'Second Industrial Revolution' was expected to secure a new degree of industrial sophistication and take Singapore out of direct competition with lower-wage countries, labour discipline (and, indeed, cost) was no less important to the PAP's new strategy. On the contrary, because of the likelihood of retrenchments, relocations and retraining due to changes in the production process, maximum labour discipline and flexibility were required. Towards this the PAP took important initiatives to enhance its political control over the labour movement. Singapore's two largest omnibus unions, the Singapore Industrial Labour Organisation and the Pioneer Industries Employees' Union, were dissolved to make way for nine smaller industry-based unions. There was a twofold purpose in this move. First, it naturally weakened the political and financial base of unions and thereby removed the possibility that the government's industry plans could be frustrated. Second, the reconstitution of unions facilitated superior technical management of the workforce by capital, particularly as it related to automation and retraining. Indeed, the government also set about introducing house unions wherever possible, the ultimate in political impotence for labour and technical management for capital. To ensure the success of these measures the PAP also tightened its direct representation in and control over the NTUC.[8] Furthermore, at the ideological level the government introduced a campaign to promote self-sacrifice and company loyalty by workers. Thus, maximum employee cooperation was institutionalised in new ways under the strategy of the 'Second Industrial Revolution'.

Singapore's 'Second Industrial Revolution'

What we see from the brief outline above is that the already-evident theme to Singapore's industrialisation, government intervention, reached new heights under the 'Second Industrial Revolution'.[9] The extent and forms of intervention were modified to consolidate and extend the state's influence in the allocation of factors of production in Singapore. This intervention was geared, however, to induce a particular response from international capital, one that would transform the Singapore economy and redefine its place in the new international division of labour.

Progress and problems

Although the problem of guest labour continued in spite of the high-wage policy and although Japanese-based capital reacted with apprehension to the new strategy, the initial experience of the 'Second Industrial Revolution' was otherwise both positive and promising. International capital did affect significant industrial restructuring towards higher-value-added production, including a number of qualitatively important developments in targeted industries and processes. Nonetheless, by the mid-1980s it became apparent that the response of international capital to the government's initiatives was not likely to gather the necessary momentum to realise official targets and objectives. International capital never quite seemed willing to accelerate its shift towards higher-value-added production to either the degree or pace required. The deepening of the global recession, and consequent reduced export demand, only compounded Singapore's economic problems. Thus, by the middle of the decade the PAP was grappling with the republic's most severe economic downturn in post-colonial history.

As Table 6.2 depicts, since 1979 there have been impressive economic gains in Singapore in a number of respects. For one thing, foreign investment rose substantially from S$6349 million in 1979 to S$11 123 million by 1983; 1980 was a record year for foreign investment with a sum of S$1171 million. Value-added per worker also improved from S$23 992 in 1979 to S$36 645 in 1983. Though this was slightly down on expectations, it was nonetheless quite significant. The definitive influence of international capital in this qualitative improvement is reflected in the fact that the value-added per worker of wholly foreign-owned companies rose from S$34 779 to S$48 995 in this period whilst that of wholly locally owned companies increased from S$16 676 to S$24 381 (Department of Statistics, Singapore, *Report on the Census of Industrial Production 1979:* 16; and *1983:* 8). Real GDP growth between 1980 and 1984 also averaged 8.5 per cent, on target with the

Table 6.2 Selected economic indicators, Singapore, 1979–85

Year	Domestic industrial exports S$ million	Manufacturing value-added per worker S$	Total real GDP growth %	Cumulative foreign investment S$ million	Unemployment rate %
1979	16 904	23 992	9.4	6 349	3.4
1980	19 875	30 027	10.3	7 520	3.5
1981	22 894	34 681	9.9	8 593	3.9
1982	22 227	34 218	6.3	9 607	2.6
1983	22 922	36 645	7.9	11 123	3.3
1984	25 993	38 881	8.2	n.a.	2.7
1985	n.a.	n.a.	−1.7	n.a.	6.0

Sources: Department of Statistics, Singapore, *Yearbook of Statistics Singapore 1984/85*: 3, 16
Economic Development Board, Singapore, *Annual Report 1984/85*: 12
Ministry of Trade and Industry, Economic Committee, Singapore (1986) *The Singapore Economy: New Directions*

economic development plan for the 1980s outlined in the 1980 budget.

In broad industry-category terms, the post-1979 period has largely seen a consolidation of international investment concentrated in the already-dominant industries of petroleum and petroleum products, electrical and electronic machinery and non-electrical machinery. However, the technology- and capital-intensive industries of industrial and non-industrial chemicals have also risen to prominence. At the same time, there has been a significant fall-off in foreign investment in Singapore's comparatively lower-value-added, labour-intensive industries.[10] This of course tells only part of the story, as the developments within industries are more illuminating.

Quite by design, the electronics industry, heavily dominated by international capital, has long been at the fore of Singapore's EOI strategy. Its fortunes in the period of the 'Second Industrial Revolution' were central to the PAP's ambitious projections. Put simply, the essential trend intended for this industry was for a general increase in the degree of mechanisation and automation in the consumer and component sectors, and a simultaneous and rapid introduction of a range of new products and processes in the industrial electronics sector.

Without question the post-1979 period has witnessed an accentuation of the trend towards greater mechanisation and automation in the consumer and component sectors, largely through investments in automatic component insertion machines in the former and automatic pattern recognition and testing equipment in the latter. Forward integration has also taken place with the introduction of the assembly of the 64-K random access memory (RAM). The high point, however, has been the decision of the Italian-based SGS-Ates to establish a semiconductor wafer diffusion plant and thereby initiate the sort of 'backward integration' long sought by Singapore's policymakers. Normally such processes are retained in the developed countries, but SGS-Ates was influenced by projections of long-term regional sales growth (Tanzer, 1983).[11] It remains to be seen how generalised such investments become.

The successful attraction of computer manufacturers to Singapore, and hence the expansion of the industrial electronics sector, is probably the highlight of the post-1979 pattern of international investment. Starting from virtually nothing in 1979, by December 1981 about S$100 million of foreign investment had gone into computer hardware (*Asian Business*, December 1981: 46). A year later this had already doubled (*Asian Business*, December 1982: 65). The surge was overwhelmingly led by US-based companies.[12] However, essentially operations involved assembly work, albeit of much higher-value-added products than had previously characterised the electronic industry.

Undoubtedly the most outstanding feature of the investment boom in computers was the spate of plants set up from 1981 by US disc drive companies. Within virtually no time Singapore has become a major world exporter of disc drives. Certainly the government's incentives and the various cost advantages of Singapore were important attractions for these companies. Furthermore, there was an element of inertia created once a few companies established themselves in Singapore and were perceived by competitors to be obtaining a competitive advantage. However, the unexpected proliferation of these companies had much to do with the speed with which the Singapore state could facilitate the implementation of investment proposals. The companies were trying to meet urgent demand in an industry characterised by rapidly changing technology. Once again though, the sort of production characterising these investments primarily involved the assembly and testing of disc drives rather than any more complete form of manufacturing process.

Due largely to the introduction of higher-value-added products and greater automation by international capital, productivity in the electrical industry also improved in the early 1980s. Amongst other developments, the rapid growth of disc drive assembly has attracted a host of foreign-based manufacturers of precision stepper and spindle motors. Lower labour costs remain the chief attraction for international capital, but events have opened up new opportunities to exploit this advantage.

Although in absolute terms the petroleum refining and processing industry continued to play a dominant role in the early 1980s, plans for the industry have run into serious problems. As elsewhere, Singapore's oil refiners have had to deal with the problem of overcapacity afflicting the industry. The strategy of multinationals in Singapore has been to further upgrade and diversify into secondary processing as a means of remaining competitive. With regional producers, particularly Indonesia, substantially increasing their processing facilities, there will need to be wholesale modifications to secure long-term viability in Singapore. Meanwhile, Singapore's fully integrated petrochemical complex has gone into production only after considerable persuasion of private companies by the Singapore government. Since the project was planned, a dramatic worldwide downturn in demand for petrochemical products, excess global capacity and the emergence of competition from Middle Eastern countries have all threatened the project's commercial viability. Thus, what was expected to be the showpiece of Singapore's new industrial phase has turned out to be an embarrassment for the republic's policymakers.

Substantial investments by international capital in production of both industrial and non-industrial chemicals occurred after 1979. In the former, interest in specialty chemicals was particularly strong owing to the backward integration of the local electronics industry. Another area of expansion was in petroleum-related chemicals, a logical complement to developments in the petroleum-refining industry. Investments continued to be motivated primarily by market opportunities in Singapore and the immediate region. Activities of the non-industrial chemicals group were largely defined by the pharmaceutical industry, particularly by the multinationals Beecham, Glaxocham and Kanegafuchi. Apart from expansion of existing product lines, new and more-sophisticated products and processes were introduced, such as augmentin, valine and phenylglycine. The activities of these companies suggested that the original attraction of labour-cost advantages in export production from Singapore remained, in spite of the 'corrective' wage policy.

Another industry that received large sums of foreign investment in the post-1979 period was non-electrical machinery.[13] There were two dominant themes to such investment. First, there was rapidly increasing investment in more-sophisticated capital equipment, especially computerised and computer-related equipment. This contributed to a substantial upgrading in the quality and efficiency of operations. Second, there has been an acceleration of industrial integration, including the actual manufacture of computerised equipment. The feasibility of these investments has been facilitated by both the general growth and the maturation of Singapore industry. This, in turn, has made it more cost-efficient for the global export of increasingly sophisticated machinery parts and components. The disappointment, however, has been the failure to attract sufficient interest by international capital in the knowledge-intensive areas of process engineering.

A major objective of the PAP's 'Second Industrial Revolution' was that Singapore become the region's major aircraft-servicing centre as well as a major component manufacturing site. It was satisfying for the government, then, that output value in aircraft equipment, repairing and servicing increased by 100 per cent, value-added by 100 per cent and exports by 137 per cent between 1980 and 1983 (Department of Statistics, Singapore, *Yearbook 1983/84*). Major investments by such international companies as Pratt & Whitney, Hawker Pacific, TRW, General Electric, Sunstrand and Garrett were heavily influenced by the cost of Singapore's relatively skilled labour—estimated at about half the equivalent cost in Europe or North America, even in the wake of the 'corrective' wage policy (Cockerell, 1984: 68).

The above discussion concentrates on those industries in which the most substantial sums of new foreign investment were located after 1979. Of course outside these areas there were other significant, qualitative developments. Some progress was made in the promotion of Singapore as a site for international sourcing by automotive component manufacturers, especially in electronic components. There were important developments in the medical equipment industry with the introduction of medical disposables. In the food industry, Nestlé's $25 million R & D project in product development and process improvement and Fuji Oil's $24 million plant to produce cocoa butter extruder and specialty fats were major advances for Singapore. In precision equipment there was also a diversification into some sophisticated product lines. Indeed, examples could be found in most industrial sectors of qualitatively significant developments by international corporations.

From the above, then, it is clear that there has been a general increase in higher-value-added production led by the investments of international capital since 1979. Motivations behind these investments vary. In some cases, regional market opportunities have prompted an upgrading of products and facilities. In other cases, investors have decided that labour-cost advantages can be gained by more fully exploiting Singapore's relatively skilled labour force. Needless to point out, there are variations between and beyond these two themes. Significantly though, labour-cost advantage remained paramount to a considerable volume of post-1979 investment. Such advantage was arrived at, however, by increasingly moving into areas of middle-level technology in which Singapore's costs were still more favourable for capital than those of alternative production sites. But does all this deem the 'Second Industrial Revolution' a success and herald the emergence of the sort of industrial economy envisaged by PAP leaders?

Impressive as the above-cited developments may appear, these must be assessed in the light of the PAP's own ambitious objectives.

Furthermore, in 1985 Singapore's economy declined in real terms by 1.7 per cent, and the government's own projections were for zero growth in 1986. In 1985 there was a net reduction of jobs of 90 000, of which 35 000 occurred in the manufacturing sector (Ministry of Trade and Industry, Economic Committee, 1986: 39). Things have obviously soured recently. It is not argued here that such a sudden turn-around in economic fortunes can be attributed solely to the policies of the 'Second Industrial Revolution'—the severity of the economic malaise is the result of a coincidence of various factors. Nonetheless, what is argued is that the PAP's active discouragement of lower-value-added production necessitated an extremely rapid and comprehensive introduction of new higher-value-added production to minimise the adversity resulting from a deepening global recession. Of course, the PAP never bargained for the degree of deterioration in the international economy characterising the mid-1980s. Just the same, the predicament that unfolded has highlighted not only the vulnerability of the EOI strategy per se, but also the insufficient pace and incomplete nature of industrial restructuring since 1979. Having put all their eggs in the one basket (higher-value-added production), Singapore's policymakers found that this exacerbated rather than reduced the effects of the global recession. In short, the PAP miscalculated the pace and degree with which international capital would usher in a qualitatively new phase in Singapore's industry. Even before 1985 there were signs of such a miscalculation.

Against the background provided above—detailing the nature and extent of restructuring led by international capital—it must be kept in mind that the rate of manufacturing growth in the early 1980s was exceeded by that of the economy at large. From the start of 1980 to the end of 1984, the rate of real manufacturing growth was 6.1 per cent compared with Singapore's overall economic growth rate of 8.5 per cent (Ministry of Trade and Industry, Economic Committee, 1986: 26). As a result, the relative contribution of manufacturing to total GDP slipped from 23.7 per cent in 1979 to 20.6 per cent in 1984 (Department of Statistics, Singapore, *Yearbook 1984/85:* 78). Thus, in spite of quantitative gains in the sector, it failed to assume the prominence expected of it under the new strategy.

Probably the most conspicuous illustration of the PAP's miscalculation of international capital's responsiveness to the 'Second Industrial Revolution' was the behaviour of Japan-based capital after 1979. Following the introduction of the higher wage policy, there was an immediate and substantial drop in its investment commitments, the 1980 level falling by 56 per cent on that of the previous year (Economic Development Board, *Annual Report 1984/85:* 14). This underlined that rising wages and labour shortages in Singapore would not inexorably lead to a universal shift in emphasis towards higher-value-added production by capital. Despite the apparent comparative advantage offered in certain higher-value-added areas in Singapore, by now the Japanese had become more concerned with circumventing trade barriers in Europe and the USA—even to the point of forgoing cost advantages in the short term. The proportion of Japanese investments in the industrialised nations has thus risen from just 27 per cent in 1974 to 42 per cent by 1984 (Hazelhurst, 1986). As Singapore's labour costs have risen, Japan-based capital has redirected much of its low-value-added investment to Hong Kong without the expected scale of extension into higher-value-added production in Singapore.[14]

The Japanese response took the PAP by surprise. Throughout the 1970s Japan-based capital had rapidly expanded investment in Singapore, and the PAP's original projections for the 1980s envisaged a continuation of this trend. It discovered, however, that the objective conditions of Japan-based capital in the international economy challenged a primary assumption of the new strategy—that comparative advantage had equal meaning for capital, in general. This has not proved to be and was clear long before 1985.

Aside from the insufficient support of Japan-based capital for the PAP's more ambitious plans, it was evident also before 1985 that, despite the best efforts of the state, international capital generally had not made the sort of qualitative reassessment of Singapore's potential role in the new international division of labour that the PAP hoped for. As we have seen earlier, the dominant form of industrial upgrading involved either the introduction of greater automation or higher-value-added products rather than a shift away from the assembly process as such. The more conceptual stages of production still tended to elude Singapore, as evidenced by the limited progress in attracting engineering and design processes. It is questionable whether Singapore can ever offer an engineering base with the sort of depth and diversification sufficient to induce international capital to establish genuinely sophisticated technology in Singapore on a large scale. The extent of investment in R & D in Singapore suggests that no qualitative leap has been made in the relocation of such processes. Despite increases, particularly after 1982, R & D expenditure in Singapore accounted for just 0.6 per cent of total GNP in 1984 and still lagged behind that of other Asian NICs (Hu, 1986: 2).

Whilst these points may have raised a few doubts in the minds of Singapore's policymakers before 1985, it was nevertheless considered that adequate progress was being made to justify optimism that by the end of the decade Singapore's economy would be transformed. In the last two years, however, events have forced the PAP to seriously re-examine its economic strategy. Not only has it become apparent to the government that the upgrading of the manufacturing sector cannot lead the economy in the way imagined, it has also become clear that the PAP's long-enjoyed and unquestioning popular support is beginning to weaken. The government's own assessment of the underlying economic problems and the initial policy direction suggests, as we shall see below, that important assumptions of the 'Second Industrial Revolution' have been revised.

Before examining the nature of the PAP's response to the economic problems besetting Singapore in the mid-1980s, it should be appreciated that the unprecedented downturn has special political significance. Over the past two decades Singaporeans have been systematically discouraged from seeking or expecting an active political culture. They have been persuaded to equate good government primarily with the ability to raise material standards of living or, more abstractly, increased GDP. The government's political legitimacy is therefore premised on the ideology of rapid economic growth, and an elitist decision-making process has helped reproduce this situation. Commitment to the PAP is thus, not surprisingly, based on pragmatism rather than any higher ideals or principles. To a greater extent than in most societies, the credibility of the government is tied to the capacity to preside over a successful economy.

The political necessity of a quick resolution to the economic problems was considered all the more important in view of the 13 per cent swing against the PAP in the December 1984 general elections. Though this in itself posed on problem for government, nor did it necessarily suggest that the PAP's long-term security was under threat, the PAP was accustomed to a complete monopoly in parliament and was determined to keep it that way.

Even before the sharp economic downturn of 1985 the government had alienated much of the electorate with policies in support of the 'Second Industrial Revolution'. One of the most unpopular of these policies was that intended to encourage selective breeding amongst Singapore's educated elite and ensure the reproduction of a suitably intelligent workforce to drive the economy. Lee Kuan Yew's notion that intelligence was primarily genetically determined served only to engender the resentment of university students and graduates, as did his social engineering designs for them. Sections of the working class also became disillusioned. Some grassroots opposition to the reconstitution of trade unions surfaced, but this was harshly dealt with (Foy, 1983). There was also concern amongst workers that the government was progressively relinquishing responsibility for public welfare. Not only had the PAP handed over some welfare responsibilities to the private sector through the Company Welfarism from Employees' Contributions (COWEC) Scheme, it had also ceased its 75 per cent subsidisation of public hospitalisation (Kulkarni, 1983). However, government suggestions that access to Central Provident Fund savings may need to be tightened caused greatest alarm. These moves reflected the state's eagerness to abdicate financially burdensome responsibilities at a time when it was outlaying considerable and increasing funds in support of the restructuring effort. Indications were, however, that Singapore's younger voters were less receptive than the previous generation to official calls for material sacrifice.

It was therefore against a background not only of unprecedented economic difficulty but also declining electoral support that the PAP came to reassess the long-term economic strategy.

Policy revision

In response to the deteriorating economic conditions, and alert to their political implications, the government set up a committee headed by the prime minister's son, acting Trade and Industry Minister Lee Hsien Loong, to investigate the report on 'Singapore's economic problems and prospects'. The report, entitled *The Singapore Economy: New Directions*, was released in early 1986 and, for the most part, has been embraced by the government. Key recommendations of the report have already been put into effect.

The report itself contained a number of themes, not all of which can be discussed here. The major theme, however, was the recognition that the manufacturing sector could not fulfil the role originally envisaged in plans for the 'Second Industrial Revolution'. The new engine of growth was expected to be the services sector (notably banking and finance, transport and communications, and international services), but manufacturing still had a role to play. According to the Economic Committee, 'as an industrial centre, we must move beyond being a production base, to being an international total business centre' (Ministry of Trade and Industry, Economic Committee, 1986: 12). The aim of attracting higher-value-added manufacturing remained, but, significantly, this should not exclude the possibility of lower-value-added, labour-intensive industries flourishing at the same time. Thus, towards enhancing the prospects of the labour-intensive service sector and restoring competitiveness in some areas of manufacturing, the committee called for a redress of the high wages policy of the 1980s and other costs. The key concern was to maximise long-term economic growth, and contrary to the objectives of the 'Second Industrial Revolution', the committee even recommended the continuation of guest labour to support this. Interestingly, the report was couched in terms of ideological support for market forces ahead of government intervention, even recommending some concrete policies to effect this.

The chief policy recommendations of the report centred on the need to restore Singapore's cost-competitiveness. These logically followed the committee's analysis of the economic downturn which identified three main structural problems with the manufacturing sector:

1 An unforeseen contraction of key industries, such as shipbuilding and petroleum refining, due to changes in global demand
2 A general decline in cost-competitiveness in international markets
3 Difficulties confronting local manufacturing companies in low-value-added, labour-intensive industries unable to respond to the restructuring policy.

The Committee argued that such problems had been compounded by the weakness of domestic demand caused by the slump in construction and the continued high rate of savings that could not be channelled into productive domestic investments.

In support of the Committee's claim that declining international competitiveness underlies much of the economy's problem, a variety of evidence was submitted. It was pointed out that unit labour costs have increased by 40 per cent between 1979 and 1984, outstripping productivity increases (see Table 6.3). This has resulted in Singapore's competitive position weakening by as much as 50 per cent against Hong Kong, 15 per cent against Taiwan and 35 per cent against South Korea. Increased rentals, interest costs, transport costs and costs of utilities were also identified. These costs, particularly labour costs, were considered responsible for a declining profitability in the private sector. According to official data, the rate of return in manufacturing in

Table 6.3 Comparison of average wage increases and productivity of Asian NICs, 1979-84

	Wage increase		Productivity growth %
	Nominal %	Real %	
Hong Kong	12.9	1.1	3.9
Taiwan	15.2	6.6	4.8
South Korea	17.7	4.1	3.9
Singapore	11.6	6.5	4.6

Source: Ministry of Trade and Industry, Economic Committee, Singapore (1986) *The Singapore Economy: New Directions*

Singapore halved from 33 per cent in 1980 to 16.5 per cent in 1984 (Ministry of Trade and Industry, Economic Committee, 1986: 44). The implications of these data are serious for an economy so heavily dependent upon the attraction of international capital intending to engage in export production at a competitive advantage as a means of increasing returns.

To illustrate its point about Singapore's declining international competitiveness the committee pointed to Singapore's relatively unsatisfactory industrial growth. Singapore's industrial production grew by an average of 4 per cent per annum between 1981 and 1984, compared to 10 per cent for other Asian NICs. Whilst the main cause of this was the decline of the shipbuilding and petroleum industries, the 1985 pattern suggests there are more general problems. In that year Singapore's industrial output declined by 8 per cent, whereas the other NICs averaged growth of 2 per cent. Eight out of Singapore's top ten industries declined in 1985, but in other NICs production continued to expand in their key industries, albeit less rapidly than before. With the value of hindsight, the committee argued that the problem of declining competitiveness was concealed by the absolute growth of the early 1980s, but exposed quite clearly once the recession deepened in 1985.

The committee's point was also underlined by export data. In the 1980–84 period, external demand for Singapore's goods and services grew at 5 per cent, half the 10 per cent rate of other Asian NICs. In 1985, Singapore's external demand fell by 2 per cent, whereas that of other NICs grew by 1–2 per cent (Ministry of Trade and Industry, Economic Committee, 1986: 27–8).

In line with the fundamental essence of the committee's report, a number of key policy recommendations have recently been implemented. Such policies are intended not only to give impetus to the services sector by advancing towards a 'broad-based, low corporate and income tax regime, with minimal selective tax incentives', but also to generally reduce the cost of doing business in Singapore. The Deputy Prime Minister, Goh Chok Tong, stated the government's revised position quite unequivocally: 'For the future, the Government will adopt a more "open arms" attitude towards all kinds of investments. Whether an investment is in high-tech or low-tech, in manufacturing or services, it is welcome.' (as quoted in *Straits Times*, 27 February 1986: 12). Thus, in the search for secure long-term growth prospects, the PAP has effectively abandoned its policy of discouragement of lower-value-added manufacturing. Certainly the measures introduced by the government to restore Singapore's international competitiveness will make life easier for those areas of the economy which are labour-intensive but which have limited opportunity or capacity to move 'upstream'.

Towards the restoration of Singapore's international competitiveness, drastic measures have been introduced by the government. Employers' costs have been attacked on three fronts. First, employer contributions to the Central Provident Fund have been cut from 25 to 10 per cent for a minimum of the next two years, and Skills Development Fund contributions have been reduced from 2 to 1 per cent. Second, a total wage freeze has also been introduced for two years, and the all-clear has been given for actual wage reductions where it is required to restore a firm's competitiveness. Third, the government has committed itself to reductions in rents, utilities, transport, communications and interest rates affecting business. At the same time, measures have been taken to render Singapore a more attractive investment proposition by lowering taxes. Corporate tax has been reduced from 40 to 33 per cent, and a post-pioneer incentive is to be introduced to ensure that companies whose pioneer status expires will still pay only an effective tax rate of 10 per cent. Apart from restoring competitiveness, the government is hopeful that some of the above measures, particularly the reduced Central Provident Fund contributions, will free up domestic savings in favour of the private sector and encourage productive investments.

These policies clearly constitute a break with the 'Second Industrial Revolution' and demonstrate the government's revised view of the role and prospects of the manufacturing sector. Indeed, according to Goh Chok Tong, the favouritism of that sector is over; and amongst other moves, the projected extension of the Capital Investment Allowances Scheme to trading and service companies testifies to this. Goh has openly acknowledged that the historical conditions under which Singapore's EOI strategy blossomed may be gone forever. He points out that automation has to some degree undermined the EOI model: 'New technology, the microchip revolution and robotic slaves that do not go on strike for better pay and working conditions, have relieved the pressures on American, European and Japanese companies to seek sanctaries outside their home.' (as quoted in *Straits Times*, 27 February 1986). This has already begun to affect Singapore. Fairchild recently returned its integrated circuit assembly operations from Singapore to Portland, USA, because developments in automated machinery have cancelled out the cost advantages of cheaper labour (Galante, 1985). Goh's fears of a maturation of such a tendency are understandable.

Goh's observation about the changing historical structures are also supported by general data on exports. The 1980s has seen an overall slowdown in the growth of exports from developing countries. Exports of manufactures from developing countries averaged an annual growth rate of 10.6 per cent between 1973 and 1980, but this fell to 6.9 per cent from 1980 to 1983 (World Bank, 1984b: 26). Moreover, for the first time, in 1985 the growth of NIC exports actually fell behind the growth of world trade (FEER *Asia Yearbook 1986*: 10). One of the reasons for this is the growing protectionist stance of the advanced economies and in particular the resort to non-tariff barriers (NTBs). NTBs have more than doubled in the US and increased by 38 per cent in the European Economic Community between 1980 and 1983 (World Bank, 1985e: 40). A resolution to the problem of protectionism is as unlikely in the near future as an end to the recession.

It is not necessary to go any further into the government's latest policy changes and public pronouncements to make the essential point that these constitute a serious revision of the 'Second Industrial Revolution'. Having miscalculated the response of international capital to the push and pull measures adopted since 1979, the PAP found itself in a difficult position. The policies of the 'Second Industrial Revolution' had compounded the problems caused by the global recession, the structural decline of key industries and the excess of savings going into non-productive investments. The degree and nature of higher-value-added investment simply wasn't a sufficient basis upon which Singapore's long-term economic strategy could be geared. On the contrary, it contradicted the goal of maximum economic growth. Singapore's policymakers also had to recognise the possibility that future opportunities available to Singapore through the structure of the new international division of labour might be constrained. In short, Singapore was beginning to confront objective limits to its 'Second Industrial Revolution'.

The path ahead

Whether the PAP's revised strategy can resolve the economic contradictions generated by the 'Second Industrial Revolution' of course remains to be seen. Naturally the extreme external dependence of the Singapore economy, whether it be in the manufacturing or services sectors, will continue to render Singapore a vulnerable economy. One thing that is much clearer, however, is that the policies recently announced by the PAP will create their own problems for the economic and political management of Singapore.

At the economic level, an obvious problem posed by the latest policies is the fiscal pressure they place on the state. To compensate for the economic slowdown, the 1986 budget has considerably expanded development expenditure allocations. Total government spending in the 1986 fiscal year is an estimated S$22.06 billion, 37 per cent higher than the revised figure for the 1985 fiscal year. Development expenditure has increased by 50 per cent and represents 60 per cent of the total 1986 budget allocation. As a proportion of GDP, government expenditure is thus expected to rise sharply from 43 to about 60 per cent. Given that these increases have taken place at a time when revenue-forfeiting reforms are being introduced to make Singapore more attractive to capital, austerity measures have been necessitated in certain areas. As a result, the government has committed itself to substantial cuts in recurrent expenditure, including a planned cut of 10 per cent in the permanent staff complement of the public sector. (Hu, 1986: 10). But this alone is not enough, and the government has announced its intention to introduce a consumption tax once it has the appropriate machinery in place. Needless to point out, both measures are unpopular.

The extent to which the PAP recognises the limitations of its low tax policy is suggested in the decision to reduce the employers' contributions to the Central Provident Fund by 15 per cent for two initial years rather than indefinitely. The role of CPF contributions in underwriting the state's aggressive infrastructural development prevents any painless parting with this source of cheap funds. Moreover, in the immediate future the level of withdrawals from the CPF will increase sharply because the first lifelong contributors are just beginning to reach retirement age. The government has not, therefore, ruled out a return to the 25 per cent level from employers. In such an event, the status of Singapore as a low tax site would suffer and might negate some of the gains made.

There is, then, an economic contradiction generated by the government's new policies: its strategy of reducing costs to capital weakens the state's long-term capacity to provide the finance and support for the costly supportive infrastructure of a modern, technologically advanced economy. But at the same time, these policies also sharpen the political contradictions of Singapore society. Whilst on the one hand easing the lot of capital, the government has adopted a policy of deliberately reducing the standard of living for workers and cutting back on public welfare spending. But the PAP may be on a dangerous course if it views welfare cuts as part of the implementation of the Economic Committee's observation that 'we have a tendency to provide too many "safety nets" in our society' (Ministry of Trade and Industry, Economic Committee, 1986: 129). For a number of reasons, the preparedness of Singaporeans to accept this situation uncritically may be a lot weaker than in the past. Not only did the corrective wage policy unintentionally raise the expectations of the masses, as evidenced in the continuing and successful pressure for wage rises after 1981, but the emergence of some form of limited parliamentary opposition has given greater vent to popular disillusionment with the government. Indeed, part of the explanation for this emergence lies in the fact that

Singapore's young generation of voters has lived only in an increasingly prosperous Singapore, and they have no genuine recollection of the political and social turmoil prior to PAP supremacy. Having been officially encouraged to judge the PAP on its ability to preside over a successful economy, these people could be more receptive to the overtures of the PAP's political opponents if conditions continue to deteriorate.

Though it is too early to assess the prospects of the services sector providing the necessary long-term economic growth sought by the PAP, we can say that this path does provide greater scope for capital accumulation by Singapore's domestic bourgeoisie than the manufacturing-oriented 'Second Industrial Revolution'. This may to some extent stifle the criticisms that this class has levelled at the government in recent times focusing on the promotion of foreign-based multinational corporations and the government's pervasive role in the economy. It remains to be seen, however, whether the government will appease these criticisms to the extent of creating a 'freer market', as recommended by the Economic Committee. Though this notion appeals to the ideology of a bourgeoisie based in the finance and property sectors of the economy, it is quite inappropriate for the further development of the manufacturing sector. As we have seen much earlier, state intervention has been central to Singapore's comparative advantage in certain areas of manufacturing. Significantly, although the government has entertained the idea of divestment of some public assets, opening up opportunities for private capital accumulation, it has not provided even a hint of withdrawing from the more consequential and substantial forms of state intervention, notably in the areas of subsidised and planned infrastructure and finance associated with the industrial programme. There are significant structural limits to the extent to which the state can withdraw from the marketplace without undermining comparative advantage in manufacturing.

In essence then, we have seen that by the mid-1980s Singapore policymakers were confronted by a number of adverse economic developments. The high point in the EOI strategy was reached with the 'Second Industrial Revolution' when the Singapore state attempted to hasten the transition towards a higher rung in the technological ladder of the new international division of labour. Serious objective limits posed by international capital and its attendant logic prevented the PAP's vision from materialising, placing the Singapore economy in a precarious position. In response, a new strategy has been devised and is now being implemented, one that rests heavily on the restoration of Singapore's cost-competitiveness in the NIDL. However, in trying to resolve the contradictions which surfaced during the period of the 'Second Industrial Revolution' policies, the Singapore state has created new economic and political contradictions. This dynamic process highlights the structural constraints associated with Singpore's incorporation into the NIDL and the inseparability of economic and political relationships.

RICHARD HIGGOTT

7
Australia: economic crises and the politics of regional economic adjustment

Only a decade ago the idea of including an essay on Australia in a book mainly about economic crisis in *Southeast Asia* would have been hard to justify. In the now-well-worn cliché of Donald Horne, Australia was the 'Lucky Country': affluent, self-sufficient in primary produce and raw materials and well able to import its capital and technological requirements. Indeed it ranked as one of the world's three or four most highly developed countries. Also at that time it was not considered part of Asia except in terms of a vague geographical proximity. In addition Australia had undergone an entirely different colonial experience to that of its regional Southeast Asian neighbours. As a settler community it saw itself as a partner in the (British) Imperial tradition rather than the victim of colonial oppression in a manner consistent with the majority of Asian opinion. Australia's interests were normally seen as being in conflict with, rather than complementary to, the rest of a region it had traditionally regarded as a potential threat in politico-strategic terms and irrelevant in economic terms.

Things have changed dramatically over the past decade or so. Writing in 1986 it is almost an understatement to suggest that Australia is in severe economic crisis. 'Recession' is becoming increasingly common amongst economic analysts in both the print and the electronic media—that is, when journalists are not resorting to more outlandish descriptions such as the 'death of the Lucky Country', 'the Land of Lost Opportunities' or the 'Latin Americanisation of Australia'. In addition, Australia is nowadays more or less continually analysed in terms of it being 'of' the Asian region or of its 'Asian future'—that is, the Asia–Pacific region generally or Southeast Asia specifically. Both issues—economic crisis and regional location—are the 'flavour of the month' with policy practitioners and analysts in Australia, many of whom pursue the issues with a zeal found only among the recently converted. It will be the purpose of this chapter, however, to argue that both trends have been a long time in the making and can be explained in historical and much less melodramatic fashion.

With regard to the nature of the economic crisis it will be argued that Australia's problems exist at two distinct, but related levels. The first level is that of the *current* crisis of confidence in virtually all spheres of the Australian economy with which the government has to deal on a day-to-day basis. The second level relates to the longer-term problems of a structural nature that *underlie* the immediate daily concerns of government.

This chapter, in keeping with the other studies in this book, will argue that the most useful way to understand the long-term structural problems faced by Australia is to examine Australia's economic position in what we call the new international division of labour (NIDL). This, the editors feel, is an analytic concept capable of providing valuable insights into the economic problems faced by all of the cases we have examined.

After providing an introductory analysis of Australia's position within the NIDL and its overall incorporation into the international political economy (IPE) in the twentieth century, the chapter will move on to a detailed analysis of Australia's structural relations at the regional level, before concluding with an examination of the policies of the current Hawke Labor government in its attempts to adjust to the regional economic imperatives as a way of mediating some of Australia's most pressing economic problems. Given that both popular and populist analysis stems from what is seen as the gravity of the immediate economic crisis, and given that we argue the connection between the immediate situation and these long-term structural questions, the dimensions of the current situation are first outlined briefly below.

Australia in economic crisis: the contemporary situation

In a recent speech that led to another rush to sell the Australian dollar, Australia's treasurer, Paul Keating, referred to Australia's status as a 'Fledgling Banana Republic' (*Australian Financial Review*, 16 May 1986: 1). As injudicous as his remarks may have been, they were based on two very real problems: the declining competitiveness of Australia as a trading nation, especially in its traditional commodity markets; and the related, and constant throughout the 1980s, severe balance of payments problems that face Australia. The increasing magnitude of these problems since about early 1985 had a bitter irony for Keating who, declared 'Treasurer of the Year' by *Euromoney* in 1984, had presided in the first two years of the Labor government, since 1983, over what many thought was an economy in the process of revivification. Labor's rhetoric of consensus and 'Accord' and its expressed commitment to introduce the necessary reforms to bring Australia into the 1980s, accompanied by a 'business-as-usual' approach to day-to-day economic management issues, hid the very real nature of Australia's financial and trading crisis—the starkness of which is revealed in the following data.

In February 1986 Australia's *gross* debt stood in excess of A$70 000 million. The increase from A$30 475 million in 1984/85 to A$52 002 million in 1985/86 represented an increase in the *net* external debt from 16.3 to 25.1 per cent of Australia's gross domestic product (*Age*, 14 February 1983: 3). The reasons for this dramatic increase were several, but the most significant factors were the increase in *private* overseas borrowing and a 40 per cent decrease in the value of the Australian dollar since its float in December 1983. The float by itself accounted for one-fifth of the total debt figure. (For a full discussion see Blundell-Wignell et al. (1985).)

Historical and comparative analysis draws out the gravity of this blow-out in Australia's debt. The six years of the 1980s have seen Australia's foreign external debt increase sixfold. Also dramatic has been the increase in debt-servicing requirements. Accounting for only 8 per cent of export earnings in 1980, debt servicing had grown to 36 per cent of export earnings in 1985/86 and was expected to be 39 per cent in 1986/87 (*Australian Financial Review*, 20 June 1986: 14). These are the highest figures for Australia since the Great Depression of the 1930s. Poland, with a current ratio of 87.7 per cent of debt-servicing requirements to export earnings, is clearly out on its own in a comparative sense, but Morocco, Nigeria and the Philippines with 39 per cent are comparable to Australia, whilst Australia's fellow OECD members are in a lesser league (UK, 28%; USA, 25%; Canada, 16.6%; France, 10.6%; West Germany, 10.4%; Netherlands, 3.9%) (*Australian Financial Review*, 20 June 1986: 14). Australia in fact currently ranks number nine in the world league of external debt borrowers behind such states as Brazil, Mexico, South Korea and Venezuela (*Australian*, 29 February 1986: 6).

The Australian debt problem has approached dimensions, not dissimilar to those in other countries, which have triggered IMF intervention. This spectre has been raised by the media in its regular bouts of sensationalism—one journalist recently argued that IMF intervention would have been visited on Australia some time ago if it had been a Spanish-speaking country (*National Times on Sunday*, 10 August 1985: 16)—but the suggestion has also come from more serious quarters such as the respected ANU economist Professor Fred Gruen, as early as June 1985.

The outpacing of export income growth by debt-servicing obligations is, of course, the major difficulty that befell many Third World states in the 1970s. This is a situation that Australia is fast approaching, and it is exacerbated not only by the declining Australian dollar but also by the uncertain, if not positively bleak, outlook for Australia's key commodity exports. The decline in the import-purchasing power of Australia's commodity exports gives Australia an export profile similar to many Third World states. This is highlighted in the recent World Bank report on *Commodity Trade and Price Trends* (1985a) which demonstrated the decline in a 'basket' of thirty-three export commodities from less-developed countries (LDCs) when measured against the import of manufactures from developed countries. This group of thirty-three commodities includes wheat, sugar, beef, bananas, copper, tin, nickel, bauxite, aluminium, iron ore, lead and zinc—all commodities of vital importance to Australia (see Table 7.3). Using an average for 1977-79 to provide a base of 100, then an index of the purchasing power of Australia's exports shows a decline from a high of 160 in 1974 to 84 in 1984. A similar set of figures illustrates the deterioration of Australia's terms of trade. Over the period from fiscal year 1978/79 to 1984/85 the terms of trade (export price index divided by import price index) declined from 115 to 94 (*Australian Financial Review*, 5 March 1986: 12).

This decline has brought Australia back to a position similar to the pre-1960s era in which solving balance of payments problems continually took precedence over the process of growth creation. As this chapter will illustrate, the mineral expansion of the 1960s and 1970s (the so-called 'resources boom') would appear to be well and truly over, and the prospects for a recovery in the commodity markets in which Australia trades are poor. It will be argued that the pressures on Australian exporters to cut export prices on many commodities may well prove overwhelming. Consequently, the days in which Australia was able to use its agricultural and mineral sectors to subsidise its protected and less-competitive manufacturing industries would also appear over. The situation is made worse by the increased competition from Europe (and the USA) which, by an ironic twist of fate, engages in the opposite practice. The core of economic practice within the European Economic Community is to carry agricultural production under the Common Agricultural Policy on the shoulders of more-efficient manufacturing industries.

The magnitude of the threat to Australia's traditional trading pattern from Europe—and of course the USA, given current farm export subsidy policies—is only now becoming apparent. As we move on towards the end of the 1980s, Australia's traditional markets, especially Japan and other Asian states, will inevitably come under increasing pressure from the more politically powerful USA and the EEC to accept their agricultural surpluses at the expense of those from states such as Australia. Agricultural subsidies for agricultural commodity *exports* (more than subsidies for *production*, as occurs in Europe) depress not only the price that competing traders, such as Australia, receive for their exports, but also the potential volume of exports. These principles apply not only in the export of farm produce, where wheat and beef are particularly important for Australia, but also in the minerals sector. The minerals sector is further affected by the success of production efficiencies and substitution policies in reducing demand. This emerging pattern is not merely one of minor market fluctuations that may at some stage restabilise, but rather what a report from Australia's major bank, Westpac, calls '...a fundamental shift in the balance of Australia's trading relationship with the rest of the world' (*Far Eastern Economic Review (FEER)*, 29 May 1986: 100). Treasurer Keating, in a statement borne out by the evidence, indicated that Australian commodity prices were 'as bad in real terms [as any time] since the Depression'.

As damaging as US wheat subsidies and the US Farm Bill may be to Australia in the short-term both economically (estimates put the cost to Australia at A$750 million in lost revenue in 1986/87 (*Age*, 18 February 1986: 15)) and psychologically, to the extent that they are sending panic waves through the Australian rural and trading communities, by far the greater long-term worry is EEC policy. In the words of the French Minister of Agriculture, Mr Guillaume, EEC surpluses are '...not a calamity but an opportunity' (*Australian Financial Review*, 26 March 1986: 12). They will be used by the EEC in the future to make inroads into new markets. The latter part of the 1980s is likely to see a 'no-holds-barred' situation in the competition to sell rural produce. There may well cease to be any such thing as a 'traditional market'. Australian exporters and the Australian government are only now beginning to realise that a policy geared to preserving their 'share' of traditional markets, based on appeals to fair play rather than keen prices, is doomed to failure.

The EEC's contempt for small peripheral traders is readily observable and contrasts sharply with its trading relations with other major traders such as the USA and Japan. These three major trading units carry on their trading relationships at a largely bilateral level, ignoring the General Agreement on Tariffs and Trade (GATT) as and when it suits them. In the absence of restraint by these powers, GATT is no defence at all to the smaller commodity-trading nations such as Australia.

These events—the crisis of the Australian dollar and the crisis in Australia's trading position—represent the high-water mark in the recent unfolding realisation of Australia's changing status in the global economy. Whilst these events are undoubtedly of an immediate, dramatic nature, they are, to the more dispassionate observer, merely the manifestations of a process that has been a long time in the making.

It is the purpose of the remainder of this chapter, therefore, to place these events in a more historically and structurally analytic framework. The first factor to consider is the evolution of a new international division of labour.

The new international division of labour (NIDL) and Australia

There is now a substantial body of literature that recognises the emergence of a new international division of labour that is qualitatively different to the division of labour that prevailed up to about the end of the 1960s. The existence of this new stage in the global political economy is recognised by scholars operating across a variety of intellectual paradigms. There is also a body of literature that attempts to locate various parts of the global political economy within NIDL and suggest the degree to which they have been favourably or unfavourably incorporated (see Higgott, 1984 and 1986a). Most attention has been on the position of the newly industrialising countries (NICs) in NIDL and particularly the extent to which the processes of industrialisation have been fostered by it (see Leaver, 1985). Australia represents a unique case study, given its location as what one scholar has referred to as the 'misplaced continent' (Grant, 1983)—white, Christian, sometime ailing capitalist 'middle' power located at the centre of the world's most rapidly developing economic region, but a region with different historical, cultural and economic impulses. Further, the Asia–Pacific region in which Australia is located has been central to the evolution of NIDL.

At its simplest, the evolution of a new international division of labour represents a qualitatively distinct stage in the process of international capital accumulation. This somewhat bold assertion may be justified, albeit briefly here, in a number of ways. Firstly, capitalism at the end of the twentieth century—and expectations of theorists of the crisis of 'late capitalism' that its demise is imminent notwithstanding—appears to be alive and well, albeit in those areas of the world that Marx himself would find difficult to imagine. Secondly, its impact on social structure seems essentially 'vertical' rather than 'horizontal'. This would appear to be the case whether we recognise the emergence of 'situses' rather than classes, as foretold by Daniel Bell (1973) or the emergence of a segmented labour market (as opposed to dual economies) cogently outlined by Caporaso (1978).

The third distinct feature of the evolution of a new international

Australia: Politics of regional economic adjustment

division of labour lies in some of its implications for political arrangements, particularly with regard to relationships between state and capital. Although only in the infancy of conceptualisation at this stage, this issue has received considerably more treatment of late. This analysis, especially concerning the relationship between the evolution of NIDL and the emergence of 'corporatist' political structures, has been carried out in European (Katzenstein, 1983 and 1985), Latin American (Collier, 1979), African (Shaw, 1982; Higgott, 1985 and 1986a), Asian (Feith, 1980; Higgott & Robison 1985) and theoretical contexts (Higgott, 1983; Evans, Rueschmeyer & Skocpol, 1985). The issue with regard to Australia is explored briefly in the last section of this chapter.

Industrialisation of the NICs of the Asia–Pacific region near Australia has to a large extent been facilitated by, indeed is characterised by, the internationalisation of production, a process that has involved the relocation of industrial activities, especially component manufacture and assembly, from industrialised to developing countries. This relocation has been enhanced by technological innovation providing for the disaggregation of the production process so that labour-intensive aspects of the production of complex products can be carried out in countries providing cheap and largely unskilled and semi-skilled labour (Frobel et al., 1978).

This stage in international capital accumulation constitutes a tendency towards redefining the position of not only developing countries but also the already-industrialised ones. The essence of the new division is greater specialisation in the production process and the ensuing facility for location and relocation of productive activity. The process of refinement still continues, with investors now drawing the distinction between varying categories of developing countries. For example, some labour-intensive industrial activities are nowadays being moved from Hong Kong and Singapore into countries of even lower wage costs such as Malaysia or, more recently, Sri Lanka. The increasing sophistication of this international specialisation has depended very much on an on-going supply of new entrants to the cause of export-oriented industrialisation (EOI) to compensate for rising production costs in already-established production sites (Rodan, 1985b). Whilst this is still a strong trend, there is some evidence to suggest that the process is not exhaustive. In a recent analysis of South Korea, S.K. Cho (1985) has suggested that there are limits to export-led industrialisation being brought about by automative advances in production, diminishing cheap labour in the NICs and an accompanying decline in the power of organised labour in some developed countries—making them once again more attractive propositions for international capital than some NICs or LDCs. In either scenario, one thing is quite clear. Production is a global, not a national process in the last quarter of the twentieth century. In this context we have seen the advanced industrial countries undergo a process of divestment of the more labour-intensive manufacturing processes to the Third World as a response to profitability considerations, although these tendencies have been offset in part by the concentration of capital and technology-intensive industries in high-wage countries (see Adam, 1971 and 1972; Plaschke, 1975; Sharpston, 1975).

Australia's economic profile exhibits a 'mix and match' of characteristics of both developed and less-developed countries. Its consequent 'location' within the NIDL is conditioned by this profile—by the fact that it is neither LDC or NIC on the one hand, nor one of the world's major industrial powers on the other. Similarly it cannot satisfactorily be compared with the small, but highly developed industrial states of Europe, given its Pacific location and the predominantly raw-material and primary-produce orientation in the structure of its economy. Like the 'small states' (see Vital, 1967; and Katzenstein, 1983) of Western Europe, it has high levels of urbanisation, high wage rates and a four-level sectoral distribution of its economy (primary through quaternary); but, as can be seen from Table 7.1 the bulk of Australia's exports, in contrast to those of other advanced industrial states, were and (despite a drop in the twenty-year period between 1960 and 1980) still are generated in the primary sector. In addition, imports traditionally show a higher proportion of manufactured goods than is typical for the other advanced industrial states (Table 7.2).

Table 7.1 Exports of primary produce and raw materials as a percentage of total exports

	1960	1981
Australia	92%	72%
Industrial market economies	34%	27%

Source: World Bank (1984b) *World Development Report* Table II, pp. 238–9

Table 7.2 Imports of manufactures as a percentage of total imports

	1960	1981
Australia	68%	77%
Industrial market economies	43%	51%

Source: World Bank (1984b) *World Development Report* Table II, pp. 238–9

Australia: Politics of regional economic adjustment

In ascertaining whether it is useful to consider Australia as a 'small state', we should remember that although it is a nation-continent (only the USSR, Canada, the USA, China and Brazil are larger in area) and its gross domestic product in 1982 was (at US$164 210 million) the eleventh largest in the world, it does suffer many of the vicissitudes of a 'small' economy in the contemporary division of labour. In particular, Australia needs to 'comply with the demands of the global economy with all the *reactive* decision-making processes and rationalization necessary to guarantee the continuing processes of national development' (quoted in Katzenstein, 1983: 92). Apart from periods of acute national crisis such as war, trade policy, as a factor in economic policy for example, can be considerably more important on a day-to-day basis than problems of security.

In formulating strategy Katzenstein suggests that a state (such as Australia) '...whose position is slipping in the international division of labour' can learn a lesson from the responses of the small developed European states to this problem, namely '...a dual strategy of international liberalisation and domestic compensation based on corporatist political structures' (Katzenstein, 1983: 93). In this context, corporatism needs to be seen less as an ideological phenomenon of either left or right wing variety, than as the '...pursuit of strategies that differ from those of either liberalism or socialism' (Katzenstein, 1983: 94). Katzenstein argues that it is the openness and vulnerability of these states to the international political economy (to a degree greater than large industrial states) that has given rise to this tendency. I plan to show later that, while openness and vulnerability are also the order of the day for Australia, the nature of these weaknesses are different; and in the final section of the chapter we shall consider how government policy in contemporary Australia reflects the dual emphasis of the small European states as outlined by Katzenstein.

In general terms, at this stage we can see that Australia's vulnerability is generated by a variety of fairly self-evident factors. Firstly, of course, with a population of only 15.5 million, Australia is unable to make the economies of scale necessary for the efficient performance of an array of industrial activities deemed central to Western developed societies. Table 7.3's analysis of Australia's imports and exports, by commodity group, demonstrates the degree of Australia's dependence on the international economy for manufactured goods; particularly important amongst these are goods of an industrial and technological nature such as cars and electronic goods, mostly of course from the USA and Japan. Secondly, this smallness has meant a specialisation in export trade in order to attain market efficiency. Yet unlike the small European states, this specialisation has been in primary produce and raw materials—products highly susceptible to global

Table 7.3 Australia's exports and imports, by commodity group, 1950–80 (annual average, per cent)

Type of trade and commodity	1950/51 to 1954/55	1955/56 to 1959/60	1960/61 to 1964/65	1965/66 to 1969/70	1970/71 to 1974/75	1975/76 to 1979/80
Imports[a]						
Food, drink, and tobacco	6.7	6.3	5.4	4.9	5.0	5.1
Minerals, fuels, and other basic materials[b]	19.7	21.1	18.5	14.3	11.6	14.6
Manufactured goods[c]	68.9	67.7	70.9	75.6	79.2	77.6
Other	4.7	4.9	5.2	5.2	4.2	2.7
Exports						
Meat	6.2	8.2	9.2	9.5	10.3	9.0
Cereals	12.8	9.9	15.6	12.4	12.1	12.1
Wool	50.7	43.2	33.9	24.3	13.8	10.3
Other rural	12.1	13.9	13.3	11.7	11.0	10.0
Unprocessed and processed minerals[d]	—	—	—	—	15.9	18.7
Coal	0.1	0.4	1.3	3.1	5.6	10.8
Metals	5.3	7.1	7.1	9.8	10.0	9.8
Simply transformed manufactures[d]	—	—	—	—	9.1	9.0
Elaborately transformed manufactures[d]	—	—	—	—	13.9	10.4

Notes: [a] After 1965/66 the classification of imports was changed from the statistical classification of imports to the Australian import-commodity classification. See notes b and c.
[b] Data from 1950/51 through 1964/65 include basic materials, fuels and lubricants. Data after 1965/66 include crude materials (inedible), mineral fuels and lubricants.
[c] Data from 1950/51 through 1964/65 include textiles, base metals, motor vehicles, electrical machinery and equipment, other machines and machinery, and other manufactures. Data after 1965/66 include chemicals, manufactured material, machinery (electric and otherwise), transport equipment and miscellaneous manufactured articles.
[d] Data begin in 1970/71.

Sources: Caves & Krause (1984): 279; Norton, Garmston & Brodie, (1982): 5, 8; Department of Trade and Resources, (1983): 23–36.

market prices. Australia is thus, at one and the same time, open and vulnerable due to this lack of diversification, which has as an inevitable outcome a degree of dependence and 'openness towards the influences of the international economy much greater than that of large countries' (Katzenstein, 1983: 96). Again, Tables 7.1 and 7.3 give an indication of the preponderance of primary produce and, of late, raw materials in Australia's export trade. By contrast, the response of the small European states has been specialised production of high-value-added goods for the international market in a manner that Australia has never even seriously considered.

In another area it is again appropriate to cite Katzenstein's study, given the lessons it holds for Australia:

> Dependence on the import of investment goods and the export of consumer goods creates, within the context of openness and vulnerability towards developments in international markets, tendencies that reinforce imbalances in the economic structures of small European states. Their economic specialisation leaves different sectors of the economy less integrated than those in large countries. [1983: 98]

Along both sectoral and spatial axes, Australia exhibits considerable asymmetries and conflicts of these kinds. While a major asymmetry within Australia is between the varying states of the Federation, this is as much a conflict between different sectors of capital as it is a spatial conflict. Conflicts between the geographically remote and sparsely populated states of the Federation (Western Australia, Queensland and the Northern Territory), on the one hand, and the smaller, more populous states of the southeastern corner (New South Wales, Victoria and, to a lesser extent, South Australia), on the other hand, reflect the different priorities of the preponderantly primary-product/raw-material exporting peripheral states—nowadays aggressively oriented towards free-trade policies—and what Head (1983: 9) calls the 'manufacturing states' of the southeastern corner. It is these manufacturing states that have, for so long, been the beneficiaries of Australia's highly protective national tariff policies. These conflicts have become particularly acute since the 'mining boom' of the early 1970s.

This was not the first mining boom in Australia's history. Mining exceeded 15 per cent of gross domestic product back in 1861 and remained at about 10 per cent in the early 1900s. Yet for a forty-year period between 1921 and 1961 mining averaged less than 3 per cent of gross domestic product, and in the twenty years since 1961 it rose above 6 per cent of gross domestic product (Helliwell, 1984: 89). Mineral exports are unlikely again to match their high point of the mid-1860s, and most of the talk of the 1970s of a new high-point of 10 per cent of

GDP by the end of the 1980s has been silenced for six years or so (Helliwell, 1984: 90). More importantly for this discussion is the degree to which a dramatic expansion in the mining sector is thought to be deleterious to other sectors of the economy.

Bob Gregory has attempted to outline the manner in which a continued increase of the importance of mining in the Australian economy might undermine the efficiency and competitiveness of other sectors (see Gregory, 1976 and 1982; Johns & MacLeod, 1977; and McQueen, 1982). At the risk of oversimplification, Gregory argued that the 'boom' of the 1970s brought not only significant increases in mineral output but also long-term implications likely to prove disruptive to the sectoral balance of the economy. The crux of Gregory's argument was that the more successful the mineral export boom (fostered by the energy-conscious world of the 1970s), then the less competitive other sectors would be. Indeed Gregory arugued that the possible impact of increased mineral exports could have a greater impact on the other importing and exporting sectors of the economy than a general reduction in tariffs of about 25 per cent (Gregory, 1976: 71-91).

The impact of these sectoral distortions, and several other consequences of the evolution of the new international division of labour outlined, form the central focus for the rest of this chapter. Particularly it will examine the nature of Australian openness and vulnerability to the international division of labour, especially in its broad Asian–Pacific regional context, before going on to suggest an emerging pattern of political behaviour characteristic of the type of corporatism described by Katzenstein. Before moving to the contemporary situation, however, a brief introduction to the process of Australia's incorporation into the global political and economic environment in the twentieth century is in order.

Australia and the emergent international political economy in the twentieth century

There are two facets to the global incorporation of Australia from the time of Federation in 1901 and its gradual emergence from British colonial suzerainty. The first is its integration into the global capitalist system. The second is the taking up of a position as an actor in the international system of states and the formulation of a national foreign policy reflecting a loosening (not severing) of the colonial bonds.

If we consider the economic process first, then this too can be bifurcated. The key to the change from the first phase to the second phase is similar, however, for the political as well as the economic process. It is, of course, represented in the changing global hegemonic fortunes of Britain and America. The Second World War saw the USA relieve Great Britain as Australia's major security partner, and the ensuing post-war period saw the USA also become one of Australia's major economic partners, to be joined in the late 1950s by Japan and in the past decade by the other rapidly developing members of the Asian–Pacific region. This last phase is the most important for the purposes of this chapter and receives full treatment in the next sections. Yet several factors from the first phase are major legacies for the contemporary situation and should be noted. Particularly important is the degree to which the period of colonialism created a nationalistic, inward-looking and highly defensive state structure which protected Australia, as best it could, from the influences of a growing world economy.

Throughout the twentieth century, Australia's historical experience has been that of a highly protectionist state, erecting barriers and providing government subsidy to secure the growth of labour-intensive manufacturing industries that would have failed to develop in the face of external competition. Given Australia's origins as a small white outpost of the British Empire subject to the 'tyranny of distance' and obsessed by a 'populate or perish' mentality, protectionism as a means of attempting to create a self-sustainable supply of manufactured goods made excellent sense—as a report on the condition of the Australian economy for the Brookings Institute recently acknowledged (Caves & Krause, 1984: 1).

Further, in the aftermath of the Second World War, indeed as late as the mid-1960s, it was as McMichael notes '... precisely the protectionist character of Australian industrialisation which attracted foreign capital investment'. This process, at the height of the US hegemony of the world economy, fostered Australia's incorporation into the global economy. Protected by tariff walls and supplied by migrant labour, transnational corporations (TNCs) 'established a pattern of investment in industrial production'. (McMichael, 1981: 49)

The changes that came about in the international division of labour in the mid-1960s, however, saw a concomitant change in the role of Australia in that division. The newly industrialising countries of the world, given the benefits of changes in technology, provided a plentiful and cheap supply of labour leading to rapid growth, especially in the wider Asian–Pacific region. It has been this rapid growth that has led to the challenge to Australian manufacturing. Whilst the Australian manufacturing sector may never had been large, or highly competitive, it did have a readymade market behind its tariff walls. As will shortly be demonstrated, whilst increasing industrialisation has made the majority of countries more open and dependent on world trade, this has not been the case for Australia—certainly not as far as trade in manufactures is concerned. Rather, Australia has become most attractive as a provider of minerals and especially energy supplies.

It is in the context of the nature of their exports that the comparison between Australia and the small European developed states breaks down. While both share an openness and vulnerability, the Europeans are involved in relatively high-level technological activities, and they have a different export pattern and a different pattern of foreign investment in their countries, especially if we look at the high rate of foreign capital invested in the Australian mining sector (Head, 1983: 5). It remains only to emphasise that these economic changes did not take place in a political vacuum. Australia was tied up in the dramatic political processes that evolved out of the Second World War. Australia has come a long way from the 1940s, when its role in world affairs was seen merely as an appendage of the British empire—when its foreign policies were merely a mirror image of Britain's world view. After the Second World War the United States was inevitably the major influence on Australia's foreign and defence policies, and many other aspects of Australia's international relations turned away from Europe.

With the benefit of hindsight many of the changes seemed inevitable (see Millar, 1977, for an overview of the period), perhaps none more so than Australia's evolving relationship with Asia following the Japanese occupation of Singapore in the Second World War (see Hamill, 1981), Australia's involvement in the Korean War (see McCormack, 1983) and the Vietnam War (see King, 1982) and more recently the arrival of the 'Boat People' refugees and the domestic debate over Asian immigration to Australia. There is insufficient space here to discuss in detail the way in which a region that was once regarded as peripheral (when it was not seen as a threat) to Australia's cultural ideology and economic interests has become central, although, as the last section of the paper will suggest, the process is far from universally understood, accepted or complete. To be sure, such changes have been a long time in the making. Since the early 1970s Gough Whitlam and Malcom Fraser set great store by improving links with Australia's regional neighbours. Since his election in March 1983, Bob Hawke, his government in general and his foreign minister in particular, have championed regionalism with both a rhetorical and practical vigour.

Australia and the Asia–Pacific region

So far this chapter has, avoiding attempts at definition, referred only loosely to the notion of an Asian–Pacific region. It should be noted that it is *Australia's* regional economic environment that is under consideration. Exact geographical definition is neither desirable nor indeed appropirate. The important factor is to appreciate the regional influences on Australia in the international political economy as opposed to global influences on Australia in the international system of states. Globalism and regionalism need not be seen as mutually exclusive orbits of the international political economy or system in which Australia operates. Rather they are two ends of a continuum at which the different activities pursued can be fairly well defined.

Briefly, at the global level in the political system, Australia's primary interests are political, diplomatic and strategic (though factors in the political economy are significant too). This is particularly so with regard to the role Australia plays, or is deemed to play, in support of the USA formally (through its membership of ANZUS) and less formally (through the less clearly defined Australian–American alliance) in the process of superpower contestation. It should of course be noted that an important element in the alliance is the role Australia plays in regional security. Then there are the various regions in which Australia has to 'live' on a day-to-day basis. At these levels different factors come into play, and it is much more useful (though again not in any exclusivist fashion) to give primacy to the political economy rather than the political system.

The criteria for defining Australia's region cannot be entirely conventional. Australia is neither part of a region with which it shares common historical and cultural links with its neighbours, nor is it part of a region sharing common current institutional links with its neighbours. Similarly its 'political culture' is different to that of the majority of its neighbours. We need to look instead to other factors, such as economic impacts on Australia, to provide the parameters of Australia's regional environments. As such, there are at least three levels for the analysis of Australia's regional position. Firstly, at its widest we have the Pacific region (a geographical not an institutional arena) containing East Asia (north and south), Japan and the western seaboard of the Americas. For the purposes of this analysis, East Asia and Japan are the key areas. Secondly, we have the immediate Southeast Asian region consisting of Australia and its ASEAN neighbours: Indonesia, Malaysia, the Philippines, Singapore and Thailand (the newest member of ASEAN, Brunei, is not relevant to this chapter). Finally, there is the Southwest Pacific region in which Australia, along with New Zealand, has something akin to regional superpower status vis-a-vis the small island micro-states of the Pacific and its former colonial territory of Papua New Guinea. The following discussion is concerned only with the first two levels.

Needless to say important political and strategic questions are to be found at all three levels, but when we focus on an examination of Australia in the international division of labour, politico/economic factors at the levels of the Pacific and ASEAN become the most important. As a final point of clarification, it should be noted that not all states of the East Asian rim are under consideration here. For example, whilst Vietnam is crucial to any discussion of Australia's regional political, strategic and diplomatic relations in the region, it is of little import for an analysis of the political economy of Australia's regional relations. Similarly, to ignore India, Burma and several other states is not to deny their 'Asianness' in regional terms but rather their significance for a study of Australia's political economy. Indeed it is the *aggregate* impact of the Asia-Pacific region on Australia's political economy, rather than specific bilateral relations, with the exception of Japan, that is under scrutiny here. It is only by analysing Australia in this context that the broader structural nature of Australia's current economic crisis can be understood.

Australia and the Pacific region

The process of dynamic economic growth in the Pacific Basin in the era after the Second World War is now sufficiently well known for it simply to be asserted here with the support of a few relevant statistics. Data are drawn from a variety of readily available secondary sources, the importance of which for this paper is the *comparative* nature of Australia's position in this regional context.

It is almost a cliché nowadays to talk of a 'shift in the world's centre of economic gravity' (Madigan, 1984: 13). For the first time in 1982, for example, US-Asian trade surpassed US trade with Europe. Japan is clearly the major factor in Pacific growth, its gross domestic product climbing from less than one-eleventh to over one-third of that of the USA between 1960 and 1982 (see Table 7.4). But also during that time Asia's share of total world gross domestic product grew from 8 to 19 per cent, whilst North America's dropped from 48 to 31 per cent. Extrapolation to 1990 sees Asia anticipated to produce 25 per cent of world gross domestic product and the Pacific Basin (as a whole) 50 per cent of total world gross domestic product (Drysdale, 1984: 1; but also see Hofheinz & Calder, 1982; and Uchida et al., 1983). Similar growth patterns have been recorded in Asia's shares of world trade with a growth from 9.5 per cent of total in 1960 to 14.4 in 1980 and an expected 22.4 per cent at the end of the millennium. (Madigan, 1984: 31b.)

A further dimension to such raw data must be the relative health of Asian growth when compared to that of the rest of the world in the second half of the 1970s, particularly the extent to which the percentage of gross domestic product made up from trade has increased. Peter Drysdale, a long-time student of the Pacific Basin economy (see

Table 7.4 Australia and the Asia–Pacific region, some selected comparative data[a]

	Total population (millions) mid-1982	Area (thousands of square kilometres)	Gross Domestic product (US$ million) 1960	Gross Domestic product (US$ million) 1982	Gross national product (per capita, US$) 1982	Gross domestic production (average annual growth, %) 1960–70	Gross domestic production (average annual growth, %) 1970–82	Exports as a share of gross domestic product (%) 1960	Exports as a share of gross domestic product (%) 1982	Gross domestic investment as a share of gross domestic product (%) 1960	Gross domestic investment as a share of gross domestic product (%) 1982	Gross domestic investment (average annual growth, %) 1960–70	Gross domestic investment (average annual growth, %) 1970–82
Australia	15.2	7637	16370	164210	11140	5.6	3.1	15	15	28	22	6.7	1.1
Indonesia	156.2	1919	8670	90160	580	3.9	7.7	13	22	8	23	4.6	13.7
Malaysia	14.5	330	2290	25870	1860	6.5	7.7	54	51	14	34	7.5	11.4
Philippines	50.7	300	6960	39850	820	5.1	6.0	11	16	16	29	8.2	9.3
Singapore	2.5	1	700	14650	5910	8.8	8.5	163	196	11	46	20.5	8.7
Thailand	48.5	514	2250	36790	790	8.4	7.1	17	25	16	21	15.8	6.4
China	1008.0	9561	42770	260400	—	5.2	5.6	—	28[b]	23	28	9.8	6.4
Hong Kong	5.2	1	950	24440	5340	—	—	82	100	18	29	6.9	13.6
Japan	118.4	372	44000	1081920	10080	10.4	4.6	11	15	33	30	14.6	3.3
South Korea	39.3	98	3810	68420	1910	8.6	8.6	3	39	11	26	23.6	11.0
USA	231.5	9363	505300	3009600	13160	4.3	2.7	5	9	19	16	5.0	1.3
New Zealand	3.2	269	3940	23820	7920	3.6	1.8	22	29	23	25	3.2	−0.1

Notes: [a] Not all states of the 'geographical' region are included. The socialist states of East Asia are ignored, as are the small states of the Southwest Pacific; Australia's former colony (Papua New Guinea) and the newest but smallest member of ASEAN (Brunei). Those included in the table are Australia's major economic partners of the Asia–Pacific region.
[b] Estimate

Source: World Bank (1984b) World Development Report Tables 1–5, pp. 218–27

Drysdale, 1986), has estimated that the percentages of gross domestic product exported from Northeast Asia and Southeast Asia has grown from 48 to 61 per cent and from 20 to 30 per cent respectively, throughout the 1970s (Drysdale, 1984: 2). Much of this growth, Drysdale notes, has come about through the growth of inter-regional trade within the Pacific to the extent that in the 1980s more than half of the Asian–Pacific trade is of an inter-regional nature.

Japan's gross domestic product, as a quick calculation from Table 7.4 demonstrates was, at US$44 billion in 1960, only slightly larger that that of Australia (US$16.3 billion) and the five ASEAN states (US$20.9 billion) combined. By 1982 the Japanese economy (US$1082 billion) had grown to be three times as large as that of ASEAN and Australia (US$370 billion) combined. The Japanese growth, moreover, has had an impact on ASEAN (see, for example, Robinson, 1985) and Australia as significant as the figures imply—as this chapter will show.

Yet as dramatic as these figures are, we need to keep some sense of perspective. The Pacific Basin has not overwhelmed the other previously developed regions of the global political economy. Rather it has joined Europe and North America as a third, fairly clearly defined, region of economic activity. In ASEAN, Australia's immediate regional neighbour, growth has been a much more recent phenomenon—largely a process of the past ten or fifteen years. Given its contiguity to Australia, its long-term importance is, however, paramount.

Currently Australia preserves a rough, but rapidly dwindling, parity with ASEAN by virtue of the relative size of its gross domestic product. Australian gross domestic product in 1982 was US$164 billion compared to the combined gross domestic product of the, then five, ASEAN states of US$208 billion. Australia's population of just over 15 million in 1982 is dwarfed, however, by an ASEAN population in excess of 270 million. As can be seen from the extrapolations in Table 7.5 however, 1970–82 growth rates repeated over the twenty-five years to 2007 and fifty years to 2032 will give Australia gross domestic products of US$352 billion and US$754 billion (at 1982 constant prices) respectively and, in sharp contrast, projected gross domestic products of US$1234 billion and US$7499 billion for ASEAN. Australia's expected population in the year 2000 is only 21 million, in contrast to an expected population of 377 million for ASEAN (World Bank, 1984b: 254–5).

Australia's decline as an economic power has been a fairly long-term process. From a position in 1870 when its gross domestic product per capita as a ratio of that of the USA was 173 per cent, it dropped by 1980 to 80 per cent (Caves & Krause, 1984: 4). Since the Second World War, per capita growth has been amongst the slowest in the developed world—notwithstanding a reasonable rate of population growth. It has,

Table 7.5 Growth projections for ASEAN and Australia, 1982–2032

	Gross domestic product (US$ billions) 1982	Average annual growth rate (%) 1970–82	Projected gross domestic product in 25 years[a] (US$ billions)	Projected gross domestic product in 50 years[a] (US$ billions)
Australia	164	3.1	352	755
Indonesia	90	7.7	575	3 673
Malaysia	26	7.7	166	1 061
Philippines	40	6.0	172	737
Singapore	15	8.5	115	886
Thailand	37	7.1	206	1 142
ASEAN total	208		1 234	7 499

Note: [a] Projected value = present value $(1 + i)^n$, where i is the annual growth rate and n is the number of years.
Source: For columns 1 and 2 the source is Table 7.4.

however, taken Australia quite a long time to wake up to this erosion. The somnambulant period of the 1950s and 1960s (the 'Menzies era') saw Australia generally quite satisfied with its performance. To be sure, for a long time Australia was fairly well sheltered from the exigencies of the global political economy behind its tariff barriers. The evolution of the new international division of labour has, however, reaped major changes in this situation. External factors (especially post-1973) are extremely influential on the Australian political economy. Since the resource boom of the early 1970s something like 80 per cent of Australian exports have been raw materials and primary produce (see Table 7.1). These exports account for approximately 15 per cent of gross domestic product. Given their subjection to price setting on world markets this means, of course, that changes in the size of Australia's gross domestic product (despite the relatively small share of gross domestic product occupied by trade compared to other developed countries) have been profoundly affected by changes in export values (Caves & Krause, 1984: 8). Australia is similarly integrated into the world's capital markets and thus exhibits exactly the kinds of vulnerabilities of 'small open economies' alluded to earlier in this chapter.

Turning specifically to Australia's trading position in the period after the Second World War, four broad major changes have come about. Firstly, and most obviously, has been the change in the direction of Australia's trade. As can be seen from Table 7.6, Europe in general and the United Kingdom in particular, have declined in importance as partners in almost direct proportion to which the Pacific in general, and Japan in particular, have risen in importance. Initially, Pacific trade saw Japan grow rapidly while the growth of importance of other Pacific states such as Hong Kong, Taiwan and Singapore has been a phenomenon of the past ten to fifteen years. Australia's ASEAN neighbours at this stage are waiting to catch the next wave but are expected to be significant in the future (Ho Kwon Ping, 1980c).

It is in the context of the increasing importance of the Pacific in world trade generally that Australia's trade with the western Pacific has increased threefold over the thirty or so years up to the early 1980s. Thirty per cent of Australia's imports come from Japan and Asia, not to mention in excess of 20 per cent coming from the USA; and over 43 per cent of Australia's exports go to Japan and the Pacific Basin (see notes to Table 7.6 for explanation). Yet this absolute growth of Australian trade with the region contrasts sharply with an actual decline in Australia's degree of penetration of Asian–Pacific markets.

The second major feature of Australian trade history is the degree to which exports as a share of gross domestic product have declined from a high point of about 40 per cent at the time of the Korean War

Table 7.6 Share of Australian exports to and imports from selected trading partners, 1949–81 (annual average, per cent)

Item and country	1949/50 to 1953/54	1954/55 to 1958/59	1959/60 to 1963/64	1964/65 to 1968/69	1969/70 to 1973/74	1974/75 to 1978/79	1979/80 to 1980/81
Imports							
United Kingdom	46.9	41.8	31.1	23.9	19.3	12.3	9.3
European Community[a]	8.8	10.1	11.2	12.2	13.4	14.1	12.6
Japan	1.9	2.7	5.8	10.1	15.5	18.8	17.4
South and Southeast Asia[b]	13.2	12.0	9.7	7.2	7.0	9.6	12.4
United States	11.1	12.9	20.0	24.9	23.0	21.2	22.1
Exports							
United Kingdom	35.0	31.3	21.3	15.4	9.7	4.4	4.4
European Community[a]	21.7	21.4	16.2	13.2	9.9	10.5	8.9
Japan	6.7	11.6	16.4	19.8	28.5	31.2	27.1
Pacific Basin[c]	8.7	9.6	9.0	11.8	12.9	14.2	16.0
United States	9.6	6.8	9.6	12.3	12.2	10.3	11.0
Canada[d]	1.5	1.5	1.7	1.7	2.7	2.5	2.1
New Zealand[d]	3.5	5.7	6.0	5.7	5.4	5.2	4.7

Notes: [a] The European Community excludes the United Kingdom. Ireland and Denmark, are included beginning in 1973/74.
[b] South and Southeast Asia include Bangladesh, Brunei, Burma, Hong Kong, India, Indonesia, Kampuchea, Laos, Macao, Malaysia, Maldive Islands, Pakistan, Philippines, Singapore, Sri Lanka, Taiwan, Thailand and Vietnam.
[c] The Pacific Basin includes Taiwan, Hong Kong, the Republic of Korea, Indonesia, Malaysia, the Philippines, Singapore, Thailand and Papua New Guinea from 1970/71. Before 1970/71, countries included are those listed in note b above.
[d] Data for Canada and New Zealand before 1974/75 are in calendar years beginning 1949.

Sources: Krause (1984): 287; Norton, Garmston & Brodie (1982: 6, 9; Department of Trade and Resources (1983): 19–22. For Canada and New Zealand before 1974/75, see International Monetary Fund, *International Financial Statistics, Yearbook 1979*, Vol. 32; and International Monetary Fund, *Direction of Trade Statistics*, computer tapes.

commodity boom of the 1950s to just under 14 per cent in 1982. As we can see from Table 7.7 the currently static nature of Australian exports as a share of gross domestic product contrasts with the more dynamic pattern of other developed countries. In 1981 exports as a proportion of gross domestic product were smaller in Australia than in any OECD countries, other than the two most economically powerful—the USA and Japan—and the four most economically weak—Greece, Portugal, Spain and Turkey (Helliwell, 1984: 91). That the share of exports in gross domestic product did not decline between 1960 and 1982 was due to the offsetting effect of the growth of services in contrast to the decline of goods as proportions of Australian trade. Explaining the static nature of Australian exports as a proportion of gross domestic product is difficult. But the range of explanations lie with the third and fourth characteristics of Australia's post-Second World War trade history: namely the nature of commodity concentration and its comparative position in world trade generally.

The chief feature of Australian exports throughout the twentieth century has been the preponderance of natural resources in these exports. With a proportion varying between two-thirds and four-fifths of total exports, Australia has a profile unique among developed countries, no others of which have such a specialisation in the export of natural resources. This degree of specialisation has varied over the years, of course, depending on the nature of world market demand, climatic conditions and technological innovation. But while the mix of the exports may have undergone significant change, the basic structural pattern has changed little. The most notable change has been in the dramatic decline of wool exports (from nearly 50 per cent of total exports in the 1950s to 10 per cent in the early 1980s) and a sharp rise in the export of minerals and metals (from about 6 per cent in the early 1950s to close to 40 per cent in the late 1970s). Manufactures as a share of exports remained fairly static in this period (see Table 7.3).

Table 7.7 Exports as a percentage of gross domestic product for selected industrial countries, 1960–82

	1960	1982
Australia	15	15
Canada	18	27
France	15	21
Germany	19	31
Sweden	23	33
USA	5	9

Source: World Bank (1984b) World Development Report p. 227

The fourth factor to note is the comparative one, that Australian trade has grown slower than world trade generally. Between 1970 and 1980 the volume of world trade grew at 5.6 per cent per annum, whilst Australian trade increased by only 3.6 per cent per annum (Krause, 1984: 278). Further, Australian trade over the period 1939–75 dropped from 2.5 to 1.25 per cent of world trade (see Johnson, 1984: 696). In short, Australia has failed to hold its own share of world trade in an era when growth through trade has been the order of the day for many countries—developed and developing.

From the Australian point of view the reasons for this in the context of the new international division of labour are somewhat alarming. In contrast to those rapidly growing NICs that are being incorporated into NIDL, but in common with many of the poorer LDCs, especially those in Africa (see Higgott, 1986a), Australia is undergoing a process of 'marginalisation' through its unfortunate specialisation in export commodities with a low-value-added component which are unable to hold their share of overall world trade. To add to this Australia appears unable to hold its own overall. For example, whilst world agricultural production between 1971 and 1981 grew at the rate of 4.2 per cent per annum, Australian agriculture only managed an average annual increase of 0.8 per cent. The figures for manufacturing over the same period were 6.7 per cent and 2.2 per cent respectively. Only in mining was the trend reversed with Australia growing at an annual rate of 7.6 per cent in contrast to world growth of 1.4 per cent (Krause, 1984: 281).

The evolution of the new international division of labour exposed the weaknesses in Australia's long-held pursuit of inward-looking manufacturing strategies behind high tariff walls. Such strategies remained largely unquestioned in Australia until the late 1960s, and it was not until Gough Whitlam's 1972 across-the-board 25 per cent reduction that tariffs had been lowered since Federation in 1901. Notwithstanding this 1972 reduction, Table 7.8 illustrates the degree to which Australia is a high tariff country.

Table 7.8 The tariff level on dutiable items, 1978 (%)

	General	Manufactured goods
USA	9	9.5
EEC	9	9
Japan	11	12.5
Canada	14	14.2
Australia	18	23

Source: Warr (1983) p. 30 n.l.

Further, the progressive slide in the efficiency of Australian manufactures would indicate that protectionism has not worked efficiently for a long time. Inward-looking strategies and the nature of assistance to industry to support production for the home market of goods in which Australia has no comparative advantage (real or engineered) has proved detrimental to a forceful approach towards production for export. In the context of the NIDL this contrasts markedly with the recent history of Japan and the NICs of the Pacific. In these states we have seen greater innovation in the use of new technologies and greater economic flexibility, especially in the pursuit of outward-oriented strategies, and perhaps most importantly the role of the state has been one geared towards intervention, but intervention to enhance export competitiveness, in ruthless fashion if necessary (see for example, Hofheinz & Calder, 1982; Robison, 1985; Rodan, 1985a and 1985b). The existence of these factors is harder to identify in the Australian context of the growth period of the 1960s and 1970s.

The importance of trade to Australia at the level of rhetoric always outstripped the facts of post-Second World War performance as Australia actually, at one level, became less of a trading nation. That Australia's trade grew in volume was in large part due to a pull effect from the new industrialisers in the region demanding Australia's raw materials, first and foremost of course being Japan. It has been growth in the Asian–Pacific region—both absolutely and relatively vis-a-vis other regions of the world—that has helped Australia's exports maintain their purchasing power against imports despite the fact that its share of world trade has declined. In a relative sense, however, the low-value-added nature of Australia's principal exports has contributed to a decline in the purchasing power of Australia's exports relative to many of the other nations of its region (see Johnson, 1984). Without the resource boom the balance of export purchasing against imports would not have been maintained. The reason for this is well documented. While the value of goods exported between 1950 and 1981 has in fact exceeded the value of goods imported for all but eight of those years, the value of services exported has *always* been exceeded by the value of services imported. Thus, whilst a surplus in visible traded goods has been achieved, a deficit has been the order of the day in invisible trade. This has meant in practice that in all but four years between 1961 and 1982 Australia has run a deficit on its current account (for discussion see Crough & Wheelwright, 1982: 166; and Dornbusch & Fischer, 1984: 32). The significance of this position becomes clear when we contrast Australia with the small European states in Katzenstein's study, which tend to run a balance of payments deficit on traded goods which they offset with a surplus on their trade in invisibles. Australia has the reverse profile.

Without its resource wealth, Australia would have had severe problems. Its resources helped it share in Japan's dramatic growth. Indeed Japanese growth was the agent of Australian export growth. From 1949–54 to 1979–81, Australian exports to Japan grew from 6.7 per cent of total to 27 per cent of total, while Japanese exports to Australia in the same period grew from 2 per cent to in excess of 17 per cent (see Table 7.6). Japan's role as Australia's major partner did, however, peak in the mid-1970s. Further, between 1972 and 1980 Australia's share of Japanese imports declined from 9.4 to 5 per cent of total.

This pattern is repeated at the wider level in Asia. While Asian trade is increasingly important for Australia, the converse is not the case. This is because Asian trade, in direct contrast to Australian trade, is growing faster than world trade overall. This disparity in the rates of Asian growth and Australian growth is more important than the barriers that protect Australian markets from Asian manufactures. The implication of this pattern of growth is quite clear. There is a growing asymmetry of need between Australia and its regional neighbours. Much more important to the growing economies of the Asian region than a healthy relation with Australia, with a market of only 15.5 million people, is an increased trading relationship with the faster-growing markets of Europe and North America. Prime Minister Lee of Singapore, for example, has shown a noticeable lack of reticence in pointing out Australia's increasing irrelevance to Asian countries in the formulation of their economic and trading policies.

In the past Australia has been cushioned by its income from resource exports, but it will in the long run need to restructure the 'mix' of its exports if it is to get a greater share of world trade. This is easier said than done. As is widely acknowledged by policymaking in all sectors in Australia, the country has a poor track record when it comes to the possession of an efficient outward-oriented manufacturing sector quick to innovate and adjust to changes in market requirements in international trade. Yet it has been those states of the Asian–Pacific region that have been successful in the process of export-oriented industrialisation that have fared best in NIDL. Australia, as the figures suggest, has undergone a process of gradual 'marginalisation'.

A further manifestation of this marginalisation is reflected in the nature of capital investment in Australia. In the current phase it seems unlikely that Australia will see a sufficiently large relocation of capital into those sectors of the economy that will produce, along with the necessary technological innovation, high-value-added goods for export. Australia's capital import pattern is in fact quite well established. Prior to the mid 1960s Britain and the USA were the major investors, primarily in the Australian manufacturing sector and spurred on by the self-contained and protected nature of the Australian market. Since that time, however, the pattern has been one of a sharp move away from investment in manufacturing towards multinational investment in Australia's mining and resource industries. This general analysis is accepted by both neo-classical analysts of the Australian economy (see Kasper et al., 1980) and analysts of a dependencia perspective on Australia's position in the global economy (see Crough & Wheelwright, 1982: 102–9). What is contested is the size of foreign investment in Australia and its impact on the Australian economy and national sovereignty. These broader issues cannot be canvassed fully here, save to say that the dependency theorists are the ones whose figures tend to be on the high side, whereas the figures in the Brookings Report, for example, are somewhat lower. Yet even if we utilise the more moderate figures, and the analytical insights that the Brookings Institute draws from them, we still find support for an interpretation of the new international division of labour which sees capital locating to specific sectors of national economies conditioned by a logic of accumulation that is global rather than national. According to the Brookings commissioned survey, up to 60 per cent of the Australian mining industry is under foreign control, whilst the level of foreign equity in Australian manufacturing currently stands at about 40 per cent of total (Krause, 1984: 302). Perhaps more significantly the increase of foreign direct investment in the Australian mining industry came at a time when foreign direct investment was decreasing from about 16–18 per cent of domestic investment in the late 1960s to 10–11 per cent at the end of the 1970s. At the risk of overgeneralisation, Australia's attractiveness to international capital was in the resources it had to offer, rather than in areas of activity with higher-value-added and technological requirements.

The nature of investment in Australia has changed not only sectorally but also in terms of the origins of investment, albeit at a slower pace. Whilst we must not underestimate the continuing importance of Australia's traditional sources of capital in Europe and North America, it is interesting to note that for the June quarter of 1984 ASEAN was the source of the largest investments in Australia, supplying A$583 million out of a total of A$1187 million. The important factor is the pattern rather than the amount. Asian investment in Australia has been, give or take fluctuations, on the rise for the past decade.

Australia and Japan

Turning from the broad Pacific region, there are two specific relationships that are important for Australia, namely those with Japan and ASEAN. Enough has been written about the evolution of the relationship with Japan not to warrant discussion here. (See, *inter alia*, Stockwin, 1972; Drysdale & Kitaoji, 1981; Whitlam, 1981: 79–94; Rix, 1982.) Several points are of importance, however. Japan's rise to the position of the world's second largest market economy was the major influence on the volume and pattern of Australia's trade throughout the 1960s and 1970s. After nearly three decades of close economic relations (Australia granted Japan 'most-favoured nation' status in 1957) the elements of a strong economic dependency of Australia on Japan are firmly in place.

Japan, in the first instance, has by far the strongest hand in the trading relationship, notwithstanding that Australia is the possessor of the raw materials and primary produce. Japan is quite successfully diversifying its sources of supply of coal and iron ore, and Australia is forced more and more to compete with other producers for its share in the Japanese market. This is not, of course, to say that Australia's importance to Japan is insignificant. The trade relationship between the two still ranks as one of the strongest bilateral trading partnerships in the world, although it has undergone a process of decline from its peak in the mid-1970s. In 1972 Australian exports to Japan represented nearly 10 per cent of Japan's total imports. By 1980 that figure had slumped to 5 per cent. This decline has been due not only to Japan's abilities to diversify sources of supply, but also because of its move into less-energy-intensive, higher-technology industries. This decline has been offset to a degree by the growth of South Korea and Taiwan as steel producers and the increase in Australia's provision of raw materials to them. China too is playing an increasingly important role in this respect. (*FEER*, 19 January 1984: 86; and Hayden, 1984.) Japan has, in Australia, a highly lucrative secondary market for its manufactured goods, especially high-value-added consumed durables such as cars and electronics.

From Japan's perspective the current relationship is very suitable. Things have changed considerably from the 1950s and early 1970s when Japan was exhorting Australia to produce all the coal and iron it could. Now Japan has a variety of sources, and Australia has been forced to adjust prices accordingly over the past few years in an attempt to maintain its proportion of the provision of Japan's iron and coal needs. Policy today is geared to the preservation of Australia's 'market share' of Japanese imports, but Japan steadfastly refuses to be drawn on such a commitment. The Japanese communique issued after Prime Minister Hawke's visit to Tokyo in early 1984 said '...the *position* of Australia as a supplier of primary products including minerals will not decline so long as these Australian products *maintain their competitiveness and their stable supply is assured*' (emphasis added).

In his visit to Australia in January 1985, Prime Minister Nakasone reaffirmed this position, placing particular emphasis on Australia's ability to be a stable, reliable deliverer of raw materials (just as a strike broke out on the railways!). In particular the visit did nothing to allay the fears of a likely diminution of Australia's market share of beef exports to Japan in the face of pressure for an increased market share from the more politically powerful USA, armed with a US$40 billion deficit on trade with Japan with which to bargain (Byrnes, 1984: 13). Australia's share fell from 75 to 60 per cent in 1984, despite 'assurances' Bob Hawke insisted he had earlier received in Tokyo. There is nothing to prevent a similar drift happening with the market shares of coal and iron ore. Japan is under pressure from the USA not only to take more beef but also to buy American West Coast coal.

Problems in the Australia–Japan relationship are also as much a matter of style as of substance. There is a qualitative asymmetry in the relationship as well as a quantitative one. Australia has never pushed itself as a trading nation, rather it has been content to be pulled along or trade only with the 'easy countries' (Ramsey, 1985: 33). Australian policy has been a 'no risk' or 'safety first' policy of doing what it is used to, rather than grasping innovative nettles.

> ...Australians in Japanese eyes, (for example) for the most part are regarded as farmers and, more recently petitioners in the technology stakes... this helps drain what little clout Australia might have in the Tokyo market place. [Byrnes, 1984: 13]

Whilst Australia's bilateral relationship with Japan is of the utmost importance it also needs to be seen in a three-way sense as well. The following discussion of Australian–ASEAN relations makes sense only if we appreciate the importance of Japan's role as an economic actor, second to none in the Southeast Asian region. Japan is the predominant economic actor in all the major states but the Philippines, where the former colonial power still holds the position as the major external economic influence. In contrast to Australia, Japan, along with the USA and Europe, holds its share of the ASEAN market. Currently Japan accounts for 21 per cent of ASEAN trade as opposed to 15 per cent for the USA, 13 per cent for Europe and only 2 per cent for Australia. Comparable levels of importance can be found in Japanese and Australian investment in ASEAN. Japan's average of 25–30 per cent of total investment in the region (except in Singapore) contrasts with an Australian average of less than 3 per cent (*Australia and ASEAN*, 1984: 127). Australia's role in the ASEAN–Japan–Australia triangle is one of increasing dependence on, but increasingly less importance to, the other parties.

There are, of course, alternative scenarios to the ones of increasing asymmetry that have been outlined. The changing pattern of Japan's industrial and economic growth in the context of the regional division of labour is going to have a strong and continuing impact. Although Japan's major involvement is in the other rapidly developing states of the western Pacific region these states are close to creating a market comparable in size to that of Japan. These regions should, according to Peter Drysdale, for example, provide opportunities for Australia comparable to that of Japan in the 1960s and 1970s. China, particularly, could be an important new buyer of Australia's raw materials. As Drysdale goes on to say: 'Australia's trade could more than double over a decade if it maintains its overall share of regional trade' (1984: 8–12). While foodstuffs and raw materials will form the lion's share of this trade, Drysdale does hope for increased exports of value-added-goods such as processed commodities and services.

Projections like these must be seen at this stage, however, as possibilities rather than probabilities. Australia has not shown the capability to maintain its regional market share in the context of overall growth over the past two decades, as Drysdale himself has noted. And up to the advent of the Hawke Labor government in March 1983, Australia had done little to convince observers of the prospects of the necessary adjustment being made to the structure of industry to suggest an inroad of any magnitude being made into regional export markets for manufactured goods of either a labour-intensive or technologically intensive nature (on Australian prospects see Tisdell, 1985).

The status, shape and prospects for economic co-operation in the Pacific Basin are sufficiently ambiguous for us not to automatically assume the emergence of a complementary regional division of labour from which *all* states will inevitably benefit—as some of the more optimistic would hope (see, for example, Duncan, 1983). Nor has Pacific Basin co-operation developed to the degree of conspiratorial sophistication that some critics of 'Pacific Rim strategies' would have us believe (see Crough and Wheelwright, 1982: 58–84). The current status of Pacific unity is in fact much more fluid than either of these two positions would suggest. Certainly Japan, strongly supported by the USA, would like to see some degree of institutionalisation of co-operation. Japan particularly, given its predominance in the region's economic growth, would benefit from this.

In contrast, the ASEAN countries, as a group and as individual states, are much less wedded to greater institutionalisation of economic co-operation at the wider Pacific level. They are currently more concerned with increasing economic activity and co-operation much closer to home (see Garnaut, 1980). Greater Pacific co-operation it is felt, especially in some of the less-developed states of the region such as Indonesia, would tie them more firmly than they would like into the predominantly lower levels of industrial activity of a regional division of labour (Sung-Joo, 1983). ASEAN states are not, however, above suggesting a specific role for Australia in the regional division of labour as a provider of raw materials for their available labour forces. Malaysian Prime Minister Dr Mahathir is, for example, an advocate of three-way co-operation between his state, Australia and Japan, in which Australia would provide the raw materials and Malaysia would provide the secondary processing of these raw materials en route to Japan for use in high-technology activities (*Australia and ASEAN*, 1984: 131–2). As attractive as this may appear to Malaysia, giving it the opportunity to maximise its comparative advantage in cheap labour, it does nothing to overcome Australia's problems as a supplier of low-value-added raw materials for international (or in this context, regional) markets.

Australia and ASEAN

> While Australia will be affected by developments in other regions of the world, and by the global interests of the superpowers, no other part of the world promises to be of more consistent importance to Australia than the region of East and Southeast Asia. (*Australia and ASEAN*, 1984: x)

Thus argues a recent high-level parliamentary report on Australian–ASEAN relations. Subtitled 'Challenges and Opportunities', the report reflects the near obsession that has been reached in policymaking circles over the management of Australia's relations with its immediate regional neighbours. If we accept the extremely small base from which the partnership began, then the growth in the trading relationship has not been insignificant. An 8 per cent growth rate per annum saw the volume of Australian trade with ASEAN grow from A$487 million in 1972–73 to A$3.43 billion in 1983–84. More importantly Australian exports to ASEAN have grown at a faster rate than Australian exports overall: 15 per cent per annum, as opposed to 11.4 per cent per annum between 1978–79 and 1983–84. During the same period ASEAN's imports to Australia grew at 14 per cent per annum. Currently ASEAN as a group (albeit most trade takes place at a bilateral level) is now Australia's fourth largest trading partner, providing just over 5 per cent of Australian imports and taking about 9 per cent of Australia's exports (*Australia and ASEAN*, 1984: 133).

When we look at the relationship from the other side of the glass a somewhat different picture emerges. Australia's importance to ASEAN is marginal. It is a market for only 2.6 per cent of ASEAN exports and a provider of only 3 per cent of ASEAN's imports. These figures recorded for 1981 have undergone a decline in the short term. The figures for 1983 are 1.7 and 2.5 per cent, respectively (*Australia and ASEAN*, 1984: 133).

Notwithstanding the fact that the economic relationship with ASEAN is essentially a six-fold bilateral relationship, there would appear to be little dispute over the asymmetry of need in the relationship being biased heavily against Australia. Further, while the economic relationships are primarily bilateral, the individual members are nevertheless able to mobilise the organisation's support in the face of a major economic dispute with a third party. The prime example of ASEAN acting as a bloc in international economic issues was the international civil aviation dispute at the end of the 1970s when ASEAN collectively supported Singapore International Airlines in its dispute with Australia (see Lawe-Davies, 1981).

A second area in which ASEAN often criticises Australia is over the trade surpluses that run heavily in Australia's favour. These, however, can turn into deficits for Australia when invisibles are taken into account. In 1981–82, for example, a A$180 million surplus, when a A$545 million flow of invisibles was taken into account, turned into a deficit for Australia of A$365 million. The three major reasons for this deficit on invisibles was profit repatriation to ASEAN, widespread Australian travel in ASEAN countries, but above all, the high cost of freight for Australian goods using non-Australian shipping services (*Australia and ASEAN*, 1984: 134). This deficit is unlikely to change in the foreseeable future, given Australia's reliance on foreign shipping to move its low value-to-weight ratio bulk commodities.

Services such as transport, travel, tourism, insurance and other commercial and technical services now make up over a quarter of world trade and are increasing rapidly. Australia has been fairly slow in recognising this growth area and indeed only in the past couple of years has its potential been given closer scrutiny (see *Report of the Committee to Review the Australian Overseas Aid Programme*, 1984; Scutt, 1985; Higgott, 1986b). Australia is not, however, expanding services as a section of its exports as quickly as some of its regional neighbours. Its 15 per cent service export as a percentage of total exports is larger than Indonesia's (7%), the same as Malaysia's (15%), but smaller than Thailand's (27%), and the Philippines and Singapore (both 35%) (*Australia and ASEAN*, 1984: 143).

We must not lose sight of the fact that ASEAN has to be disaggregated. Australia's dealings are still primarily of a bilateral nature and some quite clearly more difficult to manage than others. Australia's neighbours also differ in their levels of development. Indonesia, the largest, nearest and potentially most powerful neighbour, is still in character an LDC, as opposed to Singapore, which is one of the world's most successful NICs. Singapore's move into the second wave of industrialisation in high-technology (Rodan, 1985b), high-value-added production contrasts with Indonesia's emphasis on more rudimentary labour-intensive activities reminiscent of Singapore a decade ago.

These different levels of development and, by consequence, different degrees of integration into the global division of labour condition the nature of Australia's regional bilateral relations. So too, of course, do political and security factors which go beyond the scope of this paper (but see, *inter alia*, Brown, 1980; Lim 1980 and 1985; Mackie, 1981; Frost, 1982; Nicholas, 1983) except to acknowledge the degree to which the political and economic relationships are not mutually exclusive.

The role of government in adjusting to a regional political economy

Discussion so far has suggested a variety of structural factors to explain Australia's 'location' in the emerging division of labour in the Asia–Pacific region. This is not the same, however, as implying a total determinism of such constraints. To do so would be to ignore the complicating dimensions of governmental 'will' and 'capacity' in the face of trends in both the global and regional political economy.

It was suggested earlier, following Katzenstein's analysis of small European states, that there were a variety of political correlates to a perceived position of openness and vulnerability in the international division of labour, particularly tendencies towards corporatist forms of policymaking. Nothing has yet been written on Australia which anywhere near approaches the analytic specificity and quality of Katzenstein's study of the small European states in the international economy (but see Loveday, 1985, for a sceptical view). As he suggests, in what might hopefully prove a useful working definition for future analysis of the political responses of Australian government policy towards incorporation into the regional division of labour: 'In the areas of economic policy, corporatism can be viewed as a response to openness to, and dependence on, the world economy'. In elaborating on this definition Katzenstein goes on to highlight some of the central components of his corporatist model:

> ...the voluntary, co-operative regulation of conflicts over economic and social issues through highly structured and interpenetrated sets of political relationships by business, the unions and the state, augmented at times by political parties...Alternatively, corporatism may be viewed as a particular institutional mechanism concentrating power in the attempt to manage dependence. [Katzenstein, 1983: 116 and 128]

Whatever nomenclature one may choose to use, the election of an Australian Labor Party government led by Bob Hawke in 1983 has given rise to a rhetoric of 'consensus politics' (Katzenstein talks of 'social relationship'); the utilisation of the 'politics of summitry' leading to the 'Accord' between major groups in the economy; the establishment of bodies such as the Economic Planning Advisory Committee (EPAC) and the Advisory Committee on Prices and Incomes (ACPI); and signs of the beginning of an industry policy in the re-establishment of the Australian Manufacturing Council. These initatives, and the establishment of several other ancillary bodies, place an emphasis on the co-operation of state, capital and labour unprecedented in Australian history (see Dow, 1984).

This is not the place to analyse such initiatives, but rather to note that they are, along with a variety of other initiatives at both federal and state levels in Australia, geared towards one major end: stemming the process of national decline that is widely believed to be taking place. Two main elements in this process are perceived as essential to success. Firstly and central to this chapter, is the necessity to find a proper and prosperous niche in the regional political economy. Secondly, and the success of the first element depends on this, is the intention to bring about a process of structural adjustment of the domestic economy.

Structural adjustment: problems and prospects

Central to discussion of the Australian political economy over the past four years (largely irrespective of ideological perspective) has been the notion that Australia must adjust if it is to reverse, or even at best arrest, that process of decline down the list of affluent states. The Hawke Labor government has been much more circumspect than the previous Labor administration of Gough Whitlam (1972–75) but much more aware of the issues than the intermediate Liberal–National Party administrations of Malcolm Fraser (1975–83).

By the time the Hawke government had come to power it was evident that the supposed 'resources boom' of the 1970s (discussed earlier) was not going to provide compensatory employment opportunities for jobs in Australia's secondary manufacturing industries. There has been neither a flow-on of growth in the service industries nor vast injections of capital into technologically innovative industries, anticipated at the outset of the mining boom. Jobs lost in the secondary sector have not been dramatically replaced in the tertiary sector, which has been unable to match competition from more dynamic regional neighbours (see Bowring, 1984).

Further, the need to restructure dramatically is not universally accepted across the economic spectrum in Australia. While there is no question in government circles of the absolute necessity to restructure industry and ultimately reduce tariffs, there are objections from at least two quarters that make unlikely allies. The government position is aptly stated in the words of the foreign minister, Mr Hayden:

> ...while structural change will not be easy or painless it is going to happen. The real question is to what extent it will be foisted upon us, and to what extent we can shape it to maximize benefits and minimize negative aspects. We can seek to delay change but only at the cost of a decline in Australia's living standards, relative to those of countries which adjust more rapidly. [*Australia and ASEAN*, 1984: 171]

And again in the words of the minister for industry and commerce, Senator Button:

> ...we cannot, in general, increase our protective walls. That will lead to stagnation and withdrawal... There are sound international imperatives why we should become more closely integrated with the region, not insulate ourselves from it. [*Australia and ASEAN*, 1984: 171].

Ironically, the opposing view is articulated most clearly by the other arm of the labour movement, the Australian Council of Trade Unions (ACTU), which argues that while Australian industry has to undergo change '...neither current nor foreseeable future economic conditions justify a reduction in protection levels' (*Australia and ASEAN*, 1984: 171). This view, again ironically, but perhaps not surprisingly, is strongly supported by those sectors of the Australian manufacturing industry which get most benefit from the country's existing tariff structure. Whilst the ACTU is quite correct to say that Australia's tariff barriers are highly visible, in contrast to some of the many devices its regional partners use to protect and foster their own nascent industries (on Singapore, for example, see Rodan, 1985b), the fact nevertheless remains that even those most protected of industries (textiles, clothing and footwear) have shed many thousands of workers over the past decade. Indeed between 1974 and 1984 the general manufacturing sector's share of total employment fell by 14.8 per cent to a figure of 17.7 per cent in 1984. This would not, of course, be so drastic if a dramatic process of job-generating restructuring had occurred in other sectors of the economy. For example, whilst employment in the mining industry grew by 26.3 per cent in the same period, it represented in 1984 only 1.4 per cent of total employment. Whilst there was growth in other sectors of the workforce too, these were essentially non-wealth-generating areas such as community services, which grew by 52.5 per cent to represent 17.6 per cent of the total workforce in 1984—that is, the same proportion as manufacturing. Rapid growth in finance, property and business services (44 per cent over a ten-year period) brought it to just slightly under 10 per cent of the total workforce (Mulvey & Norris, 1985: 21).

The importance of these data for this chapter can only really be gleaned in comparative perspective. Comparing Australia with its major Pacific partner, Japan, is extremely instructive in this regard. As can be seen from Table 7.4, both countries had considerably reduced growth rates throughout the 1970s and early 1980s, compared with the 1960s: Japan's growth rate declined from 10.4 per cent per annum during 1960–70 to 4.6 per cent during 1970–82, and Australia's declined from 5.6 to 3.1 per cent over the same period. In Australia, however, this decline in growth was accompanied by a decline of almost 70 per cent in the growth rate in employment compared with a decline of only 37 per cent in Japan. In 1983 Australia's unemployment level, in excess of 9 per cent, contrasted sharply with Japan's, which was only slightly over 2 per cent (for a discussion of these issues see Henderson, 1985). A variety of factors explain the discrepancies between Australia and Japan: notably wage flexibility (contrast Japan's very free system with Australia's centralised and indexed process of wage determination); the flexibility of labour market institutions (contrast Japan's lower rate of unionisation to that of Australia's—30 per cent of the workforce, mostly in company-based unions in Japan, 55 per cent in Australia in some hundred or so trade-based unions); and the role of government and the structure of trade. Whilst all are important, the last two are particularly germane to this discussion.

There is broad agreement in both Australia and Japan of the linkage between wages, employment and international competitiveness. That the impact of this linkage is greater in Japan undoubtedly relates to the structure of Japan's trade. Manufactured goods account for 95 per cent of Japanese exports in the period 1971–82, whilst the figure for Australia in the same period was only 27 per cent. This preponderance of manufactures in exports, the export consciousness and competitiveness of Japanese industry, especially vis-a-vis the growing competition from the other Asian NICs and the lack of competition from imports into Japan, most of which are agricultural produce and raw materials, have all contributed to keep the Japanese wage structure flexible. Australia by contrast sees manufactured goods constituting about three-quarters of its imports—a good deal of which compete with locally produced goods. The lack of competitiveness of local goods has had the effect of unifying both capital and labour, in the affected industries, in seeking government support to protect wage levels and market shares. This relationship over the past 15 or so years has insulated Australian manufacturing from the realities of the global marketplace and been the major block to restructuring in Australian manufacturing industries, although in the long run probably to no avail. The policy has been described by one author 'as attempting to guard a block of ice on a hot day' (Dick, 1984).

The issue of restructuring is, however, a lot more complex than some of its most vehement advocates would suggest. This is especially the case with neo-classical advocates who see it as rational, sensible and therefore inevitable. The major deficiency in their analysis tends to be with regard to the role of government. Always keen to point to the success of Australia's rapidly developing regional neighbours, whom they perceive as advocates of some kind of late-twentieth-century 'laissez-faire', they ignore the very crucial role government has played in the development of these states. If tariffs, they argue, are abolished and market principles are allowed to apply, then 'comparative advantage' will do the rest. Such a position, articulated in a variety of forms (see, for example, Keegan, 1983) ignores a variety of important factors.

In the first instance, there is no guarantee that the abolition of protection will inevitably mean that capital which has been traditionally wasted on inefficient industries, is redirected into new, more competitive sectors of Australian industry (see Robison and Rodan, 1983: 2-5). Secondly, it is by no means clear in which industries, other than the exploration of raw materials and the production of primary produce, Australia has a comparative advantage. Could Australia compete in the computer industry against Japan, or in the production of automobiles against West Germany? This question was even recently acknowledged, in albeit somewhat different manner, in the recent *Australia and ASEAN* report (1984: 175):

> The Committee would not limit any 'comparative advantage' approach to an unimaginative fatalistic assessment of Australia's opportunities in the ASEAN region; otherwise Australia's main economic role in the region might be seen as very much limited to that of efficient primary producer and raw material supplier.

It is also possible that the removal of protective barriers on some manufactures may simply exacerbate an already-existing tendency for other nations to dump their more highly subsidised products on exposed Australian markets. The success of many of Australia's regional neighbours in pursuing outward-looking strategies has not been due to any 'natural' comparative advantage they may have had; but rather to a comparative advantage created by government through the implementation of long-term, government-financed and directed strategies. In many of the success stories of Asian development in the post-war world, the relationship between state and capital has been the crucial element in the creation of any comparative advantage (see, for example, Rodan, 1985a and 1985b on Singapore; and Haggard & Moon, 1983, and Cho, 1985, on South Korea). This state involvement in support of the creation of comparative advantage also engages in activities of a less-savoury nature in some of the regional NICs too (for example, in the suppression of organised labour or the failure to implement environmental and safety legislation).

The vital point that advocates of wholesale tariff abolition, in the cause of restructuring, invariably fail to comprehend is the degree to which the state has provided vast amounts of support to nascent industries in the rapidly developing countries of the region. Governments build infrastructures that corporations would otherwise have to build themselves, they provide long-term credits and tax incentives, they often help subsidise the restructuring of entire industries, but *above all* they provide long-term planning in the pursuit of growth. As Hofheinz and Calder note in their study of East Asia:

> The essence of a growth promoting political environment is neither the presence nor absence of state intervention. It is predictability—predictability of both leadership and commercial policy... A predictable political environment has been especially crucial for developing capital intensive basic industries such as steel and petrochemicals, where investments are so massive and complex that executives will not venture on them if the future seems cloudy and uncertain. [1982: 25–6]

The very predictability and order of many of Australia's neighbours in the Asia–Pacific region contrasts sharply with the political volatility and lack of direction and purpose of Australian governments prior to the advent of the Labor government in 1983. This is not to suggest that Australia has 'turned the corner', despite a somewhat improved economic performance over the last two years. Australia is still not sure of where its comparative advantage may be found in other than primary produce and raw material exploration. Similarly there is no consensus, despite government rhetoric, as to the role government should play in supporting the process of restructuring, although there is now an acknowledgment that any discussion of why Australia's regional neighbours are outperforming it in the regional and global economic order has to take the role of government in coordinating development strategies into very serious account. What is currently prevalent in the Australian political environment, is a recognition that if Australia does not grasp the adjustment nettle now, it may well soon be too late—as Lee Kuan Yew frequently tells Australia. Populist reportage abounds with horror stories of Australia's 'Latin American Future' (*Australian*, 2 December 1985: 2). More important, however, for students of international political economy is the growth of some very serious long-range historical analysis of Australia and, for example, Argentinian parallels (see, for example, Denoon, 1983; Duncan & Fogarty, 1984; Gerardi, 1985).

That the major burden of this adjustment will fall to those sections of the workforce whose jobs are 'restructured away' is in little doubt. It is in this context, the context of educating sectors of the labour movement to acknowledge and to accept the inevitability of job loss in the process of restructuring, that the position of a 'centrist' and 'national' leader like Hawke sitting above the party fray is supposedly important. The role of government was to be twofold in the kind of process Katzenstein describes in his case studies. Firstly, government would bring the population along in the spirit of 'social partnership' and also provide assistance in such things as retraining those who become the casualties of the adjustment process. Secondly, government will provide the ground rules for restructuring in a manner similar to the role played by MITI in Japan and its equivalents in states such as Taiwan, South Korea and Singapore. It is still too early to pass judgment on whether the 'will' and 'capacity' of the current Labor government will match the degree of commitment present in its rhetoric. What is worth considering, by way of conclusion to this section, are the constraints that would still exist and the opportunities that would be opened to an Australian economy undergoing a process of restructuring.

The nature of Australia's regional future is, at one and the same time, fairly straightforward, yet extremely complex. It is straightforward to the extent that a starting point for analysis can be pin-pointed. It is complex inasmuch as how it evolves will depend on a whole array of government policy choices over the short- to mid-term future. Australia's position in the regional environment is neither pivotal nor fixed for all time. As Grant (1983) has noted: 'Asia neither threatens nor beckons Australia, but it is there, offering Australia a chance to respond to its presence as one nation among many rather than as an alien outpost'. Similar themes are echoed extensively around Australia's immediate regional neighbourhood (see, for example, Sopiee, 1984). A widely held perception of the secondary nature of Australia's economic and political role in the region is a starting point for more measured analysis. This is not merely a populist point. It is of analytical importance too. The inability of Australian governments and scholars to recognise, until recently, the dramatic changes taking place in the region has undoubtedly been a factor, albeit an unquantifiable one in Australia's declining position (see McCawley, 1983, for a discussion).

This section has suggested that there are prospects for improvement in Australia's regional economic position, if Australia can learn the lessons of the past and adjust its production patterns in a manner that allows it to be integrated into the region other than as a producer of raw materials and primary produce. Further, while the international division of labour should in no way be seen as deterministic of Australia's (or any state's for that matter) future position, it does provide a strong structural influence which requires both governmental will and capacity to combat it.

Particularly, Australia requires the creation of a much stronger export and trading ethic which, for historical reasons outlined earlier, has traditionally been lacking. Given the trade-oriented nature of growth in the region, Australia's living standards seem destined to decline in the absence of a quantitative and qualitative leap in Australian export performance. For this to happen, a variety of problems seem to need solving: for example, the creation of an industrial economic base geared towards optimising export activity rather than just serving a domestic market is required. Similarly, the removal of an 'industrial cultural cringe' mentality which has traditionally led Australia manufacturers not to consider exporting as a vital activity must be overcome (see Ferris, 1984). If Australia's economic position is to be maintained and consequently what political influence it has not to be lost, then it has no choice but to adopt more outward-looking strategies towards the region. Australia's traditional inward-looking posture is still associated in the minds of its regional neighbours with its Eurocentric past. That there is a recognition of major change in Australia's current position, albeit that some sections of the community would resist it if it could, is a sign not only of national maturation but, perhaps more importantly, an acknowledgement of geo-political reality.

The success of Australian government policy since the change of government in March 1983 has been mixed. Rhetoric and activity have certainly set regional neighbours thinking very closely about the *bona fides* of Australia's desire to be 'of the region' as well as simply 'in the region'—particularly to the extent that Australia can, and wants to, participate in regional growth. This recognition of the economic facts of life has put relations on a more realistic footing than prior to the advent of the Labor government, deteriorating political relations with Indonesia notwithstanding. Labor has signalled a commitment to carry out policies of structural adjustment noticeably absent during the days of the Fraser administration, when Australian policy towards the region reflected more Fraser's priorities with the 'high politics' of Soviet expansionism and the degree to which ASEAN could be a check to it in Australia's neighbourhood (see Brown, 1980), regardless of Fraser's rhetoric of free trade. Despite such a shift of emphasis, it is still recognised in policymaking circles that Australia's economic prospects in the region will be conditioned by the degree to which its regional neighbours perceive Australia as being sympathetic towards, and its policies in tune with, their interests.

Conclusion

The aim of this chapter has been to analyse the nature of Australia's contemporary economic crisis. While recognising that there are a variety of levels at which such analysis can take place, it has chosen to focus not on the internal domestic concerns and responses of day-to-day Australian politics, but rather on Australia as but one actor on a wider international stage. Consequently, its thrust has been threefold: at a conceptual level it has argued the analytic utility of the concept of a new international division of labour; at an empirical level it has attempted to locate Australia within this division of labour; and at an academic-cum-scholarly level it has, by implication, argued the need for an 'international political economy of Australian foreign policy' to complement existing approaches which have tended to emphasise the politico-*strategic* dimensions of Australia's position in its international (both global and regional) environments at the expense of the politico-*economic* ones.

I have argued elsewhere how and why this tendency existed and why it was indefensible in intellectual terms (see Higgott, 1986c). In the discussion of Australia in economic crisis this chapter has demonstrated why it is doubly inappropriate in practical terms to ignore the importance of the systemic factors of the international political economy at the expense of those of the international system of states. Nothing better illustrates this assertion than the implicit declaration of 'open war' between the USA and Europe in the area of farm exports. What for several years had been a 'phoney war' has come to an end with the introduction into law of the US Farm Bill and the policy of commodity (e.g. wheat and sugar) subsidy. Whilst the target of the policies may well be the Europeans—in the words of one of the drafters of the US Farm Bill, 'We're now going to fight the Europeans head to head to change their policies' (*West Australian*, 15 August 1986: 10)—countries such as Australia will be the major victims. While space and timing preclude its discussion here, we should note that the international agricultural policy of the US may well be the catalyst for the most serious rift in American–Australian relations since the beginning of that relationship. Unlike the broader elements of the relationship, such as New Zealand's departure from ANZUS, it cannot be explained in politico-strategic terms.

I have suggested in this chapter that it is possible to isolate political and economic, and global and regional, imperatives from each other. Yet this, it needs to be stressed, is a heuristic device utilised in the interests of *analysis*. *Policymaking* is a much more complex process in which global and regional *interests* cannot be separated and in which they are subject to the two-way pull of conflicting domestic and international political and/or economic priorities—such is the nature of contemporary international interdependence and dependence where economies and societies are incorporated into the global political economy and the international system of states.

Rather, in its 'location' of Australia in the international division of labour since the Second World War, the chapter has suggested that this evolving division has provided the major structural constraint on Australian economic development. It has, however, been at pains to stress that, as crucial as a NIDL may be in 'structuring' Australia's regional economic order, Australia's position is not 'determined' by it alone. Other factors have been, and are, of major importance. Particularly significant has been Australia's colonial heritage and its contemporary political culture. The major aspects of this political culture again received only scant treatment, but several important variables in any future analysis of Australia's location in the international political economy emerged. The most notable is the degree to which Australian governments can, or cannot, exercise both 'will' and 'capacity' to adjust to regional and global economic imperatives that the kind of structural analysis conducted in this chapter indicates to be major factors in helping to explain Australia's current economic crisis.

Notes

Chapter 3

While I alone am responsible for the final product, I wish to acknowledge the advice and criticism of the following: Ben Kerkvliet, Dick Robison, Suchai Treerat, Kraisak Choonhavan, Ken Young, John Girling, Jamie Mackie and Bandid Nijathaworn. (KH)

1 For a critique of the concept of 'comparative advantage' see Rodan (1985a: 183–7).
2 EOI has never completely replaced ISI as a development strategy in Thailand. However, what is being emphasised here is that these strategies represent differing ideological orientations and the political forces that line up behind a particular political strategy.
3 It should be remembered that balance of payments figures are not necessarily an accurate indication of foreign capital flows and the activities of TNCs. Nevertheless, these figures are the best available, and confirm trends present in other sources, such as those produced by the Board of Investment.
4 These figures are certainly underestimates. For a discussion on unemployment see Apichai (1985).
5 On the F-16 issue see Surachat (1985), especially chs 10, 11 and 16.
6 While the World Bank and IMF are not identical, they were established under the same logic: Bretton Woods. In addition, in recent years, there has been a concerted effort to coordinate policies and loans. On this see World Bank (1985c: 52–53).
7 For an examination of the assets and business operations of the groups associated with the Chart Thai Party see Hewison (1983).

Chapter 4

1 To ensure that the transfer of political power did not lead to 'too much' independence, the US Congress imposed various agreements on the Philippines including the infamous Philippine Trade Act (the 'Bell Trade

Notes

Act') which even American observers were to describe as 'obvious infringements on Philippine sovereignty' (Golay, 1961).
2 The Philippine protectionist trade regime should not be equated to apparently similar measures imposed by many nationalist regimes in the Third World such as India, Burma and Tanzania. In these countries a weak indigenous industrial capitalist class—often in its embryo stage—used its control over the state in the post-independence period to reduce the penetration of the domestic market by foreign capital and to resist the related competitive pressures.
3 During the 1960-62 period, when exchange controls were relaxed, many of the foreign investors in the import-substitution industries welcomed it, as it facilitated profit repatriation (Payer, 1974).
4 Concerning industries in the export processing zones (EPZs): To the extent that they raised most of their capital within the domestic capital market and competed for other resources, they were detrimental to the protected industries. However, this adverse impact was very small. In 1983, the five operational EPZs employed a total of 30 574 workers, a tiny fraction of the workforce and certainly not large enough to exert any pressure on wage rates in other industries through a 'pull effect'. They accounted for only 11 per cent of the total non-traditional exports (less than 6 per cent of all exports) in 1982.
5 Despite this growth, however, in the Philippines the share of military expenditure as a proportion of GNP was the lowest in ASEAN. This is an indicator of the fact that the military, while of vital importance to the regime, was not the dominant power.
6 A third factor raising capital inflows to the country was the increase in remittances from Filipino workers attracted by the increased employment opportunities in the Middle East. In 1982, official estimates put this at more than US$800 million; the true figure was probably closer to US$1 billion.
7 The most quoted example is the huge loan for the inoperative Bataan nuclear power plant.
8 A plan to convert some of the debt into equity in domestic firms has been mooted but is yet to be made effective.

Chapter 6

1 Whereas according to the 1931 Census 36 per cent of Singapore Chinese were Straits-born, by 1947 the proportion was as high as 60 per cent and by the mid-1950s 70 per cent (Turnbull, 1982: 234).
2 Investment commitments increased in 1978 by S$416 million or 105 per cent on the previous year (Economic Development Board, *Annual Report 1984/85:* 14).
3 For example, the German–Singapore Institute of Production Technology (GSIPT), the Japan–Singapore Institute of Software Technology (JSIST), and the French–Singapore Institute of Electro-Technology (FSIET).
4 Priority estate projects included: the reclamation and development of Southern Islands as an international petrochemical manufacturing and distribution centre; the development of Loyang as the first centre for

aviation industries, and as an engineering base to support offshore oil and mineral exploration; the development of Seletair Air Base for aviational and aeronautical industries; and the construction of the Singapore Science Park to accommodate industrial and scientific R & D enterprises.

5 SGS-Ates, the Italian-based company which has introduced a wafer-diffusion plant to Singapore, received an interest-free loan of an undisclosed but 'substantial' sum (Duthie, 1985).

6 The Singapore Technology Corporation comprised six companies, all of which were owned by the Sheng-Li holding company which is itself the investment arm of the Defence Department.

7 The complex is comprised of an 'upstream' company which processes natural gas, naphtha and other hydrocarbon feedstocks into intermediate chemicals and four 'downstream' companies transforming these chemicals into a variety of final products. The upstream company is the Petrochemical Corporation of Singapore (PCS), a joint venture made up of 50 per cent Singapore government equity, 10 per cent Japanese government equity and 40 per cent equity by a consortium of thirty-four private Japanese companies led by Sumitomo Chemical Corporation. The downstream projects in the complex involve the Singapore government in varying degrees: 30 per cent in the Polyolefia Company; 30 per cent in Phillips Petroleum Singapore Chemical; 20 per cent in Denka Singapore; and approximately 28 per cent in Ethylene Glycols (see Leung, 1984; Koh, 1982; and *Singapore Economic Bulletin*, June 1980: 25).

8 Under the new constitutions and ties of the nine new industry-based unions, the executive councils of these unions were monitored by a 24-member advisory council consisting of at least one government MP, highly loyal union cadre members, and 'founder members', who are either PAP members or closely associated with the party. Simultaneously, there was a general increase in the number of PAP careerists taking up official positions in the NTUC.

9 For a fuller account of the various policies comprising the 'Second Industrial Revolution', see Rodan (1985b).

10 Foreign investments in textiles declined by 53 per cent, in wearing apparel by 45 per cent, in leather and rubber products by 30 per cent and in wood and cork products by 45 per cent between 1979 and 1983 (Economic Development Board, Singapore, *Annual Report 1984/85:* 12).

11 Arthur D. Little Inc., a private research company, contends that in 1981 the Asia–Pacific region's computer market was about US$73 billion, and that by 1990 this would grow to a massive US$230 billion (Anonymous (d), 1981: 43).

12 These included Apple Computer Inc., Digital Equipment Corporation, Tandon Corporation, Seagate Technology, Maxtor Corporation, and Computer Memories Inc.

13 This increased from S$448 million in 1979 to S$1027 million in 1983 (Economic Development Board, *Annual Report 1984/85:* 12).

14 In 1980 Hong Kong surpassed Singapore in terms of the volume of investment received from Japan-based capital (Hsung, 1982).

References

Abdul, Razak Abdul (1984) 'Joint Ventures Between Malaysian Public Corporations & Foreign Enterprise: An Evaluation' in Lim Lin Lean and Chee Peng Lim (eds) *The Malaysian Economy at the Crossroads: Policy Adjustments or Structural Transformation* Kuala Lumpur: Malaysian Economic Association

Abueva, Jose Veloso (1970) 'The Philippines: Tradition and Change' *Asian Survey* x (1), 56–64

Adam, G. (1971) 'New Trends in International Business: World Wide Sourcing and De-domiciling' *Acta Oeconomica* 7, 349–67

——(1972) 'Some Implications and Concomitants of World Wide Sourcing' *Acta Oeconomica* 8, 309–23

Adriano, F.D. and Adriano, L.S. (1983) 'The Development of Capitalism in Philippine Agriculture: A Critique and Redevelopment' *Philippine Social Sciences and Humanities Review* xlvii (1–4), 33–54

Agarwala, A.M. and Singh, S.P. eds. (1958) *The Economics of Underdevelopment* London: Oxford University Press

Age (various issues)

Akira Suehiro (1985) *Capital Accumulation and Industrial Development in Thailand* Bangkok: Chulalongkorn University Social Research Institute

Amnuai Petchanarong (1978) *Wiwatthanakan kan phukkhat nai prathet thai* Bangkok: Prae Pittaya

Andreff, Wladimir (1984) 'The International Centralization of Capital and the Re-ordering of World Capitalism' *Capital and Class* no. 22, 58–80

Anonymous (a) (1986) 'Chok Tong: CPF Cut and Wage Restraint Key Measures to Beating the Slump' *Straits Times* 27 February, 1

Anonymous (b) (1982) 'Computing for the Future' *Asian Business* December, 65–67

Anonymous (c) (1981) 'Software to get the Hard Sell' *Asian Business* December, 46

Anonymous (d) (1981) 'Computing Singapore's Future' *Asian Business* July, 42–3

Anonymous (e) (1980) '$200M Resin Plant to Start in Two Years' *Singapore Economic Bulletin* June, 25

Anonymous (f) (1975) '17,000 laid off in 1974' *New Nation* 24 January
Anspach, R. (1969) 'Indonesia' in F. Golay, R. Anspach and R. Pfanner (eds). *Underdevelopment and Economic Nationalism in Southeast Asia* Ithaca, N.Y.: Cornell University Press
Apichai Puntasen and others (1985) *Summary of Research Report: Education and Unemployment* Bangkok: Office of the National Education Commission
Ariff, M. and Hill, H. (1985) *Export Oriented Industrialisation: The ASEAN Experience* Sydney: Allen & Unwin
Arndt, Heinz (1975) 'P.T. Krakatau Steel' *Bulletin of Indonesian Economic Studies (BIES)*, xi (2)
——(1983) 'Survey of Recent Developments *BIES* xix (2) *Arthit–wiwat* 9–15 July 1985
Asian Business (various issues)
Asian Development Bank (various issues) *Key Indicators of Developing Member Countries of ADB*, Manila: Asian Development Bank
Asian Finance 15 November 1978
Asian Wall Street Journal (AWSJ) (various issues)
Asiaweek (various issues)
Astbury, S. 'Jakarta's First Contender for International Stardom' *Asian Business* June 1982, 20
Australia and ASEAN (1984) See below, *Report of the Joint Committee on Foreign Affairs and Defence* (1984)
Australian (various issues)
Australian Financial Review (various issues)
Balassa, Bela (1982) 'Structural Adjustment Policies in Developing Countries' *World Development* 10 (1)
Baldwin, R.E. (1975) *Foreign Trade Regimes and Economic Development: The Philippines* New York: Columbia University Press
Bandid Nijathaworn and Narit Chaisut (1985) 'Kan praman pharani tang prathet khong phak rattaban 2528–2576' in Faculty of Economics, Thammasat University (eds). *Wikhritkan nitang prathet khong rattaban thai* Bangkok: Faculty of Economics, Thammasat University, Section 8
Bangkok Bank (1983) *Annual Report 1983* Bangkok
Bangkok Bank Monthly Review (BBMR) (various issues)
Bangkok Post (BP) (various issues)
Bangkok Post (eds) (1983) *Economic Review 1983*, Bangkok, *Bangkok Post*, 31 December
Bangkok World (BW) (various issues)
Bank Negara (various years) *Annual Report* Kuala Lumpur
Bank Negara (various issues) *Quarterly Economic Bulletin* Kuala Lumpur
Bank of Thailand (1955) *Report for the Year 2496 [1953]* Bangkok
Bank of Thailand (1960) *Annual Economic Report 1958* Bangkok
Bank of Thailand Monthly Bulletin (various issues)
Bank of Thailand Quarterly Bulletin (1984) 24 (2)
Bank of Thailand Statistical Bulletin (various issues)
Bautista, Romeo M. (1980) 'Trade Strategies and Industrial Development in the Philippines: With Special Reference to Regional Trade Preferences' in Ross Garnaut (ed.) *ASEAN in a Changing Pacific and World Economy* Canberra: Australian National University Press

―――(1981) 'The 1981-85 Tariff Changes and Effective Protection of Manufacturing Industries' *Journal of Philippine Development* 8 (1-2), 1-20
―――(1984) 'Trade Liberalisation in the Philippines' (mimeo-draft) Washington, DC: IFPRI
Bautista, Romeo M. and Power, John H. & Associates (1979) *Industrial Promotion Policies in the Philippines* Manila: Philippine Institute for Development Studies
Bell, D. (1973) *The Coming of Post Industrial Society: A Venture in Social Forecasting*, Harmondsworth: Penguin
Bello, W., Kinley, D. and Elinson E. (1982) *Development Debacle: The World Bank in the Philippines* San Francisco: Institute for Food and Development Policy
Bhattacharya, A.K. (1980) 'Financial Aid and Private Banking Institutions' in Jorge Lozoya and A.K. Bhattacharya (eds) *The Financial Issues of the New International Economic Order* New York: Pergamon Press
Blundell-Wignell, A. et al. (1985) *Australia's Foreign and Public Sector Debt* Canberra: Economic Planning Advisory Council, paper 6
Boonkong Hunchangsith (1974) Economic Impact of the US Military Presence in Thailand, 1960-72, Ph.D. thesis, Claremont Graduate School
Boonsong K'thana and Chris Sherwell (1985) 'Battle Ahead for Finance Strongman' *Australian Financial Review* 3 September, 14
Booth, Anne (1984) 'Survey of Recent Developments' *Bulletin of Indonesian Economic Studies* xx (3)
Bowring, P. (1982) 'ASEAN's Dark Horse' *Far Eastern Economic Review*, (*FEER*) 22 October, 85
―――(1984) 'Stop Waltzing Matilda' *FEER* 19 January, 79
Broad, Robin (1984) 'The Transformation of the Philippine Economy' *Monthly Review* 36 (1), 11-21
Browett, J. (1985) 'The Newly Industrializing Countries and Radical Theories of Development' *World Development* 13 (7)
Brown, C. (1980) 'Australia-ASEAN Relations' *Australia-Asia Papers* no. 8 Nathan, Qld: Griffith University, Centre for the Study of Australian-Asian Relations
Bryan, Richard (1983) 'Xenophobia or Theory Phobia: Economic Nationalism and the Question of Foreign Investment' *Australian Outlook* 37 (2), 68-73
Buchanan, Iain (1972) *Singapore in Southeast Asia* London: G. Bell & Sons
Business Day (various issues) Manila
Business in Thailand (various issues)
Business Review (1972) December
Byrnes, M. (1984) 'Japan: The Biggest but Maybe not the Best' *Australian Financial Review* 30 August, 13
Caporaso, J. (1978) 'Dependence, Dependency and Power in the Global System: A Structural Analysis' *International Organisation* 32 (1), 13-29
Caves, R.E. and Krause, L.B. (eds) (1984) *The Australian Economy: A View From the North* Sydney: Allen & Unwin for the Brookings Institute
Chai-Anan Samudavanija (1982) *The Thai Young Turks* Singapore: Institute of Southeast Asian Studies
Cheong Kee Cheok and Lim Kok Cheong (1981) 'Implications of the Transfer of Technology and Primary-Ancillary Linkages: A Case Study of the

Electronics and Electrical Industries in Malaysia' in H. Osman-Rani et al. (ed.) *Development in the Eighties* Bangi: Universiti Kebangsaan

Chesada Loohawenchit (1983) *Fiscal Policy Issues in Thailand* Bangkok: Thammasat University, discussion paper series no. 89

Chira Charoenloet (1971) *The Evolution of Thailand's Economy* Bangkok: Thai Watana Panich

Cho, S.K. (1985) 'The Dilemmas of Export-led Industrialization: South Korea and the World Economy' *Berkeley Journal of Sociology* 30, 65–94

Cockerell, Nancy (1984) 'Aerospace Firms Soar Upwards' *Asian Business* November, 68–71

Collier, D. (ed.) (1979) *The New Authoritarianism in Latin America* Princeton: Princeton University Press

Constantino, Renato (1979) *The Nationalist Alternative*, Quezon City: Foundation for Nationalist Studies, Philippines

Coxhead, I.A. (1984) 'The Economics of Direct Seeding: Inducements to and Some Consequences of Some Recent Changes in Philippines Rice Cultivation', unpublished Masters thesis, Australian National University

Crouch, Harold (1976) *The Army and Politics in Indonesia* Ithaca, N.Y.: Cornell University Press

——(1984) *Domestic Political Structures and Regional Economic Co-operation* Singapore: Institute of Southeast Asian Studies, ASEAN Political Studies

Crough, G. and Wheelwright, E. (1982) *Australia: A Client State* Ringwood, Vic: Penguin

Darling, Frank C. (1980) 'Thailand in the 1980s' *Current History* 79, (461), 185–8 and 195

Daroesman, Ruth (1981) 'Survey of Recent Developments' *Bulletin of Indonesian Economic Studies*, xvii (2)

David, C.C. (1983) *Economic Policies and Philippine Agriculture* Working paper 83–02, Philippines Institute for Development Studies, Manila

De Dios, Emmanual S. et al. (1984) *An Analysis of the Philippine Economic Crisis* Quezon City: University of the Philippines Press

Denoon, D. (1983) *Settler Capitalism: The Dynamics of Dependent Development in the Southern Hemisphere* Melbourne: Oxford University Press

Department of Statistics, Malaysia (1981) *Industrial Survey, 1981*

——(1983) *Report on the Financial Survey of Limited Companies, Malaysia, 1983*

Department of Statistics, Singapore *Report on the Census of Industrial Production 1979*

——*Report on the Census of Industrial Production 1983*

——*Yearbook of Statistics Singapore 1983/84*

——*Yearbook of Statistics Singapore 1984/85*

Department of Trade and Resources (Economic Policy Division) (1983) *Pattern of Australian Exports/Imports 1970/71 to 1980/81* Canberra: Australian Government Publishing Service

Dibb, P. (ed.) (1983) *Australia's External Relations in the 1980s: The Interaction of Economic Political and Strategic Factors* Canberra: Croom Helm

Dick, Howard (1982) 'Survey of Recent Developments', *Bulletin of Indonesian Economic Studies* xviii (1)

References

——(1984) 'Restructuring: A Bridge Too Far?' *National Times* 24 February-1 March, 46

——(1985) 'Survey of Recent Developments', *BIES*, xxi (4)

Diebold, W. (1980) *Industrial Policy as an International Issue* New York: McGraw-Hill for the Council on Foreign Relations

Doranilla, Amando (1985) 'The Transformation of Patron-Client Relations and its Political Consequence in Postwar Philippines' *Journal of Southeast Asian Studies* xvi (1), 99–116

Dornbusch, R. and Fischer, S. (1984) 'The Australian Macroeconomy' in R.E. Caves, and L.B. Krause (eds). *The Australian Economy: A View From the North*, Sydney: Allen & Unwin for the Brookings Institute

Dow, G. (1984) 'The Case for Corporatism: A Second Look at the Hawke Government's Tendencies Towards "Corporatism"' *Australian Society* 3 (11), 22–4

Drysdale, P. (1984) *Pacific Growth and Economic Interdependence*, Perth: Australian Institute of International Affairs, May mimeo

——(1986) *The Economics of International Pluralism: Economic Policy in the Pacific Community* Sydney: Allen & Unwin for the Australian Institute of International Affairs

Drysdale, P. and Kitoaji, H. (eds) (1981) *Japan and Australia: Two Societies and Their Interaction* Canberra: Australian National University Press

Duncan, T. and Fogarty, J. (1984) *Australia and Argentina: On Parallel Paths* Melbourne: Melbourne University Press

Duncan, W. (1983) 'Towards a Pacific Community' *Canberra Times*, 31 May, 8

Duthie, Stephen (1985) 'Economic Problems Plague Singapore' *Asian Wall Street Journal* 21 May

East, M.A. (1973) 'Size and Foreign Policy Behaviour: A Test of Two Models' *World Politics* 25 (4)

ECAFE (1959) *Economic Survey of Asia and the Far East 1958*, Bangkok: ECAFE

——(1964) *Economic Survey of Asia and the Far East 1963*, Bangkok: ECAFE

Economic Development Board, Singapore *Annual Report 1981/82*

——*Annual Report 1982/83*

——*Annual Report 1983/84*

——*Annual Report 1984/85*

Edwards, C.B. (1975) Protection, Profits and Policy: An Analysis of Industrialization in Malaysia, Ph.D thesis, University of East Anglia

Edwards P.G. (1983) *Prime Ministers and Diplomats: The Making of Australian Foreign Policy* Melbourne: Oxford University Press

Evans, P.B., Rueschemeyer, D. and Skocpol, T. (eds) (1985) *Bringing the State Back In* Cambridge: Cambridge University Press

Far Eastern Economic Review (eds) (1986) *Asia Yearbook 1986*

Far Eastern Economic Review (*FEER*) (various issues)

Feith, H. (1980) 'Repressive Developmentalist Regimes in Asia: Old Strengths, New Vulnerabilities' *Prisma* 19 December, 39–55

Ferris, W.D. (1984) *Lifting Australia's Performance as an Exporter of Manufactures and Services* Canberra: Australia Government Publishing Service

Foy, Choy Peng (1983) 'Don't Block Moves to Form House Unions' *Singapore Monitor* 27 July

Frank, Charles R. and Cline, William R. (1970) 'Debt Servicing and Foreign Assistance' *Development Digest* 8 (1), 102–13

Frobel, Folker (1982) 'The Current Development of the World Economy' *Review* V, spring

Frobel, F., Heinrichs, J. and Kreye, O. (1978) 'The New International Division of Labour' *Social Science Information* 17, 123–42

——(1980) *The New International Division of Labour* Cambridge: Cambridge University Press

Frost, F. (1982) 'ASEAN and Australia' in A. Broinowski (ed.) *Understanding ASEAN* London: Macmillan

Galante, Steven (1985) 'Chip Automation is Hitting Jobs in Asia' *Asian Wall Street Journal* 20 August

Gamble, A. (1981) *Britain in Decline* London: Macmillan

Garnaut, R. (ed.) (1980) *ASEAN in a Changing Pacific and World Economy* Canberra: Australian National University Press

Gerardi, R.E. (1985) *Australia, Argentina and World Capitalism 1830–1945* Sydney: Transnational Corporations Research Project

Girvan, Norman and Bernal, Richard (1982) 'The IMF and the Foreclosure of Development Options: The Case of Jamaica' *Monthly Review* 33 (9), 34–48

Glassburner, Bruce (1971) 'Economic Policy-Making in Indonesia 1950–57' in Glassburner (ed.) *The Economy of Indonesia* Ithaca, N.Y: Cornell University Press

——(1986) 'Survey of Recent Developments' *Bulletin of Indonesian Economic Studies* xxii (1)

Goh, Chok Tong (1981) *Towards Higher Achievement* budget speech by Minister for Trade and Industry, 6 March (Singapore: Information Division, Ministry of Culture)

Golay, Frank H. (1961) *The Philippines: Public Policy and National Economic Development* Ithaca, N.Y: Cornell University Press

——(1983) 'Taming the American Multinationals' in Norman G. Owen (ed.) *The Philippine Economy and the United States: Studies in Past and Present Interactions* Ann Arbor, Mich: Michigan Papers on South & Southeast Asia No. 22, Ctr. S & SE Asian, University of Michigan

Government of Malaysia *Financial Statements 1984*

Grant, B. (1983) *The Australian Dilemma: A New Kind of Western Society*, Sydney: Macdonald Futura

Gray, Clive S. (1982) 'Survey of Recent Developments' *Bulletin of Indonesian Economic Studies* xviii (3)

Green, Rosario (1980) 'Trends of Public External Debt of Developing Countries' in Jorge Lozoya and A.K. Bhattacharya (eds). *The Financial Issues of the New International Economic Order* New York: Pergamon Press

Gregory, R. (1976) 'Some Implications of the Growth of the Mineral Sector' *Australian Journal of Agricultural Economics* 20 (2), 71–91

——(1982) 'Inter-sectoral Links' in S. Harris and G. Taylor (eds) *Resource Development and the Future of Australian Society* Canberra: Australian National University, CRES monograph no. 7

References

Griffith-Jones, Stephany and Rodriguez, Ennio (1984) 'Private International Finance and the Industrialization of LDCs' *Journal of Development Studies* 21 (1)

Habibie, B.J. (1983) *Some Thoughts Concerning a Strategy for the Industrial Transformation of a Developing Country* Jakarta: Department of Research and Technology, 14 June

Haggard, S. and Moon, C. (1983) 'The South Korean State in the International Political Economy: Liberal, Dependent or Mercantile?' in J. Ruggie (ed.) *The Antinomies of Interdependence: National Welfare and the International Division of Labour* New York: Columbia University Press

Hamill, I. (1981) *The Strategic Illusion: The Singapore Strategy and the Defence of Australia and New Zealand* Singapore: Singapore University Press

Hamilton, Clive (1983) 'Capitalist Industrialization in East Asia's Four Little Tigers' *Journal of Contemporary Asia* 13 (1)

Hartato, (1985) 'Menumbuhkan Pohon Industri dan Keterkaitnya' *Prisma* (5)

Hayden, W.G. (1984) 'Australia and China' *Australian Journal of Chinese Studies* 1, 83–97

Hazelhurst, Peter (1986) 'Asia's Share of Japanese Investment Cut' *Straits Times* 14 March

Head, B. (ed.) (1983) *State and Economy in Australia* Melbourne: Oxford University Press

Helliwell, J.F. (1984) 'Natural Resources and the Australian Economy' in R.E. Caves and L.B. Krause (eds) *The Australian Economy: A View From the North* Sydney: Allen & Unwin for the Brookings Institute

Henderson, A.G. (1985) 'A Comparison of Australian and Japanese Labour Markets' *Australian Bulletin of Labour* 12 (1), 22–45

Hewison, Kevin J. (1981) 'The Financial Bourgeoisie in Thailand' *Journal of Contemporary Asia* 11 (4), 395–412

——(1983) The Development of Capital, Public Policy and the Role of the State in Thailand, Ph.D. thesis, Murdoch University

——(1985) 'The State and Capitalist Development in Thailand', in R. Higgott and R. Robison (eds) *Southeast Asia: Essays in the Political Economy of Structural Change* London: Routledge & Kegan Paul

Higgott, R.A. (1983) *Political Development Theory* New York: St Martins Press

——(1984) 'Export-Oriented Industrialisation, the New International Division of Labour and the Corporate State: An Essay in Conceptual Linkage' *Australian Geographical Studies* 22, 58–71

——(1985) 'The State in Africa: Some Thoughts on the Future Drawn From the Past' in T. Shaw (ed.) *Africa Projected: From Recession to Renaissance by 2000?* London: Macmillan

——(1986a) 'Africa and the New International Division of Labour' in J. Ravenhill (ed.) *Africa in Economic Crisis* New York: Columbia University Press

——(1986b) 'Structural Adjustment and the Jackson Report: The Nexus Between Development Theory and Foreign Policy' in P. Eldridge, D. Forbes and D. Porter (eds) *Australia's Overseas Aid: Future Directions* Canberra: Croom Helm

——(1986c) 'The Dilemmas of Interdependence: Australia and the International Division of Labour in the Asia-Pacific Region' in J. Caporaso (ed.) *The International Division of Labor: International Political Economy Yearbook* vol. II Boulder, Colorado: Lynn Reinner Publications

Higgott, R.A. and Robison, R. (eds) (1985) *Southeast Asia: Essays in the Political Economy of Structural Change*, London: Routledge & Kegan Paul

Hill, Hal (1984a) 'Survey of Recent Developments' *Bulletin of Indonesian Economic Studies* xx (2)

—— (1984b) 'High Time for High Tech—or is it?', *Far Eastern Economic Review* 12 July

Hill, Hal and Jayasuriya, Sisira (1985) 'The Philippines: Growth, Debt and Crisis: Economic Performance during the Marcos Era', working paper no. 85/3 Canberra: Development Studies Centre, Australian National University, p. 92

Hill, Hal and Rice, R. (1977) 'Survey of Recent Developments' *BIES*, xiii (2)

Hill, Hal and Johns, Brian (1985) 'The Role of Direct Foreign Investment in Developing East Asian Countries' *Weltwirtschäftliches Archiv* 121 (2), 355–81

Ho Kwon Ping (1979) 'A Bitter Pill for Thailand' *Far Eastern Economic Review* 14 December, 94–96

—— (1980a) 'Thailand Puts an Aid Plan on Ice' *FEER* 22 February, 40–41

—— (1980b) 'Thailand Inc: An Open Door to the World's Multinationals' *FEER* 23 May, 40–43

—— (1980c) 'The Implications of Export-Oriented Industrialization for Southeast Asia' paper presented to the National Conference on Trade, Australian National University, 1980

—— (1981) 'Thailand Faces a Hard Choice' *FEER* 13 February, 40–44

Hofheinz, R. and Calder, K.E. (1982) *The Eastasia Edge* New York: Basic Books

Hsung, Bee Hwa (1982) 'Big Jump in Japan's Investment in Singapore' *Straits Times* 31 August

Hu Tsu Tan, Richard (Finance Minister) *Budget Statement 1986* delivered 7 March 1986, Singapore: Information Division, Ministry of Communication and Information, n.d.

Hughes, H. (1983) 'Global Economic Relations' *Australian Outlook* 37 (3), 132–7

—— (1985) 'Australia and the World Environment: The Dynamics of International Competition and Wealth Creation', in J. Scutt (ed.) *Poor Nation of the Pacific: Australia's Future?* Sydney: Allen & Unwin

Hymer, Stephen (1975) 'The Multinational Corporation and the Law of Uneven Development' in Hugo Radice (ed.) *International Firms and Modern Imperialism*, Harmondsworth: Penguin

Inamura, Raiji (1978) 'Philippine Industrialization: Plant Imports and the United States' *Monthly Report*, Research Institute of Overseas Investment, Export-Import Bank of Japan, Tokyo (special issue: March 1978)

Indonesian Commercial Newsletter (ICN) (various issues)

Ingram, James C. (1971) *Economic Change in Thailand, 1850–1970* Stanford: Stanford University Press

International Bank for Reconstruction and Development (1959) *A Public*

Development Program for Thailand Baltimore: Johns Hopkins University Press
——(1974) *Current Economic Position and Prospects for Thailand* Washington, DC: IBRD, East Asia and Pacific Department
——(1980) *Industrial Development Strategy in Thailand*, Washington, DC: East Asia and Pacific Regional Office
——(1983) *Thailand: Managing Public Resources for Structural Adjustment* Washington, DC: IBRD
International Labour Organisation (ILO) (1974) *Sharing in Development: A Programme of Employment, Equity and Growth for the Philippines* Geneva: ILO
International Monetary Fund (IMF)/World Bank (1979) *Aspects of the Financial Sector: The Philippines* (Joint Mission Report) Washington, DC
Janssen, Peter (1983) 'Watershed for Readjustment Period' *Business in Thailand* September, 23–8
Jenkins, Rhys (1984) 'Divisions Over the International Division of Labour' *Capital and Class* (22), 28–57
Johns, D.S. and Macleod, B. (1977) 'The Gregory Chant' *Australian Quarterly* 2, 92–105
Johnson, M. (1984) 'The Search for a New Japanese Locomotive', in R. Catley (ed.) *Australia and Asia: Towards New Horizons* Adelaide: Australian Institute of International Affairs
Jomo Kwame Sundaram (1986) *A Question of Class: Capital, the State and Uneven Development in Malaysia* Singapore: Oxford University Press
Jomo K.S. & Ishak Shari (1986) *Development Policies and Income Inequality in Pensinsular Malaysia*, Kuala Lumpur: Institute of Advanced Studies, University of Malaya
Jufri, Fikri (1984) 'Pemimpin Baru-Untuk Sebuah Era Baru di Pertamina' *Tempo* 23 June
Jurong Town Corporation, Singapore *Annual Report 1979/80*
——*Annual Report 1982/83*
Kanitha Srisilpavongse (1984) 'Export Promotion' *Bangkok Bank Monthly Review* 25 (8), 311–15
Kaplinsky, Raphael (1984) 'The International Context for Industrialization in the Coming Decade' *Journal of Development Studies* 21 (1)
Kasper, W. et al. (1980) *Australia at the Crossroads: Choices to the Year 2000* Sydney: Harcourt Brace Jovanovich
Katzenstein, P. (1983) 'The Small European States in the International Economy: Economic Dependence and Corporatist Politics', in J. Ruggie (ed.) *The Antinomies of Interdependence: National Welfare and the International Division of Labour* New York: Columbia University Press
——(1985) 'Small Nations in an Open International Economy: The Converging Balance of State and Society in Switzerland and Austria' in P.B. Evans, D. Rueschemeyer and T. Skocpol (eds) *Bringing the State Back In* Cambridge: Cambridge University Press
Keegan, D. (1983) 'Business Delivers the Real Message' *Australian* 12 April, 2
Keesing, Donald (1967) 'Outward Looking Policies and Economic Development' *Economic Journal* 77 (306)
Kenichi Ohmae (1985) 'Rethinking Global Corporate Strategy' *Asian Wall*

Street Journal 1 May, 10

Kerkvliet, Benedict J. (1979) *The Huk Rebellion: Study of Peasant Revolt in the Philippines*, Quezon City: New Day Publishers

Khor Kok Peng (1983a) *Recession and the Malaysian Economy* Penang: Institut Masyarakat, Penang

——(1983b) *The Malaysian Economy: Structures and Dependence* Kuala Lumpur: Marican

——(1986) 'Industrial Policy in Malaysia: Problems and Prospects' *Kajian Ekonomi Malaysia* xxiii (1)

——(1987) 'Implications of the External Debt and Capital Position' in Jomo K.S. et al. (ed.) *Crisis and Response in the Malaysian Economy* Kuala Lumpur: Malaysian Economic Association.

King, P. (ed.) (1982) *Australia's Vietnam* Sydney: Allen & Unwin

Koh, Frieda (1982) 'Launch late and Lose', *FEER*, 24 September, 138–140

Kompas (various issues) Jakarta

Kraisak Choonhavan (1984) 'The Growth of Domestic Capital and Thai Industrialisation' *Journal of Contemporary Asia* 14 (2), 135–46

Krause, L.B. (1984) 'Australia's Comparative Advantage in International Trade', in R.E. Caves and L.B. Krause (eds) *The Australian Economy: A View From the North* Sydney: Allen & Unwin for the Brookings Institute

Kreuger, Anne (1982) 'Newly Industrializing Economies' *Economic Impact* (40)

Krirkkiat Phipatseritham (1981) *Wikhro laksana kan pen chaokhong thurakit khanat yai nai prathet thai* Bangkok: Thai Khadi Research Institute

Kulkarni, V.G. (1983) 'Patient, Heal Thyself' *Far Eastern Economic Review* 15 September, 30–2

Lacaba, Jose F. (1982) *Days of Disquiet, Nights of Rage* Manila: Salinlahi Publishing House

Lal, Deepak (1983) 'Real Wages and Exchange Rates in the Philippines, 1956–1978' Washington, DC: World Bank Staff Working Papers no. 604

Lall, Sanjaya (1978) *Transfer Pricing in Assembly Industries* Commonwealth Economic Paper No 11, Industrial Cooperation, Commonwealth Secretariat, London

Lawe-Davies, J. (1981) 'The Politics of Protection: Australia-ASEAN Economic Relations 1975 to 1980' *Australia-Asia Papers* no. 13, Nathan, Qld: Griffith University, Centre for the Study of Australian-Asian Relations

Leaver, R. (1985) 'Reformist Capitalist Development and the New International Division of Labour' in R.A. Higgott and R. Robison (eds) *Southeast Asia: Essays in the Political Economy of Structural Change* London: Routledge & Kegan Paul

Ledesma, A.J. (1982) *Landless Workers and Rice Farmers: Peasant Subclasses under Agrarian Reforms in Two Philippine Villages* Los Banos, Philippines: International Rice Research Institute

Leung, James (1984) 'Singapore Petrochemical Complex Starts Up With Prediction of Loss' *Asian Wall Street Journal* 20 February

Lim Chin Choo (1979) A Comparative Analysis of the Shah Alam and Senawang Industrial Estates, M.Ec. thesis, University of Malaya

Lim, R. (1980) 'Current Australian-ASEAN Relations' in *Southeast Asian Affairs* Singapore: ISEAS

References

——(1985) 'The Debate on the "Political-Economy" of Australian-ASEAN Relations', in R.A. Higgott and R. Robison (eds) *Southeast Asia: Essays in the Political Economy of Structural Change* London: Routledge & Kegan Paul

——(1986) 'The Regularization of Military Bureaucratic Regimes: The Philippine Case', paper prepared for the Asian Studies of Australia Conference held in Sydney, 11–16 May 1986 (mimeo)

Lo Sum Yee (1972) *The Development Performance of West Malaysia, 1955–1967: With Special Reference to the Industrial Sector* Kuala Lumpur: Heinemann

Lindsey, Charles W. and Valencia, Ernesto M. (1982) 'Foreign Direct Investment' in *Surveys of Philippines Development Research II* Manila: Philippine Institute of Development Studies

Loveday, P. (1985) 'Corporatist Trends in Australia' *Politics* 19 (1), 46–51

McCawley, P. (1978) 'Some Consequences of the Pertamina Crisis in Indonesia' *Journal of Southeast Asian Studies* ix (1)

——(1983) 'Australia's Misconceptions of ASEAN' in P. Dibb (ed.) *Australia's External Relations in the 1980s: The Interaction of Economic, Political and Strategic Factors* Canberra: Croom Helm

——(1985) 'Survey of Recent Developments' *Bulletin of Indonesian Economic Studies* xxi (1)

McCormack, G. (1983) *Cold War, Hot War: An Australian Perspective on the Korean War* Sydney: Hale & Iremonger

McCoy, Alfred W. (1985) 'Rural Philippines: Technological Change in the Sugar Industry' in R.J. May and Francisco Nemenzo (eds) *The Philippines After Marcos*: Croom Helm

McCue, Andy 1978 'Shortage of Workers Pinches Development of Singapore' *Asian Wall Street Journal* 31 October

Mackie, J.A.C. (1981) 'Australia and Southeast Asia' in C. Bell (ed.) *Agenda for the Eighties* Canberra: Australian National University Press

——(1985) 'Economic Growth in the ASEAN Region: The Political Underpinnings', paper, Workshop on Explaining the Success of Industrialisation in East and Southeast Asia, Canberra, Australian National University, August

McMichael P. (1981) 'Redivisions of World Labour and Australian State Formation' Nathan, Qld: Griffith University, Conference on Economy Organisation and Society (mimeo)

McQueen, H. (1982) *Gone Tomorrow: Australia in the 1980s* Sydney: Angus & Robertson

Madigan R. (1984) 'Australia and Asia in the 1980s' in B. Catley (ed.) *Australia and Asia: Towards New Horizons* Adelaide: Australian Institute of International Affairs

Mahathir bin Mohammed (1970) *The Malay Dilemma* Singapore: Donald Moore for Asia Pacific Press

Makin, John H. (1984) *The Global Debt Crisis* New York: Basic Books

Magallona, Merlin M. (1982) 'The Economic Content of Neo-Colonialism' in Vivencio R. Joser (ed.) *Mortgaging the Future: The World Bank and the IMF in the Philippines* Quezon City: Foundation for Nationalist Studies

Malaysia Department of Statistics (1973) *Mid-Term Review of the Second Malaysia Plan 1971–1975* Kuala Lumpur: Government Printers

——(1981) *Fourth Malaysia Plan 1981–1985* Kuala Lumpur: Government Printers
——(1984) *Mid-Term Review of the Fourth Malaysia Plan 1981–1985* Kuala Lumpur: Government Printers
——(1986a) *The Fifth Malaysia Plan 1986–1990* Kuala Lumpur: Government Printers
——(1986b) *The Industrial Master Plan*, Kuala Lumpur: Malaysian Industrial Development Authority
Marx, Karl (1975) 'The Eighteenth Brumaire of Louis Bonaparte' in Karl Marx and Frederick Engels *Selected Works* Moscow: Progress Publishers
Millar, T.B. (1977) *Australia in Peace and War* Canberra: Australian National University Press
Ministry of Finance, Malaysia, *Economic Report* (various years), Kuala Lumpur
Ministry of Trade and Industry, Economic Committee, Singapore (1986) *The Singapore Economy: New Directions*, Singapore: Singapore National Printers
Mulvey, C. and Norris, W.K. (1985) *Labour Market Efficiency in Australia*, Canberra: Bureau of Labour Market Research, monograph no. 9, Australian Government Publishing Service
Nangsuphim ho kam kha thai (various issues)
Narongchai Akrasanee (1973a) The Manufacturing Sector in Thailand: A Study of Growth, Import Substitution, and Effective Protection, 1960–1969, Ph.D. thesis, Johns Hopkins University
——(1973b) 'The Structure of Industrial Protection in Thailand During the 1960s' *Economic Bulletin for Asia and the Far East* 24, (2/3), 36–57
Nation (various issues)
National Economic and Development Authority (NEDA) (1983) *Philippine Statistical Year Book 1983* Manila
——(1985a) *Philippine Statistical Year Book 1985* Manila
——(1985b) *The National Income Accounts of the Philippines 1983–1985 (Advance Estimates as of December, 1985)* Manila
Nations, Richard (1979) 'An Electrifying Controversy' *Far Eastern Economic Review* 14 December, 96–9
Nemenzo, Francisco (1984) 'Rectification Process in the Philippine Communist Movement' in Lim Joo-Jock and S. Vani (eds) *Armed Communist Movements in Southeast Asia* Singapore: Institute of Southeast Asian Studies
——(1985) 'The Left and the Traditional Opposition' in R.J. May and Francisco Nemenzo (eds) *The Philippines after Marcos*: Croom Helm
New Nation 24 January 1975
Nicholas, R. (1983) 'Misperception and Muddled Thinking in Australian-ASEAN Relations' *Contemporary Southeast Asia* 5 (2), 153–71
Niksch, Larry (1981), 'Thailand in 1980: Confrontation with Vietnam and the Fall of Kriangsak' *Asian Survey* 21 (2), 223–31
——(1982) 'Thailand in 1981: The Prem Government Feels the Heat' *Asian Survey* 22 (2), 191–9
Norton, W.E., Garmston, P. and Brodie, M.W. (1982) *Australian Economic Statistics, 1949/50 to 1980/81* Canberra: Reserve Bank of Australia, Occasional Paper 8a
Ofreneo, Rene E. (1980) *Capitalism in Philippine Agriculture*, Quezon City:

Foundation for Nationalist Studies
—— (1984) 'Contradictions in Export-led Industrialization: The Philippine Experience' *Journal of Contemporary Asia* 14 (4)
Palmer, Ingrid (1978) *The Indonesian Economy Since 1965* London: Cass
Pante, Filologo (1982) 'Exchange Rate Flexibility and Intervention Policy in the Philippines, 1973-81' *Philippine Economic Journal* 21 (1-2), 3-36
Pasuk Phongpaichit (1980) *Economic and Social Transformation of Thailand, 1957-1976* Bangkok: Chulalongkorn University Social Research Institute
Patrick, Hugh and Moreno, Honorata (1981) 'The Evolving Structure of Philippine Private Domestic Commercial Banking System from Independence to 1980: In Light of Japanese Historical Experience' (mimeo), cited in De Dios (1984)
Payer, Cheryl (1974) *The Debt Trap: The IMF and the Third World* Penguin
Petras, James (1984), 'Towards a Theory of Industrial Development in the Third World' *Journal of Contemporary Asia* 14 (2), 182-203
Philippine Institute of Development Studies (PIDS) (1985) *A Review and Appraisal of the Government Response to the 1983-84 Balance of Payments Crisis* Manila: Philippine Institute of Development Studies
Ping H.K. (n.d.) *The Implications of Export-Oriented Industrialization for Southeast Asia* Canberra (mimeo)
Plaschke, H. (1975) 'International Sub-contracting' *Instant Research on Peace and Violence* 2, 88-97
Pool, John C. and Stamos, Stephen C. (1985) 'The Uneasy Calm: Third World Debt—The Case of Mexico' *Monthly Review* 36 (10), 7-19
Power, John H. and Sicat, Gerardo P. (1971) *The Philippines: Industrialization and Trade Policies* London: Oxford University Press
Prachammit 30 May 1981
Prannee Thinnakon and Direk Pathomsiriwat (1985) 'Nitang prathet khong prathet toi phatthana lae karani suksa nitang phak rattaban khong thai' in Faculty of Economics, Thammasat University (eds) *Wikkhritkan Nitang Prathet Khong Rattaban Thai*, Bangkok: Faculty of Economics, Thammasat University, Section 1
Puthucheary, J.J. (1960) *Ownership and Control in the Malayan Economy* Singapore: Eastern Universities Press
Rahardjo, M. Dawam (1985) 'Evolusi Struktur Pajak dan Proses Domokrataisasi' *Prisma* (4)
Rao, V.V. Bhanoji (1976) *National Accounts of West Malaysia, 1947-1971* Singapore: Heinemann
Ramsey, A. (1985) 'The Cowards of Asia' *National Times* 1-7 February, 33
Remolona, Eli M. and Lamberte, Mario B. (1985) 'Financial Reforms and Balance of Payments Crisis: The Case of the Philippines 1980-83' Dilima: paper presented at the Seminar on Economic Development in the Philippines: Analysis and Perspectives, School of Economics, University of the Philippines, 5-6 December 1985
Report of the Committee to Review Australia's Relations with the Third World (1979) Canberra: Australian Government Publishing Service
Report of the Committee to Review the Australian Overseas Aid Programme (1984) Canberra: Australian Government Publishing Service

Report of the Joint Committee on Foreign Affairs and Defence (1984) Australia and ASEAN: Challenges and Opportunities, Canberra: Australian Government Publishing Service

Report of the Senate Standing Committee on Foreign Affairs and Defence (1980) The New International Economic Order: Implications for Australia Canberra: Australian Government Publishing Service

Rice, R. and Hill, H. (1977) 'Survey of Recent Developments' *Bulletin of Indonesian Economic Studies* xiii (2)

Richter, H.V. and Edwards, C.T. (1973) 'Recent Economic Developments in Thailand' in Robert Ho and E.C. Chapman (eds) *Studies of Contemporary Thailand* Canberra: Department of Human Geography, Research School of Pacific Studies, Australian National University

Rivera, Temario, Magallona, Merlin M., Tiglas, Rigoberto D., Valencia, Ernesto M. and Magno, Alex R. (1982) *Feudalism and Capitalism in the Philippines: Trends and Implications* Quezon City: Foundation for Nationalist Studies

Rix, A. (1982) 'Australia and Japan' in P.J. Boyce and J. Angel (eds) *Independence and Alliance: Australia in World Affairs 1976-80* Sydney: Allen & Unwin

Robinson, W. (1985) 'Imperialism, Dependency and Industrialisation: The Case of Japan in Indonesia' in R.A. Higgott and R. Robison (eds) *Southeast Asia: Essays in the Political Economy of Structural Change* London: Routledge & Kegan Paul

Robison, Richard (1985) 'Class, Capital and the State in New Order Indonesia', in R.A. Higgott and R. Robison (eds) *Southeast Asia: Essays in the Political Economy of Structural Change* London: Routledge & Kegan Paul

——(1986) *Indonesia: The Rise of Capital* Sydney: Allen & Unwin

Robison, R. and Rodan, G. (1983) 'Restructuring Australian Industry: The Case for a More Active State Role' *Discussion Papers in Public Policy* no. 2 Perth: Murdoch University

Rodan, Garry (1985a) 'Industrialisation and the Singapore State in the Context of the New International Division of Labour' in R. Higgott and R. Robison (eds) *Southeast Asia: Essays in the Political Economy of Structural Change* London: Routledge & Kegan Paul

——(1985b) *Singapore's 'Second Industrial Revolution': State Intervention and Foreign Investment*, Canberra: ASEAN-Australia Economic Papers, no. 18

Roepstorff, Torben, M., 1985 'Industrial Development in Indonesia: Performance and Prospects' *Bulletin of Indonesian Economic Studies* xxi (1) Far

Rowley, Anthony (1982) 'Clausen and a More Worldly World Bank' *Far Eastern Economic Review* 26 March, 131-7

——(1984) 'Picking up its Skirts to Dance to Washington's Tune' *FEER* 27 February, 65-7

Ruggie, J. (ed.) (1983) *The Antinomies of Interdependence: National Welfare and the International Division of Labor* New York: Columbia University Press

Sangsit Phiriyarangsan (n.d.) *Thunniyom khunnang thai (ph.s. 2475-2503)* Bangkok: Sangsan

Santi Mingmonkol [pseud.] (1981) 'The World Bank and Thailand: New Wine in an Old Bottle' *Southeast Asia Chronicle* (81), 20-4

References

Schmitz, H. (1984) 'Industrialization Strategies in Less Developed Countries: Some Lessons of Historical Experience' *Journal of Development Studies* 21 (1)
Scutt, J. (ed.) (1985) *Poor Nation of the Pacific: Australia's Future?* Sydney: Allen & Unwin
Sharpe, Willard D. (1985) 'Asia's Debt Danger Zones' *Asian Wall Street Journal* 8 August, 8
Sharpston, M. (1975) 'International Subcontracting' *Oxford Economic Papers* (New Series) 27, 94–135
Shaw, T.M. (1982) 'Beyond Neocolonialism: Varieties of Corporatism in Africa' *Journal of Modern African Studies* 20 (2), 239–61
Siam Rath Weekly Review (1962) 1 November, 4
Sicat, Gerardo P. (1972) *Economic Policy and Philippine Development* Quezon City: University of the Philippines Press
Sidhiphol Vichaidist (1972) 'Import Substitution and Thailand' *Bangkok Bank Monthly Review* 13 (10), 429–39
Sinar Harapan (various issues)
Singapore Economic Bulletin (1980) June
Sjahrir (1985a) 'Ekonomi Politik Undang Pajak' *Prisma* (4)
Sjahrir (1985b) 'Privatisasi Menuju Efisiensi?' *Prisma* (7)
Soehoed, R. (1977) 'Commodities and Viable Economic Sectors' *Indonesian Quarterly* 5 (1)
——(1981) 'Japan and the Development of the Indonesian Manufacturing Sector', paper given at the Seminar on Industrialisation, Jakarta, Centre for Strategic and International Studies
——(1982) 'Industrial Development During Repelita III', *Indonesian Quarterly* 10 (4)
Sopiee, N. (1984) *Australia and ASEAN: Down the Road to Disengagement* Kuala Lumpur: Institute for Strategic and International Studies
Souter, K. (1983) 'Australia and the Third World' *Third World Quarterly* 5 (4), 861–73
Stockwin, J.A.A. (ed.) (1972) *Japan and Australia in the Seventies* Sydney: Angus & Robertson
Straits Times (various issues)
Suchitra Punyaratanabandhu-Bhakdi (1983) 'Thailand in 1982: General Arthit Takes Center Stage' *Asian Survey* 23 (2), 172–7
——(1984) 'Thailand in 1983: Democracy, Thai Style' *Asian Survey* 24 (2), 187–94
Suhartoyo (1981) *Penanaman modal dan Industrialisasi* paper given at a seminar on industrialization, Jakarta: Centre for Strategic and International Studies
Sung-Joo, H. (1983) *Pacific Economic Co-operation: The Next Phase* Jakarta: Centre for Strategic and International Studies
Surachat Bamrungsuk (ed.) (1985) *F-16 kap kanmuang thai* Bangkok: Institute of Strategic and International Studies
Tan, N. (1983) 'The Structure, Causes and Effects of Manufacturing Sector Protection in the Philippines', paper presented at a seminar on Protection in ASEAN and Australia, Canberra, Australian National University
Tanzer, Andrew (1983) 'Cashing in on Chips' *FEER*, 21 July, 65–6
Tempo (various issues) Jakarta, esp. 'Mendorong Swasta Ke Mana' 25 February

1984; and 'Pri, "Non Pri" dan Investasi Rp. 67.5 trilyun' 31 March 1984
Tetzlaff, Rainer (1979) 'The World Bank: The Way it Functions and its Political Importance for the Third World' *Economics* 19, 118–35
Thailand (1984) *Thailand's Budget in Brief: Fiscal Year 1984* Bangkok: Bureau of the Budget
Thailand Investment Bulletin (1980) 5 (1), 1–14
Thailand *National Income of Thailand* (various issues)
Thailand *Statistical Yearbook* (various issues)
Thailand Yearbook 1975–76, esp. 'The Third National Economic and Social Development Plan (1972–1976)' Ivan Mudannayake and others, Bangkok: Temple Publicity Services
Thoburn, J.T. (1973) 'Exports and the Malaysian Engineering Industry: A Case Study of Backward Linkages' in David Lim (ed.) *Readings on Malaysian Economic Development* Kuala Lumpur: Oxford University Press
Thomas, K.D. and Panglaykim, J. (1973) *Indonesia: The Effect of Past Policies and President Suharto's Plans for the Future* Melbourne, Committee for the Economic Development of Australia (CEDA)
Tilman, Robert O. (1971) 'The Philippines in 1970: A Difficult Decade Begins' *Asian Survey* xi (2), 139–8
Tisdell, C. (1985) 'Technological Change and Transfer in the Pacific: The Position of Australia and Japan' in *Australian Outlook: The Australian Journal of International Affairs* 39 (1), 39–43
Tolley, Howard E. (1964) 'World Bank Operations in Thailand' *Bank of Thailand Monthly Report* 4 (9), 1–6
Trairong Suwanakiri (1970) The Structure of Protection and Import Substitution in Thailand, M.A. thesis, University of the Philippines
Tsuda, Mamoru (1978) *A Preliminary Study of Japanese-Filipino Joint Ventures* Quezon City: Foundation for Nationalist Studies
Turnbull, C.M. (1982) *A History of Singapore 1819–1975* Singapore: Oxford University Press
Twatchai Yongkittikul (1979) *Trends in RTG Revenue Generation and Budget Expenditures* Bangkok: Thailand University Research Association, report no. 3
Uchida, T. et al. (1983) 'Forecast of Growth Potential and Factors Influencing Asian Development' in T. Haseyama et al. *Two Decades of Asian Development and the Outlook for the 1980s* Tokyo: Institute for Developing Economies
United States Department of Commerce (1981) *US Direct Investment Abroad, 1977* Washington, DC: Bureau of Economic Analysis
van Rijnberk, W.L. (1961) *Industrial Development Policy and Planning in Thailand* New York: Commissioner for Technical Assistance, Department of Economic and Social Affairs, United Nations report no. TAO/THA/14
Viksnins, George J. (1973) 'United States Military Spending and the Economy of Thailand, 1967–1972' *Asian Survey* 13 (5), 441–57
Villegas, Edberto M. (1982) 'Debt Peonage and the New Society' in Vivencio R. Jose (ed.) *Mortgaging the Future: The World Bank and IMF in the Philippines* Quezon City: Foundation for Nationalist Studies
——(1984) *Studies in Philippine Political Economy* rev. edn. Manila: Silangan Publishers

References

Virabongse Ramangkura and others (1983) *The Behaviour of the Trade Balance and Current Account* vol. 1, Main Report *A Study Undertaken as a Part of the SIAM Project on Macro-Economic Management of the Thai Economy* Bangkok: A report submitted to the National Economic and Social Development Board and the World Bank, October

Vital, D. (1967) *The Inequality of States* Oxford: Clarendon Press

Warr, P.G. (1983) *Structural Effects of Increasing Australia's Imports from Less Developed Countries* Canberra: Australian National University, Centre for Economic Policy Research, Discussion Paper 72

——(1984) 'Export Promotion via Industrial Enclaves: The Philippines' Bataan Export Processing Zone' (mimeo) Canberra: Australian National University

Whitlam, E.G. (1981) *A Pacific Community* Cambridge, Mass: Harvard University Press

Wilson, David A. (1970) *The United States and the Future of Thailand* New York: Praeger Publishers

World Bank (1980) *Aspects of Poverty in the Philippines* Washington, DC

——(1981) *Indonesia: Selected Issues of Industrial Development and Trade Strategy* Jakarta

——(1983) *The World Development Report 1983* Washington DC

——(1984a) *Indonesia: Policies and Prospects for Economic Growth and Transformation* Jakarta

——(1984b) *World Development Report* New York: Oxford University Press

——(1985a) *Commodity Trade and Price Trends* Washington, DC: World Bank

——(1985b) *Indonesia: Policies for Growth and Employment* Jakarta

——(1985c) *World Bank Annual Report 1985* Washington, DC: World Bank

——(1985d) *World Debt Tables 1984-85* Washington, DC: World Bank

——(1985e) *World Development Report 1985* New York: Oxford University Press

Index

'Accord', the, 179, 209
ACPI, 209
ACTU, 210
Advisory Committee on Prices and Incomes (Australia), *see* ACPI
Affan, Wahab, 38
Agency for the Assessment and Application of Technology (Indonesia), *see* BPPT
agriculture, in Australia, 181, 191; in Indonesia, 20, 22; in Malaysia, 114, 119, 121, 135; in Philippines, 83, 84, 85, 86, 89, 101–3; in Thailand, 52, 53, 54, 78; *see also* landed oligarchy
aid, foreign, 45, 58, 63, 64
aircraft industry, 38, 165
Alliance Party (Malaysia), 113
Amnuay Viravan, 72
ANZUS, 191, 216
Aquino, Benigno, 82, 88, 92, 97, 110
Aquino, Corazon, 80, 100, 110, 111
Arthit Kamlang-ek, 73, 74
ASEAN, 2, 52, 191, 192, 194, 195, 196, 202, 204–8
automobile industry, 30, 35, 38–9, 41, 42, 51, 165
Australia, 4, 9, 11, 177–217; and Asean, 204–8; and Japan, 202–5; and the Pacific region, 190–202, 205
Australian economic policies, 2, 14–15, 177–217
Australian Labor Government, 178, 179, 205, 209, 213, 214, 215
Australian Liberal-National Party Government, 209
Australian Manufacturing Council, 209

automation, 162, 172, 183
Ayala Corporation, 109

balance of payments, 9, 13, 14; in Australia, 178, 180, 200; in Indonesia, 21, 49, 51; in Malaysia, 113, 122–4, 125, 145; in Philippines, 88, 101; in Thailand, 55, 60, 66–7, 70
Bandung, 37
Bangkok Bank, 56, 61
Banjurd Cholvicharn, 55
Bank Negara (Malaysia), 144
bankruptcy, 60, 61, 105, 107
'banks, political', 106
Bappenas, 19, 25, 44
Barisan Sosiatis, *see* BS
Bataan Export Processing Zone, 96
Bayan, Partido ng, 112
Beecham, 164
beef, 181, 204
Benedicto, Roberto, 105
Benguet Mining Corporation, 109
BKPM, 46
Boonchu Rojanastien, 70, 71, 72, 79
borrowing, *see* loans
BPPT, 37, 38
Brazil, 9, 45, 93
Britain, 152, 189, 190
Brookings Institute, 202
BS, 153
Button, Senator, 210

Capital Assistance Scheme (Singapore), 155, 159
capital-intensive production, 116, 117, 155, 157, 164

238

Index

capital, international, *see* investment, foreign
Capital Investment Allowances Scheme (Singapore), 172
Capital Investment Board (Indonesia), *see* BKPM
capitalism, 13; in Australia, 182, 188; in Indonesia, 18, 42, 43, 50; in Malaysia, 133, 137, 145, 147; in Philippines, 89, 91, 92, 106; in Thailand, 56, 58, 60, 62, 76, 77, 78; *see also* crony capitalism, domestic capitalist groups, investment, TNC
capitalism, crony, 97, 101, 105, 107, 108, 109, 111
Central Bank (Philippines), 106, 107
Central Provident Fund (Singapore), *see* CPF
Chart Thai Party, 72, 74
China, 203, 205
Chinese, 54, 114, 151
Church, Roman Catholic, 109, 110
Ciputra, 36, 48
Citibank, 100
CKD packs, 141
Clausen, A.W., 73
coal, 203, 204
coconut growing, 102, 105, 109, 112
Cojuanco, Eduardo, 105, 109
colonialism, 4, 114, 115, 151, 189
Commission for Asia and the Far East, *see* ECAFE
Communist Party, 18, 90, 101, 112
Communist Party of the Phillippines, *see* CPP
communists, 65, 80, 82, 90, 91, 92, 103
Company Welfarism from Employees' Contributions Scheme, *see* COWEC
computer manufacture, 163
competitiveness, international, 170–5, 178, 211
completely knocked down packs, *see* CKD
computer manufacture, 163
Concepcion, Jose, 111
Construction and Development Corporation of the Philippines, 105
corporations, business, *see* domestic capitalist groups, multinational corporations, TNC
COWEC, 168
CPF, 155, 160, 169, 172, 174
CPP, 101, 102, 103, 104
Cuenca, Rodolfo, 105
Customs, department (Indonesia), 33–4

Dasaad, 18, 38
debt, foreign, Australia, 179; Indonesia, 28, 29, 46, 49; Malaysia, 113, 125–33; Philippines, 80, 87, 88, 104, 108, 111; Thailand, 61, 62, 63, 65, 66, 73, 74; *see also* loans
debt, public, 124–33, 146
Dee, Dewey, 106, 107
defence, national, 66
defence spending, *see* military
devaluation, currency, 31, 26, 50, 66, 73, 74, 89, 91, 95, 98, 144
Development Bank of the Philippines, 106
Development Bank of Singapore, 155
Diokno, Jose W., 90, 92
Disini, Herminio, 106
domestic capitalist groups, in Indonesia, 26, 35, 37, 38, 42, 43, 48, 49, 51; in Thailand, 53, 56, 57, 58, 59, 60
Drysdale, Peter, 192, 194, 205
DSP, 25, 35, 46

ECAFE, 55
Economic Development Board (Singapore), 154, 159
Economic Expansion Incentives (Amendment) Act (Singapore), 155
economic nationalism, 17, 18, 19, 25, 39, 41, 42, 43, 50, 51, 76
Economic Planning Advisory Committee (Australia), *see* EPAC
EEC, 173, 180, 181
electrical industry, 139, 162, 163
electronics industry, 117, 135, 139, 157, 158, 159, 162, 163, 165
Eman, Fritz, 49
employment, 8, 49, 52, 53, 116, 137, 155, 211; *see also* labour
Employment Act (1968) (Singapore), 154
Enrile, Juan Ponce, 105, 109, 110
EOI, 4–12, 13, 114; in Australia, 183, 201; in Indonesia, 16, 25, 41, 43, 50; in Malaysia, 115–17, 134, 139, 142, 147; in Philippines, 98, 99; in Singapore, 149, 150, 151, 153–8, 162, 166, 172, 175; in Thailand, 56, 57, 60, 62, 66, 67, 68, 69, 70, 71, 72, 76, 77, 78
EPAC, 209
EPZ, 99
European Economic Community, *see* EEC
exchange rate, 39, 55, 87, 98, 101
export-oriented industrialisation, *see* EOI
export processing zones, *see* EPZ
exports, Australia, 179, 180, 181, 184,

185, 186, 187, 188, 190, 196, 197, 198, 200, 201, 203, 204, 206, 207, 215, 216; Indonesia, 22, 39–44; Malaysia, 117, 119–22, 123, 138, 139, 140, 144, 145, 148; Philippines, 85, 95, 102, 112; Singapore, 155, 157, 171, 173; Thailand, 57, 66, 67; *see also* EOI

Fairchild, 8, 172
Farm Bill, US, 181, 216
farming, *see* agriculture
Federal Industrial Development Authority (Malaysia), 115–16
Fernandez, Jose, 111
forestry, 25, 84, 119, 121
Fraser, Malcolm, 190, 209, 215
free-market policy, 6, 11, 19, 35, 38, 42, 44, 49, 50
free-trade policy, 6, 16, 36, 41, 42, 75
free-trade zone, 116, 117, 140
Frobel, 11
Fuji Oil, 165

gas, liquefied, *see* LNG
gas, natural, 65, 73, 114
GATT, 157, 181
Gaya, 38
GDP, 192, 193, 194; of Australia, 179, 185, 195, 196, 197; of Indonesia, 20, 26, 49; of Malaysia, 113, 118, 119, 142, 144, 145; of Philippines, 84, 85, 86; of Singapore, 161, 162, 166, 168, 174; of Thailand, 53, 56
General Agreement on Tariffs and Trades, *see* GATT
General Electric, 165
Generalised System of Preferences, *see* GSP
Ginanjar Kartasasmita, 30, 36, 41, 42
Glaxocham, 164
GNP, 193; in Indonesia, 45; in Malaysia, 116, 118, 125, 130, 143, 144; in Philippines, 80, 81, 87; in Thailand, 52, 63
Goh Choh Tong, 171, 172
Gregory, Bob, 188
growth rate, annual, in Australia, 195, 206, 211; in Indonesia, 26; in Malaysia, 113, 116, 118, 145; in Philippines, 84, 85–6; in Singapore, 172; in Thailand, 52, 53; *see also* GDP, GNP
Gruen, F., 157
GSP, 157

Habibie, B.J., 30, 32, 34, 37, 41
Hartato, 30, 41
Hawke, Bob, 178, 190, 204, 209, 214
Hawker Pacific, 165
Hayden, Bill, 210
higher-value-added production, in Australia, 187, 201, 202, 203; Singapore, 157, 158, 159, 161, 165, 167, 169, 173, 208
Hon Sui Sen, 155
Hong Kong, 170, 196
Hukbalahap movement, 82, 90

IBRD, 12, 55, 152
ILO, 99
Ilocanisation, 93
IMF, 1, 9, 10, 13; and Australia, 179; and Malaysia, 147; and Philippines, 88, 91, 94, 96, 99, 100–1, 104, 108, 109, 110, 111, 112; and Thailand, 69, 70, 71, 73, 74, 75, 76, 77, 79
immigrant, Asian, 190
IMP, 113, 137–42
import-substitution policies, *see* ISI
imports, 40, 41, 66, 67, 115, 186, 187, 197, 200, 201, 203, 211
income, 50, 80, 104, 116; *see also* wages
Indocement group, 48, 49
Indonesia, 2, 3, 6, 7, 9, 12, 16–51, 92, 195, 207, 208; Bank of, 32; University of, 44
Industrial Estates, 154, 155
Industrial Master Plan (Malaysia), *see* IMP
Industrial Relations Act (1969) (Singapore), 154
'Industrial Revolution, Second' (Singapore), *see* 'Second I.R.'
industrialisation, 11, 14; in Indonesia, 18, 25, 41; in Malaysia, 113, 114, 115–17, 134, 138; in Singapore, 152, 153, 158–61, 208; in Thailand, 52–7; *see also* EOI, ISI
inflation, 18, 50, 56, 70, 71, 80, 90, 91, 110
Inpres, 4, 34, 39
interest rates, 65, 101, 109
International Bank for Reconstruction and Development, *see* IBRD
International Labour Organisation, *see* ILO
International Monetary Fund, *see* IMF
International Political Economy, *see* IPE
International Trading Company (Singapore), *see* INTRACO

Index

INTRACO, 155
investment, foreign, 8, 10; in Australia, 190, 200, 202; in Indonesia, 18, 26, 30, 35, 46, 50, 51; in Malaysia, 114–15, 117, 123, 124, 134, 140–1, 143, 144, 148; in Philippines, 94–5, 96–7, 99, 108; in Singapore, 155, 157, 161, 162, 164, 165, 166, 167; Thailand, 58, 59, 60, 63, 64
Investment Incentives Act (Malaysia), 115
Investment Promotion Act (Thailand), 57
investment, state, in Indonesia, 26, 29, 36, 37, 38, 39, 45, 46; in Malaysia, 118; in Singapore, 160
IPE, 178
iron ore, 203, 204
irrigation, 114
ISI, 2, 3, 4–13, 57; in Indonesia, 16, 18, 25, 26, 28, 34, 35, 41, 42, 43, 50; in Malaysia, 113–14, 115–17, 138, 142; in Philippines, 83, 95, 98, 99, 100; in Singapore, 149, 152, 153, 154; in Thailand, 55–7, 58, 60, 66, 67, 68, 69, 70, 72, 74, 75, 76

Japan, 8, 9, 14, 39, 166–7, 180, 181, 185, 191, 194, 196, 198, 201, 202–5, 206, 211
Joint Industrial Training Centres, 159
joint ventures, 96–7, 100
Jurong Town Corporation, 154, 159

Kanegafuchi, 164
Katzenstein, P., 185, 188, 200, 208, 209, 214
Keating, Paul, 178
Kilusan Mayo Uno, see KMU
KMU, 103, 112
Korea, 11, 14; see also South Korea
Korean War, 55, 58
Kraivixien, Thanin, 65
Krakatau Steel, 18, 19, 36, 37, 38, 42, 48
Kriangsak Chomanan, 64, 70, 72
Krirkkiat Phipatseritham, 68

labour, control of, 154, 158, 160
labour costs, 158–9
labour-intensive production, 8, 11, 14; in Australia, 183, 184, 189, 205; in Indonesia, 26, 50, 208; in Malaysia, 116, 117, 138; in Philippines, 85; in Singapore, 150, 155, 157, 159, 169; in Thailand, 57, 62

labour, low-wage, 10, 40, 59, 62, 71, 78, 117, 156, 158, 163, 172, 183, 189
labour, migrant, 189
labour, nationalisation of, 157
labour, new international division of, see NIDL
labour shortage, 157
land reform, 90, 101, 102
landed oligarchy, 89, 92, 105, 106
Laya, Jaime, 94
LDC, 180, 183, 199, 207
Lee Hsien Loong, 169
Lee Kuan Yew, 152–3, 168, 201, 213
less developed countries, see LDC
Liberal-National Party Government, 209
Liem Sioe Liong, 18, 36, 37, 38, 48
life expectancy, 80
liquefied natural gas, see LNG
living standards, 90, 152, 168, 174, 215
LNG, 9, 13, 18–19, 22, 25, 28, 40, 44, 119, 121, 123
loans, 9, 10, 13; to Australia, 179; to Indonesia, 19, 25, 28, 44, 45, 46, 51; to Malaysia, 124, 125–33, 146; to Philippines, 87, 88, 93, 94, 105; to Thailand, 60, 63, 64, 65, 66, 68, 69, 73, 75; see also debt, IMF, SAL, World Bank
loans, government, 48, 159
Lopez, Fernando, 90, 92, 105
Luzon, 101, 102

Magsaysay, Ramon, 90
Mahathir, Mohamad, 113, 133, 134, 135, 136, 143, 147, 206, 207
Makati Business Group, 109
Malays 114, 151; see also UMNO
Malaysia, 2, 3, 4, 6, 7, 8, 12, 13, 40, 113–48, 152, 153, 183
Malaysia Plans, 113, 116, 118, 123, 142–5, 195
Malaysian Chinese Association, see MCA
Malaysian Common Market, 153
Malaysian Indian Congress, see MIC
Marcos, Ferdinand, 2, 13, 80, 81, 88, 89, 90, 91, 92, 93, 98, 100ff
marginalisation, 199, 201
martial law (Philippines), 13, 86, 87, 91, 92, 93, 94, 96, 99, 101, 110
MCA, 146
MIC, 146
middle classes, 92, 103, 152
military power, 19, 25, 92, 93, 103

military spending, 65–6, 104
Mindanao, 102
minerals, 9, 20, 22, 47, 53, 119, 180, 181, 187, 190, 198, 199, 202, 203, 210
mining, *see* minerals
MNLF, 103
monopoly, 19, 25, 35, 37, 38, 42, 43, 48, 49, 102, 105, 136, 139
Monsod, Solita, 111, 112
Moro National Liberation Front, *see* MNLF
motor car industry, *see* automobile
multinational corporations, 36, 95, 100, 108, 163–4, 202; *see also* TNC
Murtopo, Ali, 25
Muslims, 80, 92, 103

NAP, 135–6
NASUTRA, 105
National Agricultural Policy of Malaysia, *see* NAP
National Democratic Front (Philippines), *see* NDF
National Economic and Social Development Board (Thailand), *see* NESDB
National Economic and Development Authority of the Philippines, *see* NEDA
National Economic Planning Board (Indonesia), 19, 25, 44
National Sugar Trading Corporation, *see* NASUTRA
National Trades Union Congress (Singapore), *see* NTUC
National Wages Council (Singapore), 154
nationalism, 14, 41, 51, 54, 83, 90, 91, 92, 96, 99, 189; economic, 10, 12, 17, 18, 19, 25, 39, 42, 43, 51, 152
Nationalista Party (Philippines), 90, 92
NDF, 104
NEDA, 98
NEP, 116, 124, 134, 136, 141, 142–3, 145
Neptune Orient Lines, 155
NESDB, 55, 61
new economic division of labour, *see* NIDL
New Economic Policy of Malaysia, *see* NEP
New Order (Indonesia), 18, 26, 32, 34, 35, 38, 43, 45, 49
New People's Army (Philippines), *see* NPA
newly industrialising country, *see* NIC
NFPE, 123, 124, 125

NIC, 1, 6, 52, 60, 62, 133, 134, 150, 172, 182, 183, 189, 207, 211
NIDL, 6, 11, 14; and Australia, 178, 182, 183, 188, 189, 191, 196, 199, 200, 201, 202, 217; and Indonesia, 16, 30, 37, 39, 50, 51; and Malaysia, 117; and Singapore, 149, 150, 151, 157, 158, 161, 166, 176
Ning, Hashim, 18, 38
non-financial public enterprises (Malaysia), *see* NFPE
non-tariff barriers, *see* NTB
NPA, 101, 102, 103, 104
NTB, 173
NTUC, 154, 157, 160
Nurtanio, 37

OBA, 123, 124, 125
OECD, 96, 115, 125, 147, 148
off budget agencies, *see* OBA
offshore banking, 100
oil, 7, 9, 12, 13; and Indonesia, 2, 16, 18–19, 20, 21, 25, 28, 30, 32, 33, 39, 40, 44, 45, 49, 51; and Malaysia, 114, 119, 120; and Philippines, 104; and Thailand, 68, 72
oil, palm, 114, 117, 119, 120
oligopoly, 19, 89, 92, 105, 106; *see also* landed oligopoly
Ongpin, Jaime, 109, 111
OPEC, 9, 33, 40, 62, 64, 87
Organisation for Economic Cooperation and Development, *see* OECD
Organisation of Petroleum Exporting Countries, *see* OPEC
Osmena, Sergio, 90

Pacific region, 190–202
PAL, 37, 38
Palau Ayer Marbau, 160
Panggabean, 38
PAP, 3, 8, 14, 149–51, 152–8, 162, 164, 166, 167, 168, 171, 173, 174, 175
Partido ng Bayan, 112
People's Action Party (Singapore), *see* PAP
Pertamina, 18, 19, 25, 32, 33, 37, 38, 42
petroleum industry, 25, 119, 138, 162, 163, 164, 171; *see also* oil, OPEC
Phibun Songkhram, 3, 54
Philippine National Bank, 100, 106
Philippines, The, 2, 3–4, 6, 7, 9, 12, 13, 80–112, 195, 207
Phisit Pakkasem, 70

Index

politico-bureaucrats, 16, 17, 19, 28, 33, 34, 41, 43, 50, 51
population, 185, 193, 194
populist movements, 70, 77, 91, 93
Prachakon Thai Party, 74
Pratt and Whitney, 165
Prawiro, Radius, 32, 33
Prem Tinsulanonda, 68, 71, 72, 76
price control, 64, 70, 73
prices, rising, 69, 70, 72, 73, 86
priority investment lists (Indonesia), *see* DSP
private enterprise, *see* domestic capitalist groups, multinational corporations, TNC
privatisation, 48, 64, 136, 143, 147
Probosutejo, 38
protectionism, 3, 6, 7, 9, 10; in Australia, 189, 200, 210, 212; in Indonesia, 18, 19, 26, 30, 34, 35, 36, 40, 41, 42, 43, 49; in Malaysia, 122, 125, 138, 139, 142; in Philippines, 83, 89, 96, 98, 99, 100, 111, 112; in Singapore, 173; in Thailand, 55, 56, 59, 71, 78; *see also* tariffs

Quasha Decision 91

R & D, 159, 165, 167
Rahman, Tunku Abdul, 113
Raja Mohar, 115
Ramly, General, 33
Ramos, Fidel, 110
recession, 10, 60, 61, 74, 78, 150, 156, 161, 166, 177
refugees, 190
regionalism, 190, 191
research and development, *see* R & D
rice production, 86, 102, 114
rubber, 113, 114, 119, 120, 123, 151

Sabah, 113
Saha Phattanapipul group, 61
SAL, 10, 71, 73, 75, 99
Samak Sundaravej, 74, 75
Sanchez, Augusto, 112
SAP, 71, 72, 76
Sarawak, 113
Sarit Thanarat, 54, 55, 58, 69
'Second Industrial Revolution' (Singapore), 8, 150, 158–61, 162, 164, 165, 166, 168, 169, 172, 173, 175
Semen Madura, 48
shipbuilding industry, 37–8, 41, 138, 171
Sicat, Geraldo, 94

Silverio Ricardio, 106
Sin, Cardinal Jaime, 109, 110
Singapore, 2, 3, 7–8, 10, 11, 14, 149–76, 195, 196, 207, 210
Sison, Jose Maria, 112
Skills Development Fund (Singapore), 159, 172
Snoh Unakul, 61
Social Action Party (Thailand), *see* SAP
Soehoed, R., 25
Soerjadjaja, Willem, 18
Sommai Hoontrakul, 74, 75, 76
Sophonpanich family, 56
South Korea, 7, 10, 11, 134, 170, 179, 203
specialisation in exports, 198, 199
Sri Lanka, 183
state intervention, 30, 38, 104–10, 145, 147, 149–50, 160, 161, 175
steel industry, 18, 19, 25, 30, 35, 36, 37, 38, 41, 42, 51, 138, 203
strikes, 103, 104, 154, 172
structural adjustment loans, *see* SAL
student militancy, 90, 91, 93
Subroto, 32
subsidies, 26, 29, 30, 31, 32, 34, 35, 39, 45, 49, 78, 102, 160, 169, 181, 189
Sudharmono, 30, 32
sugar, 89, 102, 105, 112, 181
Suharto family, 48
Suharto, President, 33, 49, 92
Suhartoyo, 25
Sukarno, President, 3, 18, 19
Sumarlin, 32
Sumbono, Judo, 32, 33
Sumitro, Professor, 41, 43
Surabaya, 37
Surayajaya, 38
Surwarma, 38
Suthee Singhasaneh, 76
Sutowo, Ibnu, 18, 19, 25, 32, 36, 38
Swan, Tan Koon, 146

Taiwan, 7, 10, 11, 134, 170, 196, 203
Tanjung Priok, 33
tariffs, import, 41, 42, 55, 85, 100, 196, 199, 210, 213; *see also* protectionism
taxation, 19, 24, 31–2, 44–5, 68, 159, 172, 174
technocrats, 30, 32, 70, 71, 72, 93, 94, 98, 99, 101, 104
Technology Corporation, Singapore, 160
technology, transfer of, 135, 141
Thai Farmers Bank, 61
Thai Industries Association, 56

Thailand, 1, 3, 6, 7, 9, 12, 40, 52–79, 195, 207; Bank of, 55, 66, 69, 73, 74
tin, 113, 121, 123, 151
TNC, 5, 30, 58, 59, 60, 62, 78, 117, 135, 139, 141, 142, 189
trade unions, 15, 103, 112, 137, 154, 160, 168, 210
transnational corporations, *see* TNC
TRW, 165

UMNO, 133, 146
unemployment, 7, 10, 61, 74, 90, 150, 152, 155, 156, 211
United Malays National Organisation, *see* UMNO
United Nations, 55, 58
urbanisation, 184
USA, 8, 9, 11; and Australia, 180, 181, 185, 189, 191, 192, 194, 196, 198, 204, 216; and Malaysia, 147; and Philippines, 82, 89, 90, 91, 94, 95, 98, 103; and Singapore, 172; and Thailand, 58, 62, 63, 64, 65, 71, 78
USA Farm Bill, 181, 216

Vellu, Samy, 146

Vietnam, 190, 192
Virata, Cesar, 94, 108

wage freeze, 172
wage-labour, *see* labour
wage policy, 'corrective', 158
wages, 5, 104, 154, 156, 170, 184, 211
welfare state, 15
welfare spending, 174
wheat, 181
Whitlam, Gough, 190, 209
wool, 198
World Bank, 1, 9, 10, 12, 13; and Australia, 180; and Indonesia, 17, 19, 29, 31, 34, 35, 39, 45; and Malaysia, 115, 147; and Philippines, 94, 96, 98, 99, 100–1, 104, 108, 109; and Thailand, 55, 57, 58, 64, 65, 69, 71ff
World War II, 189, 190, 194

'Young Turks', 77
youth militancy 103; *see also* student militancy

Zainuddin, Daim, 146
Zobel, Enrique, 109